Chaos, Criminology, and Social Justice

Chaos, Criminology, and Social Justice

THE NEW ORDERLY (DIS)ORDER

EDITED BY
Dragan Milovanovic

PRAEGER

Westport, Connecticut
London

Library of Congress Cataloging-in-Publication Data

Chaos, criminology, and social justice : the new orderly (dis)order /
  edited by Dragan Milovanovic.
    p.   cm.—(Criminology and crime control policy, ISSN
  1060–3212)
    Includes bibliographical references and index.
    ISBN 0–275–95707–1 (alk. paper).—ISBN 0–275–95912–0 (pbk.)
    1. Criminology.   2. Chaotic behavior in systems.   3. Law.
  4. Social justice.   5. Social change.   I. Milovanovic, Dragan,
  1948–   .   II. Series.
  HV6030.C48   1997
  364—DC21   96–37114

British Library Cataloguing in Publication Data is available.

Library of Congress Catalog Card Number: 96–37114
ISBN: 0–275–95707–1
      0–275–95912–0 (pbk.)
ISSN: 1060–3212

First published in 1997

Praeger Publishers, 88 Post Road West, Westport, CT 06881
An imprint of Greenwood Publishing Group, Inc.

Printed in the United States of America

The paper used in this book complies with the
Permanent Paper Standard issued by the National
Information Standards Organization (Z39.48–1984).

10 9 8 7 6 5 4 3 2 1

Contents

Introduction

Dragan Milovanovic

Once upon a time everything seemed so clear and certain. Newtonian physics and Euclidean geometry, for a time, seemed to clearly map the modernist terrain. The cosmos was orderly, linear, and predictable: "God does not play dice." Humans were seen as self-determining, reflective, conscious, and in control. *Cogito, ergo sum*—I think, therefore I am. The individual was celebrated. And, it was said, the newly discovered global logic of rationalism would transform society into a higher form. Post-Enlightenment thought was a time for optimism. But this fairyland ideal has been fundamentally challenged.

Postmodernist thought was to question these presuppositions and truth claims. The 1990s saw various threads of a postmodernist perspective develop. Psychoanalytic semiotics of Jacques Lacan was one key development which was to be influential with many progressive thinkers. Catastrophe theory, quantum mechanics, topology theory, and Godel's theorem were other emerging threads. But chaos theory has emerged as one of the key threads of postmodernist analysis that fundamentally challenges the assumption of an orderly world.

The world is more disorderly, uncertain, non-linear, and unpredictable. But it is not without a form or structure: rather, the notion of an orderly disorder was the basis of an alternative metaphysics. Chaos should not, therefore, be seen as purely randomness and chance events: rather, "what makes chaos confounding is the way measurement uncertainties expand," and "statements clarifying the limits and likelihoods of future behaviors can still be made for a chaotic process" (Peak and Frame, 1994: 158). Here, Nietzsche has emerged as a key thinker confronting much of structural functionalists' analysis which incorporated the modernist ideals in the social sciences. According to Nietzsche,

The astral order in which we live is an exception; this order and the relative duration that depends on it have . . . made possible an exception of exceptions: the formation of the organic. The total character of the world, however, is in all eternity chaos—in the sense not of a lack of necessity but of a lack of order, arrangement, form, beauty, wisdom, and whatever other names there are for our aesthetic anthropomorphisms. (Nietzsche cited in Babich, 1996: 109, 168)

For Nietzsche, we are more likely to engage in the development of "semiotic fictions" that provide us an illusory sense of understanding and mastery of the universe. He has emphasized that rather than the search for "truth" resting on Logos, the search for a seemingly underlying logic, rationality, and certainty, we should focus on Pathos—struggle, contradiction, the unexpected, surprise, and the emergent.

Chaos theory has arrived as a new vision in doing critical inquiry that celebrates the unexpected, surprise, ironic, contradictory, and emergent. It does not dismiss otherwise seen inconsequential inputs, noise, or deviation, as is often the case in modernist analysis. In fact, very small differences in starting conditions, when iterated (feedback), could produce dramatic results. This "butterfly effect" has it that, yes, an otherwise seen small input by a person can indeed make a difference.

In the early 1990s, several studies began to emerge applying chaos theory to criminology and law. T.R. Young (1991a, 1991b) was to take the lead in this development. His work was to have an immense influence on a number of scholars doing postmodernist research in criminology (Arrigo, 1994; Milovanovic, 1992). It has also been integrated into a peacemaking perspective (Pepinsky, 1991). In law, the works of Brion (1991), Arrigo (1995a, 1995b), and Milovanovic (1992, 1996, 1997) have established a body of scholarly work engaging the task of integrating chaos theory with other strands of critical analysis. We have recently developed a "constitutive" approach in criminology and law that attempts an integration of various perspectives within postmodern analysis (Henry and Milovanovic, 1996; Milovanovic, 1996, 1997). In social movement theory and community building, Schehr (1996a, 1996b) and Young (1992) have been pacesetters. Their innovative analysis has challenged conventional thought on the subject. A number of accomplished scholars as well as Ph.D. students across the country are beginning to actively consult this perspective as an alternative to the entrenched structural functionalism and empiricism rooted in linear science. Chaos is seen as providing something new and refreshing, an approach that provides novel analytical and conceptual tools for critical inquiry. The chapters in this book attest to the fruitful lines of inquiry that may take place.

Young (Chapter 4, this volume) has outlined the key elements in doing a chaos-informed postmodern analysis. The foci are:

1. To locate the attractors hidden in complex data sets.
2. To determine how many attractors exist in that data set.
3. To find the change point(s) at which new attractors are produced.

And for purposes of social control,

4. To identify the key parameters which drive the system into ever more uncertainty.

And for purposes of social policy,

5. To determine which setting of those key parameters is acceptable to the whole society.

This book brings together some of the key thinkers applying chaos theory to criminology, law, and social change. It provides both the interested but yet not-well-versed reader and the initiated reader with some contemporary approaches in doing a critically informed, postmodernist analysis with chaos theory as one of its main constitutive threads. Accordingly, this book is organized into three parts. Part I, "Chaos Theory: Conceptual Contributions to a Postmodern Criminology and Law," is meant to provide the reader with: (1) a sensitivity to how chaos theory *fits* within the postmodern perspective and how it is fundamentally at odds with much of the modernist framework; and (2) an understanding of some of the key conceptual tools of chaos theory. This part, therefore, is meant to acquaint the reader with how chaos theory is situated in contemporary critical thought in criminology and law. Part II, "Chaos, Criminology, and Law: Critical Applications," provides chapters on doing critical criminology and law from a predominantly chaos perspective. It also suggests further integration, that is, with discourse analysis (psychoanalytic semiotics), peacemaking, and critical legal studies. Part III, "Chaos Theory, Social Justice, and Social Change," presents applied studies in chaos-informed perspectives on new social movement theory, social change, and the development of social justice. It is also suggestive as to establishing vistas for a society based more on orderly (dis)order principles.

Part I consists of two chapters. In Chapter 1, "Postmodernist versus the Modernist Paradigm: Conceptual Differences," Milovanovic outlines some of the key differences between postmodernist and modernist thought. He focuses on eight dimensions: society and social structure, social roles, subjectivity/agency, discourse, knowledge, space/time, causality, and social change. In each case we should view a continuum rather than dichotomies. Only for presentational and clarification purposes are we dividing the two approaches into separate categories. Some differences, however, such as in the notion of causality and subjectivity, tend toward mutual exclusivity. Chaos theory will be situated within postmodernist analysis. It will become clear that within postmodern analysis the many threads (psychoanalytic semiotics, catastrophe theory, topology, Godel's theorem, chaos, etc.) have not been, to this day, integrated into a grand theory that can call itself *the* postmodern approach. Rather, we have various integrations that remain dynamic and continue toward refinement.

In Chapter 2, "Challenges: For a Postmodern Criminology," Young acquaints the non-initiated reader to the core concepts of chaos theory. Explicated are the ideas of attractors (point, limit/cyclic, torus, and strange), causal basins, fractals, bifurcation theory, feedback (iteration), non-linearity, self-similarity, and phase space. Compared to the modernist framework inherited from the Enlightenment theory, chaos theory is providing a new language for research. Young also provides many examples for each of the concepts developed. Having read this chapter, a reader will have an understanding of the necessary critical tools of chaos theory to appreciate the various applications to criminology, law, and social change.

Part II consists of six chapters that apply chaos theory to criminology and law. The first three chapters apply chaos to criminology, the last three to law. In Chapter 3, "Chaos and Modeling Crime: Quinney's *Class, State and Crime*," Forker has applied chaos theory to Richard Quinney's theory of the relationship between the development of capitalism and crime. A bifurcation diagram was developed situating his linear thesis as well as how various attractors emerge. Forker develops the notion of a "phase space" which maps complex, dynamic systems in movement. She questions the linear developments predicted in Quinney's model that specify the causes of crime and how transformations will progress from unconscious criminal behavior often supportive of the dominant capitalist order, or "crimes of accommodation," into "crimes of resistance" and "political rebellion." She suggests the need for modifications to the evolutionary model presented in Quinney's classic study as well as other treatises in criminology which privilege linearity.

In Chapter 4, "The ABCs of Crime: Attractors, Bifurcations, and Chaotic Dynamics," Young develops specific applications of chaos theory to criminology. Many of the conceptual tools explained in chapters 1 and 2 are integrated into a critical analysis of crime. He focuses on forms of crime in rural areas (banditry, rustling, kidnapping, highway robbery), urban crimes (property and violent crimes), and gender violence, as well as corporate, organized, white-collar, and political crimes. Chaos theory is shown to offer new ways of conceptualizing onsets of harm in their various forms. He identifies various methods for managing uncertainties, and he provides some suggestive ideas concerning how to reduce the incidence of harm.

In Chapter 5, "Geometric Forms of Violence," Pepinsky integrates chaos with a "peacemaking perspective" in indicating how state violence emerges. He extends on his earlier work (1991) on the "geometry of violence." He outlines how, with concentrations of state violence, turbulence will develop culminating in a social order where peacemaking practices will prevail. He sees this as a process of democratizing our lives and of learning to live in partnership with our fellow humans in an increasingly diverse society. His recognized ongoing work in the peacemaking perspective (Pepinsky and Quinney, 1991) and critical criminology (MacLean and Milovanovic, 1996) has discovered conceptual tools from chaos theory worthy of integration in developing vistas for the better society.

Chapter 6, "Law and Social Change: The Implications of Chaos Theory in Understanding the Role of the American Legal System," begins the three chapters focusing on applying chaos theory to law. In this chapter, Simons and Stroup outline how chaos theory can contribute to and enhance our understanding of the relationship between law and social change by incorporating some of the differing ideas of the functionalist and conflict perspectives. These two perspectives have often been polarized in the literature. The writers show how concepts from chaos theory, including iterative processes, bifurcations, and attractors, can provide additional insights into this relationship, which helps correct for deficiencies in earlier approaches. In so doing, this chapter helps to dispel two commonly held myths regarding the applicability of chaos theory in the social sciences, namely: (1) that *either* "order" or "conflict" is the "normal" state of a society, and (2) that the concepts of chaos theory are irrelevant or incompatible with other social theories.

In Chapter 7, "Chaos, Law, and Critical Legal Studies: Mapping the Terrain," Schulman applies chaos theory to decision-making in law. She draws from Brion's work (1991) and integrates the bifurcation diagram and the various attractors in specifying the dynamic process involved in law-finding (decision-making). She indicates how critical legal studies can benefit by an understanding and incorporation of the conceptual tools provided by chaos theory. She points out that a number of ideas already are shared, by different nomenclature, between chaos theorists and critical legal studies theorists, such as indeterminacy, anti-formalism, contradiction, and marginality. In recent years, theorists from critical legal studies have gone beyond their earlier conceptual boundaries, and surely could find chaos theory a useful perspective in their ongoing challenge of the legal order.

In Chapter 8, "The Chaotic Law of Forensic Psychology: The Post-modern Case of the (In)Sane Defendant," Arrigo integrates two main themes in a postmodern approach: (1) psychoanalytic semiotics, which explains the relationship between language and subjectivity, and (2) the findings of chaos theory. He first lays out some principles of psychoan-alytic semiotics and Lacan's theory of the four discourses, which are said to be the basic organizational framework through which communication takes place. Arrigo then makes a case for the applicability of chaos prin-ciples. This is followed by applying an integrative approach in the ex-amination of legal discourse dealing with the disordered criminal defendant. He closes with insights concerning the potential development of replacement discourses. Chaos theory, Arrigo shows, provides useful conceptualizations for bringing out the complex dynamics at play in con-structing various "realities" in law.

Part III, "Chaos Theory, Social Justice, and Social Change," consists of three chapters focusing on theorizing new approaches in new social movement, community building, and social justice.

In Chapter 9, "Surfing the Chaotic: A Non-Linear Articulation of Social Movement Theory," Schehr provides an alternative vision to the litera-ture in social change and community building. Contemporary social movement literature, he argues, finds three paradigms: collective behav-ior, resource mobilization, and, from Europe, new social movement the-ory (NSM). Schehr suggests that a fourth model can be developed. This model would integrate chaos theory with new social movement litera-ture. He notes that the conceptual tools of NSM, by itself, are too limiting in providing forms of resistance. For example, much of it is predicated on linear analysis. We need to go beyond, he argues. His model of the "intentional community" certainly is a welcomed change to limiting con-temporary models of social change and organization. Chaos theory and other ideas from postmodernist analysis provide us with conceptual tools for better theorizing social struggle, change, and the emerging new community.

In Chapter 10, "Dimensions of Social Justice in an SRO (Single Room Occupancy): Contributions from Chaos Theory, Policy, and Practice," Arrigo applies chaos theory to community building and the development of social justice. Although some efforts in recent days have been focused on the viability of single room occupancy (SRO), little if any attention has been brought to the conceptual dimension of community building. Arrigo draws from his ethnographic data, and by using postmodern in-quiry, particularly the concepts of chaos theory, indicates that orderly disorder practices and non-linear dynamics were at the core of the SRO neighborhood's social ecology. He links these conceptual micro-properties (the level of community) to a more macro-model of building a social, just, participatory, and empowering milieu. The impact of the dynamics of chaos among the disenfranchised constituencies in his study is explained. He especially focuses on several key chaos concepts: non-linearity, fractional space, attractors, self-similarity, bifurcations, and dissipative structures. The implications for community systems theory, policy, and practices are discussed. Chaos theory is shown to be integral to contributing to the development of new vistas for the emergence of social justice and for community building. Arrigo provides a case study for the emerging "fourth paradigm" in social movements that Schehr is developing.

In Chapter 11, "Visions of the Emerging Orderly (Dis)Order," Milovanovic outlines a theoretical model for the development of an alternative society based on the principles of chaos theory. He provides some suggestions as to the possible basis of an alternative social structure, political economy, community, agency, criminology, law, and replacement discourses. The many contributors in this book directly or indirectly address these various issues. This chapter applies chaos theory to social change and to the development of an alternative (dis)order where an alternative replacement discourse, a language of possibility, will be the medium for social encounters and narrative constructions. What is indicated is how a social structure such as the one assumed by the modernists (one in which order, equilibrium, bureaucracies, determinism, global rationality, and logic prevail) can undergo transformation to a society conceptualized by chaos theorists as far-from-equilibrium, where orderly disorder prevails (here chance, uncertainty, spontaneity, and the unpredictable are privileged). In other words, in this vision of social transformation and social justice, "dissipative structures" highly sensitive to their environment would be ubiquitous.

Dissipative structures, unlike rigid bureaucracies, undergo constant change as they actively interact with their environments. Here the disenfranchised, disempowered, and marginalized will have a discourse within which to regain their denied voices. Indicated is how these denied voices can find expression at various stages of social intervention practices and in the criminal justice system. Chaos theory provides some crucial links in developing thoughts on a social structure that is more dynamic, open, diverse, open to the unexpected, and, ultimately, humanistic. And contrary to earlier, more nihilistic/fatalistic forms of postmodern analysis that often seemed to advocate "the death of the subject," the contemporary, affirmative postmodern view conceptualizes a dynamic subject-in-process.

This book's emphasis is on sensitizing readers to the usefulness of the conceptual tools offered by chaos theory. Surely, much good research awaits those willing to integrate an alternative view to doing critical criminology and law. The ultimate criteria hinge on how helpful chaos theory is in providing vistas for understanding the contemporary social

scene and for the development of the new just society. Theory building
by itself, of course, does not suffice: the purpose is not merely to theorize
but to engage in transformative practices in building a just society.

REFERENCES

Arrigo, B. 1994. "The Insanity Defense." Pp. 57–83 in R. Kevelson (ed.), *The Eyes
    of Justice*. New York: Peter Lang.
———. 1995a. "Deconstructing Classroom Instruction." *Social Pathology* 1(2): 115–
    48.
———. 1995b. "The Peripheral Core of Law and Criminology: On Postmodern
    Social Theory and Conceptual Integration." *Justice Quarterly* 12(3): 447–72.
Babich, B. 1996. "The Order of the Real: Nietzsche and Lacan." Pp. 43–68 in D.
    Pettigrew and F. Raffoul (eds.), *Disseminating Lacan*. Albany, NY: State
    University of New York Press.
Brion, D. 1991. "The Chaotic Law of Tort: Legal Formalism and the Problem of
    Indeterminacy." Pp. 45–77 in R. Kevelson (ed.), *Peirce and Law*. New York:
    Peter Lang.
Henry, S. and D. Milovanovic. 1996. *Constitutive Criminology*. London: Sage.
MacLean, B. and D. Milovanovic. 1996. *Thinking Critically About Crime*. Vancou-
    ver, Canada: Collective Press.
Milovanovic, D. 1992. *Postmodern Law and Disorder*. Liverpool, England: Deborah
    Charles.
———. 1996. "Postmodern Criminology." *Justice Quarterly* 13(4): 567–609.
———. 1997. *Postmodern Criminology*. New York: Garland.
Peak, D. and M. Frame. 1994. *Chaos under Control*. New York: W.H. Freeman.
Pepinsky, H. 1991. *The Geometry of Violence and Democracy*. Bloomington: Indiana
    University Press.
Pepinsky, H. and R. Quinney (eds.). 1991. *Criminology as Peacemaking*. Blooming-
    ton: Indiana University Press.
Schehr, R. 1996a. *Communities of Resistance*. New York: Lang.
———. 1996b. *Dynamic Utopia: Establishing Intentional Communities as a New Social
    Movement*. Westport, CT: Praeger.
Young, T.R. 1991a. "Chaos and Crime Part II: The ABC of Crime: Attractors,
    Bifurcations, Basins and Chaos." *Critical Criminologist* 3(4): 3–4, 13–14.
———. 1991b. "Chaos and Crime." *Critical Criminologist* 3(2): 3–4, 10–11.
———. 1992. "Chaos Theory and Human Agency." *Humanity and Society* 16(4):
    441–60.

PART I

Chaos Theory: Conceptual Contributions to a Postmodern Criminology and Law

CHAPTER 1

Postmodernist versus the Modernist Paradigm: Conceptual Differences

Dragan Milovanovic

INTRODUCTION

Much, in recent days, has been said of a postmodernist analysis in the social sciences. Accordingly, this chapter is more didactic and pedagogical in orientation. We have identified eight dimensions as a basis of comparison. Although presented as dichotomies, the differences often fall along a continuum—some tending toward further polarization, others becoming discontinuities, such as the differences between the centered and decentered subject, the privileging of disorder rather than order, the emphasis on Pathos rather than Logos, and so on.

Postmodern analysis assumes a number of threads (discourse analysis, critical theory, topology, Godel's theorem, quantum mechanics, catastrophe theory, chaos theory, etc.). Chaos theory has recently emerged as a prominent thread in need of further integration into emerging scholarly postmodern studies. The chapters in this book are especially focused on this emerging thread.

A considerable amount of literature from those who are committed to the modernist approach is of a defensive sort when confronted with the epistemological directions advocated by postmodernist analysis. The first tactic generally is to dismiss its claims as old wine in new bottles, followed by incorporating the postmodernist premises and concepts within the discourse of modernist thought. Much effort, then, is taken to undo the postmodernist's concepts by way of a discursive reorientation, at the conclusion of which modernist thinkers hope to say, "There, I told you so! Old wine in new bottles!" This attempt fails, however, even though it is the case that in some instances several modernist thinkers did in fact anticipate some aspects of the postmodern paradigm. What is necessary to recognize is that postmodernist analysis is indeed premised on radically new concepts, and discursive redefinitions will not help further progressive thought in the social sciences.

Modernist thought had its origins in the Enlightenment period. Celebrated here were the liberating potentials of the social sciences, the materialistic gains of capitalism, new forms of rational thought, due process safeguards, abstract rights applicable to all, and the individual—it was a time of great optimism (Milovanovic, 1992a, 1994d; Dews, 1987; Sarup, 1989; Lyotard, 1984; Baker, 1993).

Postmodernists are fundamentally opposed to modernist thought. Sensitized by the insights of some of the classic thinkers, ranging from Marx, to Weber, to Durkheim, Freud, and the critical thought of the Frankfurt School, postmodernist thought emerged with a new intensity in the late 1980s and early 1990s. "Let us wage a war on totality," states one of its key exponents (Lyotard, 1984: 82). Most of the key concepts of modernist thought were critically examined and found to be wanting. Entrenched bureaucratic powers, monopolies, the manipulative advertisement industry, dominant and totalizing discourses, and the ideology of the legal apparatus were seen as exerting repressive powers. In fact, the notion of the individual—free, self-determining, reflective, and the center of activity—was seen as an ideological construction, nowhere more apparent than in the notion of the juridic subject, the so-called "reasonable man in law." Rather than the notion of the individual, the centered subject, the postmodernists were to advocate the notion of the *decentered subject*.

Postmodernist analysis had its roots in French thought, particularly during the late 1960s and 1970s. Here, with the continued disillusionment with conventional critical thought, a transition from Hegelian to Nietzschean thought took place. Deleuze, Guattari, Derrida, Lyotard, Baudrillard, Foucault, Kristeva, and many others were to emerge bearing the banner of postmodernist thinking. Feminists from the postmodern tradition were to become key thinkers. Such theorists as Irigaray, Moi, and Cixous were to apply much of this thought to gender construction. The central figure in developing alternative notions of the subject, the determining effects of discourse, and the nature of the symbolic order was Jacques Lacan.

New wave postmodernist thinkers are likely to draw from chaos theory, Godel's theorem, catastrophe theory, quantum mechanics, and topology theory. Novel conceptions of space, time, causality, subjectivity, the role of discourse, desire, social structure, roles, social change, knowledge, and the nature of harm, justice, and the law were developed and continue to be developed in postmodernist thought. The call is for the abandonment of a center, privileged reference points, fixed subjects, first principles, and an origin (Sarup, 1989: 59).

This chapter will outline the differences between the modernist and the postmodernist paradigm. As Thomas Kuhn told us many years ago, paradigms tend to crystallize around key validity claims that become premises for scientific thought. "Normal science" tends to work out the implications of this general body of knowledges through, for example, deductive logic. Occasionally, as in the case of postmodernist thought, a revolutionary new science with entirely new premises develops and becomes the body of knowledge from which new questions are asked and entirely new discoveries are made.

POSTMODERNIST VERSUS THE MODERNIST PARADIGM

To clarify some of the more salient differences, we have selected eight dimensions for comparison. These dimensions include the nature of: (1) society and social structure, (2) social roles, (3) subjectivity/agency, (4) discourse, (5) knowledge, (6) space/time, (7) causality, and (8) social change.

Society and Social Structure

Much has been written over the years concerning how society is structured. What keeps it together? Why are there recurring themes? How are variability and stability maintained? Postmodernist thought has a different image of how society is held together than the modernist ideal.

Modernist Thought. Much of the dominant literature of modernist thought can be traced to the work of structural functionalism or totalizing theory. Theorists such as Emile Durkheim, Talcot Parsons, and Niklas Luhmann stand out as exemplary. A good part of this literature rests on an underlying homeostatic, tension-reduction, or equilibrium model. Freud, for example, rests his views on some conception of tension-reduction as the operative force in social structural development. Perhaps we can trace much of this to Newtonian physics and its influence. The central question is one of order. It is seen as desirable without further explanation. In fact, some, such as Parsons, define deviance in terms of distance from some assumed acceptable standard of normativity.

Modernist thought is focused on totalizing theory—the search for overencompassing theories of society and social development. Some discoverable foundation was said to exist. At the center, a logos was said to be at play; whether, for example, as in Weber's forces of rationalization, Freud's homeostasis, or as in Hegel's Absolute Spirit. These logics slumbered in anticipation of their correct articulations. These were the transcendental signifiers that were discoverable.

Much of the often-mentioned consensus paradigm in the social sciences, too, can be placed within the modernist paradigm. Thus, meta-narratives are still replete with assumptions of homogeneity, desirability of consensus, order, and so on.

Postmodernist Thought. Postmodernist thought, although still emerging, and which initially found its basis in its critique of modernism, has found grounding in the insights of chaos theory, Godel's theorem, catastrophe theory, quantum mechanics, emerging cosmological insights, topology theory, and Lacanian thought—to name a few.

Postmodernists begin their analysis with privileging disorder rather than order. Their starting point is *paralogism*: privileging instabilities (Lyotard, 1984). Accordingly, this model begins with far-from-equilibrium conditions as being the more "natural" state, and places a premium on flux, non-linear change, chance, spontaneity, intensity, indeterminacy, irony, and orderly disorder. No permanent stable order is possible or even desirable. No center or foundation exists. Godel's theorem (1962), describing the impossibility of formal closure, dictates that the search for an overall, all-encompassing, totalizing theory is an illusory exercise. Any attempt to create a formal system that encompasses all cases of phenomena will ultimately find some that do not "fit." In fact, as we shall show below, since no precise center exists, or since no possibility exists for precisely specifying initial conditions, then, the process of iteration, or continuously feedbacking information into some algorithm, will produce disproportional and unanticipated effects.

"Dissipative structures," dynamic systems that are simultaneously disintegrating and emerging, are offered as relatively stable societal structures that remain sensitive and responsive to their environment (Baker, 1993; see also Unger's suggestion for the establishment of criticizable institutions, 1987; see also Leifer on organizational transformations, 1989). This concept implies both relative stability as well as continuous change (i.e., order and disorder). Contrary to structural functionalism and its privileging of homeostasis, postmodernists see the desirability of ongoing flux and continuous change captured by the notion of far-from-equilibrium conditions. It is within these conditions that dissipative structures flourish.

Accordingly, some have offered the notion of *structural coupling* and *constitutive theory* to explain the movement of information between structure and environment (Luhmann, 1992; Hunt, 1993; Jessop, 1990; Henry and Milovanovic, 1991, 1996). Here all is interconnected, interlocking, interpenetrating, and "reality" is co-constructed and produced. Implied is the coexistence of multiple sites of determinants whose unique historical articulations are never precisely predictable. Due to inherent uncertainties in initial conditions (starting values are always imprecise), iterative practices produce the unpredictable. Even a small difference of .0001, when continuously recomputed (iterated), will produce disproportional effects, called the "butterfly effect." Here, the focal concern is on tolerance and support for the spontaneous and incommensurable. Assumed is the existence of perpetual fragmentation, deconstruction, and reconstruction. Advocated is the facilitation of the emergence of the voices of the marginalized, disenfranchised, alienated, and disempowered.

Noteworthy in the analysis of societal structure by way of postmodernist analysis is Unger's work on an empowered democracy (1987), even if he didn't explicitly state his affinity with postmodernist thought. In his offerings, orderly disorder should be privileged. During the 1960s and 1970s, the development of the conflict paradigm in the social sciences marked some movement toward the postmodernist approach, but the promise fell short.

Chaos theory is increasingly becoming a key element in postmodern analysis. The founding figures include Ilya Prigogine, Henri Poincaré, Mitchell Feigenbaum, Benoit Mandelbrot, and Edward Lorenz (see the overview by Briggs and Peat, 1989; Gleick, 1987; Stewart, 1989). We find application of chaos theory to psychoanalysis (Deleuze and Guattari, 1987; Milovanovic, 1992a, 1993b); to literature (Serres, 1982a, 1982b; Hayles, 1990, 1991); to criminology (Young, 1991b; Pepinsky, 1991); to law (Brion, 1991; Milovanovic, 1993b); to psychology (Butz, 1991, 1992a, 1992b); to sociology (Young, 1991a, 1992; Baker, 1993); to business and management (Leifer, 1989); and to political science (Unger, 1987). Others, such as Charles Sanders Peirce, anticipated some dimensions of this approach (see especially his essay on the doctrine of chance and necessity, 1940: 157–73; and his notion of *Pure Play* or *musement*, 1934: 313–16).

Nietzschean and Lacanian thought, rather than Hegelain, stand as inspirational for postmodernist thinkers. Feminist postmodernists traced to the former have perhaps contributed the most important insights. Julia Kristeva, Luce Irigaray, Helene Cixous, and Toril Moi, to a considerable extent, have borrowed ideas from them in their elaborations of given phallocentric social structures and their possible alternatives (a useful overview is found in Sellers, 1991; Grosz, 1990; for an application in law, see Cornell, 1991, 1993; Milovanovic, 1994d: ch. 6; 1994b).

Roles

The question of how people play out their respective "parts" with an assumed "script" in front of various audiences has been the subject of much sociological inquiry. Postmodernist and modernist inquiry differ as to how much variability exists in the roles assumed by people in their everyday interactions in various settings.

Modernist Thought. The modernist view tends to rely on a Parsonian construct of a role in which centripetal forces of society socialize the person into accepting the obligations and expectations that pertain to them. This, then, becomes the question of functional integration. Accordingly, roles tend to become dichotomized—male/female, employer/employee, good guy/bad guy. In the specified balance of the I-me that many social theorists advocate (Durkheim, Mead, etc.), great weight is placed on the dominance of the "me," that part of the self which dresses itself up with the persona of the situation, struts upon the stage, and plays its part with various degrees of success to various audiences. A person is relegated to role-taking. The operative metaphor we offer is a member of a symphony orchestra.

Postmodernist Thought. Postmodernists see things differently. Roles are essentially unstable and are in a dialectical relationship between centrifugal and centripetal forces. And this is desirable. Whereas roles in the modernist view would be similar to what chaos theorists refer to as *limit attractors* (they tend toward stereotypical closure), roles in postmodernist analysis would be very much like *torus* or *strange attractors*. A strange attractor can appear as two butterfly wings where instances of behavior may occur in one (i.e., a person's conduct is situated in the illegal underworld), and in the other (i.e., a person's conduct is in the legitimate world). Where the two cross, maximal indeterminacy prevails. When instances of behavior are plotted in *phase space* (a diagrammatical depiction), what appears over time is some degree of global patterning (the distinct wings of the butterfly), but at any instance, that is, at any specific location, variability and indeterminacy prevail (from quantum mechanics' uncertainty principle, one cannot at the same time predict location and momentum). There exists, in other words, local indeterminacy but a relative global stability, an orderly disorder. A person's fate is relegated to role-making (Young, 1994).

In George Herbert Mead's framework, role-making would indicate the active contribution of the "I." Unger's notion of *role-jumbling* would be another example (1987). Haraway's idea of a postmodernist identity would be another (1991). Others have advocated a simultaneous disidentification and identification with various discursive subject positions, a process by which reidentifications are produced (JanMohammed, 1993; McLaren, 1994). "It is . . . a process of forming affiliations with other positions, of defining equivalences and constructing alliances" (JanMohammed, 1993: 111). In fact, Lacan's view is that the person is decentered and is always subject to imaginary and symbolic play and therefore a stable *moi* is illusory and stability can only be maintained by the impositions of external forces (i.e., manipulative powers of the political and the advertisement industry; the violence of a phallocentric symbolic order, etc.). For the postmodernist view, the call is to be a jazz player and poet.

Subjectivity/Agency

The person has been conceptualized differently throughout the ages. The crucial question has focused on how much independence and consciousness to assume for the acting subject. This ranges from the notion of the individual (the centered subject) assumed by modernist inquiry to the notion of the (decentered) subject assumed by postmodernist inquiry.

Modernist Thought. Modernist thought has privileged the idea of the individual, a person that is assumed to be conscious, whole, self-directing, reflective, unitary, and transparent. In its extreme we have what had been characterized in the 1960s by Dennis Wrong and picked up in the critical literature as the "oversocialized conception of man." Other conceptions cling to a homo-duplex view in which human nature is said to be a balance of egoism and altruism. Here individual desires are said to be in need of synchronization with given socio-political systems. Alternatively, we have *homo economicus*. Here rational utility theory is said to guide the subject. The person is guided by the pursuit of pleasure and benefits rather than pains and costs. The Enlightenment period was one in which the individual or the centered subject was discovered. This conception of the transcendental self, the Cartesian subject, has been incorporated in the legal sphere as the juridic subject, the reasonable man/woman in law. Nowhere better has it been expressed than in *Cogito, ergo sum*—I think, therefore I am.

Desire, the unique psychic energy seeking expression by each person, for the modernists, is inscribed on the body; it is *territorialized* (Deleuze and Guattari, 1987). As Foucault would point out, the desiring subject becomes a body of passivity and economic/political utility (1977). Desire must be tamed, captured within the coordinates of various dominant discourses. Here desire begins with a lack (the various psychic deficiencies), the price it pays for its inauguration into the Symbolic Order, and the biography of the self is one in which repetition drives the organism in its attempt to fill the void (see also Dews, 1987: 132, 135). In the more passive form of adaptation, the person is driven toward homeostasis, tension-reduction, catharsis, and so on. The subject is said to be interpellated (i.e., constituted) into her/his discursive subject-positions necessitated by the imperatives of a smoothly functioning socioeconomic political order. By discursive subject-positions we assume a person finds various positions within which to take up a speaking position. Thus, we have the *interpellated* (Althusser, 1971), *spoken* (Silverman, 1983), or the *good* subject (Pecheux, 1982). In the more active form of adaptation, expressions of alienation, despair, resistance, and opposition produce the oppositional subject caught within the *discourse of the hysteric* (Lacan, 1991; Milovanovic, 1993b).

Postmodernist Thought. Postmodernist thought has offered the idea of the decentered subject. The subject is more determined than determining, is less internally unified than a desiring subject caught within the constraints of various discourses and their structuring properties. Kristeva has referred to the person as the subject-in-process; Lacan, *l'être parlant* or the *parlêtre* (the speaking being, or the speaking); and much African-American feminist analysis in law, for example, has argued for the polyvocal, polyvalent nature of consciousness (Harris, 1991: 235–62; Matsuda, 1989; Williams, 1987; Williams, 1991; Bartlet, 1991: 387–89).

Perhaps the clearest exposition of the decentered subject has been provided by Lacan in his Schema L (1977). This four-cornered schema proposes two diagonally intersecting axes: one represents an unconscious/symbolic axis, the other the imaginary axis. Here the subject is drawn over all four corners of this schema; s/he is simultaneously caught in the working of the symbolic and imaginary axes. The unconscious/symbolic axis has at one end of the pole the grammatical "I"; at the other end, the Other, the sphere of the unconscious structured like a language. The second axis, the imaginary axis, has at one end the imaginary construction of the self (*moi*); at the opposite end that the *other*, the entity through whom the self establishes itself as a coherent (be it illusory), whole being. Lacan's more dynamic models of Schema L appear as the *graphs of desire* and Schema R (1977; see also Milovanovic's expose, 1992a; on Schema R, see Milovanovic, 1994d).

The modernist's view of the subject often centers on the idea that desire emerges from "lack," and is predicated on the desirability of keeping desire in check—its free-flowing expression being said to be inherently subversive or disruptive in ongoing social activity. The postmodernists add that the desiring subject is imprisoned within restrictive discourses; at one extreme in *discourses of the master*, where subjects enact key master signifiers producing and reproducing the dominant order; at the other, in the *discourses of the hysteric*, where despairing subjects find no adequate signifiers with which to embody their desire (Lacan, 1991; Bracher, 1988, 1993; Milovanovic, 1993a, 1993b). Oppressive discursive structures interpellate subjects as supports of system needs (Althusser, 1971; see also Silverman's analysis of the manipulative media effects, 1983). In either case hegemony is easily sustained.

Postmodernists offer both a more passive and a more active form of disruptions. In the more passive form we have the notion of disruptive voices, such as in the notion of *délire*, a disruptive language of the body (Lecercle, 1985, 1990), or in *minor literature* and the *rhizome* (Deleuze and Guattari, 1986, 1987), or in the notion of *noise* or the *parasite* (Serres, 1982a: 65–70; Hayles, 1990: 197–208), or in the non-linear discursive disruptions of the *enthymeme* that intrude on any linear discursive constructions (Knoespel, 1985), or, finally, in Lacan's notion of an alternative form of *jouissance*, a jouissance of the body, a view that initiated much debate over the desirability of an *écriture féminine* (1985: 145). In the more active form, postmodernists offer a dialogically based pedagogy whereby the cultural revolutionary or revolutionary subject enters a dialogical encounter with the oppressed in co-producing key master signifiers and replacement discourses which more accurately reflect the given repressive order (see Lacan's discourse of the analyst in combination with the discourse of the hysteric, Milovanovic, 1993b; see also Freire, 1985; McLaren 1994; Aronowitz and Giroux, 1985).

For postmodernists, desire can "be conceived as a forward movement, a flight toward an object which always eludes our grasp, the attempt, never successful but never frustrating, to reach the unattainable by exploring the paths of the possible" (Lecercle, 1985: 196). Here desire, contrary to merely responding to lack and being a negative, conservative force, is seen as equated with positive processes (Dews, 1987: 132, 135–36); a will to power, defined as "the principle of the synthesis of forces" (Deleuze, 1983: 50). Nietzsche, not Hegel, is the key figure. Deleuze and Guattari's notion of the *rhizome* brings out the non-linear paths taken by desire seeking expression at each level of semiotic production (Milovanovic, 1992a: 125–33).

For postmodernists, desire is liberating, joyous, ironic, playful, and a positive force. Ultimately, the "hero" (or Nietzsche's *overman*) as opposed to the *common man* (woman) must avow her/his desire and act in conformity with it (Lacan, 1992: 309, 319–21; Lacan, 1977: 275; Lee, 1990: 95–99, 168–70; Rajchman, 1991: 42–43).

Discourse

Many differences exist between postmodernist and modernist thinkers as to how to conceive of discourse. Is it merely a neutral instrument by which we speak? Does the social construction of reality change as we move from one more stable discourse to another? Are there words (signifiers) that attain universal meaning (transcendental signifiers)? Does discourse speak the subject? To what degree are we determined by the very discourse within which we insert ourselves to speak?

Modernist Thought. The modernist paradigm assumes that discourse is neutral; it is but an instrument for use to express rationally developed projects of an inherently centered subject. In fact, some transcendental signifiers exist at the center of social structure and phenomena which are discoverable. Assumed, most often, is an ongoing dominant discourse that is seen as adequate for providing the medium for expression, whether for dominant or subordinate groups.

The couplet, the signifier (the word), and the signified (that which it expresses) are said to stabilize and crystallize in conventional understandings (uni-accentuality). Signifiers are more often said to be referential: they point to something outside themselves—to some "concrete" reality (naturalism). Modernists are more likely to assume these natural categories, rather than treating them as semiotically variable concepts (the Sapir-Whorf linguistic relativity principle anticipated many of the insights of postmodernist analysis). Modernist discourse celebrates the noun rather than the verb forms (Bohm, 1980). It is much more likely to make use of master signifiers such as prediction, falsification, replication, generalization, operationalization, objectivity, value freedom, and so on: these are "givens" in investigations (Young, 1994).

Modernists are more likely to focus on the most conscious level of semiotic production. Consciously constructed discourses are coordinated by two axes: the paradigmatic axis, which is a vertical structure, if you will, provides word choices, a dictionary of sorts. The horizontal axis, the syntagmatic axis, stands for the grammatical and linear placement of signifiers. The two axes work together to produce meaning. Debates that do question the nature of dominant discourses often are centered on the differences between an oppressive master discourse versus an ostensibly liberating discourse of the university (on the nature of the four main discourses—master, university, hysteric, and analyst, see Lacan, 1991; Bracher, 1988, 1993; Milovanovic, 1993b). The evolution of history, for the modernist thinker, is often seen as the progressive victory of the discourse of the university over the discourse of the master.

Discursive production, in modernist thought, is much more likely to produce the *readerly text* (Barthes, 1974; Silverman, 1983) and *major literature* (Deleuze and Guattari, 1986). This text is a linear reading (or viewing) with the organizing principle of non-contradiction. The passive subject is offered reasonably coherent inferences which lead to a continuous linear flow in meaning production. Its goal is closure. Its effect is the production and reproduction of conventionality. Interpreters and viewers are encouraged to assume conventional discursive subject-positions and fill in gaps by use of dominant symbolic forms.

Postmodernist Thought. Postmodernist thought does not assume a neutral discourse. There are many discourses reflective of local sites of production (i.e., multiculturalism), each, in turn, existing with a potential for the embodiment of desire in signifiers and for the constructions of realities. The sign, composed of signifier and signified, finds its natural state as being in flux. The signified is multiaccentual, the site of diverse struggles (Volosinov, 1986). The paradigm-syntagm semiotic axis is only the most manifest level of semiotic production, the most conscious. Two other levels have been identified and work at the unconscious level: the condensation-displacement semiotic axis, and the metaphoric-metonymic semiotic axis (Milovanovic, 1992b, 1993a).

Desire, it is argued, is activated and mobilized at a deeper level of the psychic apparatus and undergoes embodiment—for Freud, "figuration"; for Lacan, essentially "fantasy," $\$ \Diamond a$. This takes place by the contributory work ("overdetermination") of the condensation-displacement axis: it is the coordinating mechanism which provides temporary anchorings to the floating signifiers (i.e., the more loosely connected signifiers to signifieds or meanings), found in the Other, the sphere of the unconscious. The emerging embodied desire finally reaches the level of a particular historically rooted and stabilized discourse or linguistic coordinate system. It is here where final embodiment must be completed in the paradigm-syntagm semiotic axis (i.e., a particular word or utterance is vocalized). It was Freud who began this analysis with his investigation of *dream work* as the "royal road to the unconscious." It was Lacan who added the metaphoric-metonymic semiotic axis. Much of the investigation of the effects of language by modernists is focused merely on the surface structure of paradigm-syntagm (in law, for example, see Greimas, 1990; Jackson, 1988; Landowski, 1991).

Postmodernists identify the *violence of language* (Lecercle, 1985, 1990). Linguistic repression and alienation are the results of historically situated hegemonic discourses (see also the notion of the *regime of signs* of Deleuze and Guattari 1987, and their notion of *minor* versus *major literature*, 1986; see also Foucault's notion of discursive formations and the epistemes, 1973; Milovanovic's notion of *linguistic coordinate systems*, 1992a, 1992b; Pecheux's notion of discursive formations, 1982).

Critically, as we have previously said, Lacan has offered four intersubjectively structured discourses (1991; Bracher, 1988, 1993; Milovanovic, 1993b; Arrigo, 1993). Desire, it is argued, has various forms of embodiment in these structured discourses. Different discourses may, on the one hand, be manipulative and repressive in the expression of desire; and, on the other, offer greater possibilities of expression to these same desires.

Postmodernists would celebrate the *writerly text* (Barthes, 1974; Silverman, 1983). This text is seen as being more subversive than a readerly text. Here non-linear meaning production is at work. Encouraged in the viewer/interpreter is "an infinite play of signification; in it there can be no transcendental signified, only provisional ones which function in turn as signifiers" (Silverman, 1983: 246). For the writerly form, deconstruction of the text is celebrated with the purpose of uncovering hidden or repressed voices (consider the feminist's celebration of investigating her/ story rather than history). This strategy, the postmodernists would say, is particularly important in a contemporary society characterized as producing the non-referential and autonomous *hyper-real* (Baudrillard, 1981), and the new order of *cyberspace* (Gibson, 1984).

Similarly, Deleuze and Guattari (1986) have offered the idea of *minor literature* which tends toward a deterritorialization, manifest in the carnivalesque genre or other forms expressive of *délire* (Lecercle, 1985) such as in the writings of e.e. cummings, Franz Kafka, and James Joyce. In this spirit, David Bohm (1980) has advocated the privileging and the further development of the verb over the noun form; this would allow us to transcend the limiting metaphysics and meta-narratives embedded in subject-verb-object discursive forms (consider, too, Benjamin Whorf's investigations of the Hopi language, 1956).

Knowledge

The question of how knowledge develops, how it is transmitted, its degree of universality, and for whom it serves finds differences in explanation with the postmodernist and modernist scholars.

Modernist Thought. Enlightenment thought tended toward a totalizing Truth centered on an ostensibly discoverable Logos. Driven by formal rational methods, one inevitably dominant and globalizing thought would result. Lyotard, for example, has explained how *scientific knowledge* has usurped *narrative knowledge* (1984; see also Sarup, 1989: 120–21; Hayles, 1990: 209–10; see also Habermas's point concerning the establishment of new *steering mechanisms* based on power and money that fuel *purposive rational action*, 1987). Narrative knowledge, on the other hand, is based on myth, legend, tales, stories, and so on, which provided the wherewithal of being in society (see also Habermas's idea of communicative or symbolic communication, 1987). Whereas scientific knowledge tends toward closure, narrative knowledge embraces imaginary free play.

Lacan has provided the mechanism for the production of knowledge and the reconstitution of Truths in his analysis of the *discourses of the master and university*. For the former, knowledge and ideology are embedded in dominant discourse. Since this discourse is the one which is seen as relevant and since subjects must situate themselves within it, they, too, are subject to its interpellative effects (Althusser, 1971; Milovanovic, 1988). Thus, conventional knowledge is more likely to be reconstituted by way of the *readerly text, major literature*, or the *discourse of the master and university*.

The search for Truth by the modernists was inevitably guided by the ideal of establishing Absolute Postulates from which all other "facts" can be explained by linear, deductive logic. Efficiency and competency in the educative process are geared toward a *banking education* whereby con-

ventional master signifiers or their derivatives are stored to be capital-
ized (Freire, 1985).

Postmodernist Thought. Postmodernists, on the other hand, view knowledge as always fragmented, partial, and contingent (see also Sarup, 1989;
Dews, 1987; Lyotard, 1984). It always has multiple sites of production
(Geertz, 1983). It is derived from a dialogic pedagogy where novel signifiers are co-produced in the process of critique and the development
of a *language of possibility* (Freire, 1985). It is more likely to reflect Pathos,
human suffering, than Logos. Since there are many truths and no overencompassing Truth is possible (following Godel's undecidability theorem, 1962), knowledge defies closure or being stored passively as in a
banking education. In fact, following the chaos theory idea of iteration,
the unpredictable and unanticipated are likely to continuously appear.

Postmodernists celebrate local knowledge. Dominant and global
knowledge always subverts voices that otherwise seek expression, either
directly or indirectly, by the demand that all desire must be embodied
within dominant concepts, signifiers, and linguistic coordinate systems,
or by way of translation (intertextuality) from their more unique, concrete form into abstract categories of law and bureaucracy. Postmodernists, however, view local knowledges as not necessarily subsumable
under one grand narrative or logic (Godel's theorem).

Postmodernists view subjects within a social formation as thwarted in
their attempts to be true to their desires. Even so, "space" does exist for
possible articulation of desire. The destabilizing effects of *noise*, the *parasite*, the work of the *rhizome, minor literatures*, the non-linear disruptions
of *enthymemes*, and the subversive *writerly* text always threaten dominant
forms of knowledge. Denied subjects may be oppositional, as in the discourse of the hysteric; or revolutionary, as in the discourse of the ana-
lyst/hysteric (Milovanovic, 1993a, 1993b).

For postmodernists, knowledge is always both relational and posi-
tional (Kerruish, 1991). Accordingly, standpoints are always situated in
social relations and within ideologies (p. 187). Power and knowledge are
intricately connected and hierarchically arranged (see Dew's useful discussion of Foucault, Nietzsche, Lyotard, 1987). To enter a discursive formation (legal, medical, scientific, political, etc.) is to enter the logic and
rationality embedded within it (Foucault, 1973; Pitkin, 1971); thus, truth
is discourse-specific.

Feminist postmodernist analysis has been poignant as to the explanation of the construction of the phallic symbolic order, gender roles,
and possible alternative knowledges (see especially Cornell, 1991, 1993;
Brennan, 1993). Investigations on the contribution of the imaginary
sphere and its possible impact on reconstructing myths have been illu-
minating (Arrigo, 1992, 1993). Constitutive theory has also offered the
notion of replacement discourses (Henry and Milovanovic, 1991; Milo-

vanovic, 1993a, 1993b). This new knowledge is based on contingent and provisional truths, subject to further reflection and historicity.

The notion of *abduction* offered by Charles S. Peirce is more accurately reflective of the postmodernist epistemology than deductive logic. Here, Absolute Postulates or major premises never achieve stability; rather, creative free play guides the formulation of tentative propositions. As Nancy Fraser and Linda Nicholson have said, "postmodernist critique floats free of any universalist theoretical ground. No longer anchored philosophically, the very shape or character of social criticism changes; it becomes more pragmatic, ad hoc, contextual, and local . . . [t]here are no special tribunals set apart from the sites where inquiry is practiced, [but only] . . . the plural, local, and immanent" (cited in Bartlett, 1991: 388).

Space/Time

Explaining how space and time can be conceptualized finds differences between postmodernist and modernist thinkers. An assumption of dimensionality and the "arrow of time" is embedded in different paradigms. And this has important implications in creating knowledge.

Modernist Thought. Modernist thought rests on Newtonian mechanics. This classical view in physics rests on notions of absolute space and time. This in turn is connected with the existence of determinism within systems: if we know the positions, masses, and velocities of a particle at one time we can accurately determine their positions and velocities at all later times (Bohm, 1980: 121).

Newtonian physics and Euclidean geometry, with its use of Cartesian coordinates, are the map or blueprint of space on which modernists construct the social world. It is what Deleuze and Guattari refer to as *striated space* (1987: 488): it consists of space with whole-number dimensions where constant direction can be describable and end-states predictable. Drawing from Descartes' coordinate grid of an x-axis perpendicularly intersecting with a y-axis, a point could be located anywhere in two-dimensional space (similarly, with 3-D space, with an added z-axis). Thus, the equation $y = 3x$ can be identified on this graph. At one stroke geometry and algebra are linked. And Newton refined this further with his calculus with its differential equations. Now a continuous change in one variable can be shown to produce a calculable change in the other. And just as time flows forward, it can flow backward in a predictable way: the romantic past, the "good old days," can be recreated.

This model has been incorporated in the social sciences. A person's life course, for example, could be plotted with precision if we discover appropriate determinants. This is the basis of positivism. It is by a *striated space* (Deleuze and Guattari, 1987) that science progresses and by which desire can be territorialized on the body (1986) by a political economy. But striated space needs its discrete variables with whole-number dimensions.

Postmodernist Thought. Postmodernists see things differently. Quantum mechanics, non-Euclidean geometry, string theory, twister space, topology theory, and chaos theory, to name a few of the most prominent approaches, have offered alternative conceptions. The question of a dimension and prediction becomes problematic.

Nuclear physicists, for example, faced with trying to reconcile general relativity theory with quantum mechanics have come up with infinities. By adding space dimensions to their equations these begin to drop out of the equation. At 10-D in one model, and 26-D in another they disappear (Peat, 1989; Kaku, 1994). The 3-D model we see is perhaps just an explicate order with the rest of the dimensions rolled up tightly (compactified). This compactified order is the *enfolded* or *implicate order* (Bohm, 1980), said to have its origins moments after the Big Bang.

Chaos theory has developed the idea of *fractal* dimensions. Rather than having whole dimensions, we can refer to a space with one and one-half dimensions, one and three-quarters and so on. (A point has a dimension of 0, a line a dimension of one; a plane, two; a volume, three.) A coastline, for example, can have a fractal dimension between one and two. So, for example, contrary to the boolean logic of doctrinal legal analysis (yes/ no answers), truths are always fractal in form (i.e., shades of grey always exist). Deleuze and Guattari have developed the idea of a *smooth space* which is continuous, not discrete. The notion of fractals is in accord with smooth space (1987), and, as we shall show below, fields. It is within smooth space that becoming occurs; but progress and conventional science are done in striated space (p. 486; see also Serres, 1982a, 1982b).

Yet others, such as the noted mathematician Penrose, have constructed a view of space in terms of imaginary numbers, a *twister space* (Peat, 1988: Chapter 8; Penrose, 1989: 87–98). Chaos theorists, such as Mandelbrot, made use of complex numbers in the form of $z = x + iy$, where i is an imaginary number (the square root of -1). By further plotting $z = z^2 + c$ and by taking the result and reiterating (continuously feeding back the result) by the use of the same formula, they were to find enormously complex and esthetically appealing figures (see Penrose, 1989: 92–94). Yet others have relied on the hologram to indicate how inscriptions of phenomena are encoded and how they can be revealed with their multidimensional splendor (Bohm, 1980: 150; Pribram, 1977). Finally, we note the field of topology, the qualitative math which offers alternative ways of conceptualizing phenomena without the use of math. Here, in what is often called the "rubber math," figures are twisted, pulled, and reshaped in various ways. Breaking and gluing are not legitimate operations. Breaking produces entirely new forms. Much current thinking in nuclear and astro-physics relies on topology theory (Peat, 1988; Kaku, 1994).

Lacan has made use of topology to explain such things as the structure of the psychic apparatus by using borromean knots, Mobius bands, the torus, and projective geometry (the cross-cap) (see also Milovanovic, 1993a, 1994a, 1996, 1997; Granon-Lafont, 1985, 1990; Vappereau, 1988; for an introduction to topology theory, see Hilbert and Cohn-Vossen, 1952; Weeks, 1985; for non-Euclidean geometry, see Russell, 1956). In fact, in 4-D space the borromean knot of Lacan is no longer knotted. The cross-cap, which topologically portrays the working of Schema R and how desire is embodied as a result of the effects of the Symbolic, Imaginary, and Real Orders, can also be presented in 3-D or 4-D space (Milovanovic, 1994a, 1996; Hilbert and Cohn-Vossen, 1952). It is not without effect when we move from 3-D to 4-D space (Rucker, 1984; Banchoff, 1990; for the contributions of non-Euclidean geometry and 4-D space on cubism in art, see Henderson, 1983). Much needs to be done in the analysis of the effects of these novel conceptions.

Thus, for the postmodernists, several notions of space are currently being explored and incorporated in their analysis of the subject, discourse, causality, and society: multidimensional (Peat, 1989), fractal (Mandelbrot, 1983), holographic (Talbot, 1991; Bohm, 1980: Pribram, 1977), enfolded/implicate order (Bohm, 1980; Bohm and Peat, 1987), cyberspace (Gibson, 1984), hyper-real (Baudrillard, 1981), smooth space (Deleuze and Guattari, 1987), twister space (Penrose, 1989; see also Peat, 1989), and topological (Lacan, 1975, 1987; Peat, 1989; Granon-Lafont, 1985, 1990; Vappereau, 1988; Milovanovic, 1993a, 1994a, 1996; Lem, 1984). Young has been succinct in indicating the relevance of these notions in that an alternative space is open for the development of conceptions of "human agency in ways not possible in those dynamics privileged by Newtonian physics, Aristotelean logic, Euclidean geometry, and the linear causality they presume" (1992: 447). And there can be no return to the nostalgic "good old days": time is irreversible; since initial conditions are undecidable, then, with the passage of time and iteration, there can be no return to some decidable state.

Causality

Much fundamental disagreement exists between postmodernist and modernist scholars as to how phenomena develop. Attributing cause to some "independent variable" or combination of variables becomes problematic. A critical question revolves around the idea of linearity (versus non-linearity) and proportional (versus disproportional) effects.

Modernist Thought. Modernist thought rests on the determinism of Newtonian physics. It appears most often in the form of positivism.

Modernist thought assumes that given some incremental increase in some identified cause or determinant, a proportional and linear increase in the effect will result. The basic unit of analysis is the particle (i.e., assumed autonomous individuals, social "elements," and discrete categories) and its contributory effects. Cartccian coordinates, whole-number dimensions, calculus, and so on, in other words, striated space, is what makes possible a mathematics that has high predictive powers. Even Einstein refused to accept much of quantum mechanics that came after him, particularly the notion that God plays dice.

Postmodernist Thought. Postmodernists see things differently. Chaos theory and quantum mechanics stipulate that proportional effects do not necessarily follow some incremental increase of an input variable. Uncertainty, indeterminacy, and disproportional (non-linear) effects are all underlying assumptions and worthy of inquiry in explaining an event (genealogy). In the extreme, a butterfly flapping its wings in East Asia produces a hurricane in Warren, Ohio. Key thinkers here are Edward Lorenz, Benoit Mandelbrot, and Stephen Smale (see the excellent overview by Gleick, 1987; Briggs and Peat, 1989). In fact, in the extreme, something can emerge out of nothing at points identified as *singularities;* this is the sphere of order arising out of disorder.

Two current approaches within chaos theory are making their impact: one, focused more on order that exists in an otherwise apparently disorderly state of affairs (Hayles, 1991: 12; see Feigenbaum, 1980; Shaw, 1981); the second, focused more on how in fact order arises out of chaotic systems—order out of disorder or self-organization (Hayles, 1991: 12; 1990: 1–28; see also Prigogine and Stengers, 1984; Thom, 1975). A growing number of applications is taking place. See particularly Unger's application in his prescription for an empowered democracy (1987) and other applications to criminology, law, social movements, and social change (this volume).

The notion of iteration is a central concept of postmodernism. Simply, it means continuously recomputing with answers obtained from some formula. Continuous feedback, or iteration, produces disproportional (non-linear) effects. Derrida has applied it to how words obtain new meaning in new contexts (1973; see also Balkan, 1987); in law, for example, the "original intent" of the "founding fathers" undergoes modification over time and cannot be reconstructed. The point being made is that because of minute initial uncertainties (however small—consider Godel's theorem), when iteration proceeds these are amplified producing indeterminacies (Hayles, 1990: 183; Lyotard, 1984: 55). Thus, rather than celebrating global theory, chaos theorists and postmodernists look to local knowledges where small changes can produce large effects (Hayles, 1990: 211). In other words, postmodernists see otherwise small contributions as having profound possibilities. Yes, "small" persons' actions can make a difference! One person's involvement in a demonstration, petition signature, act of civil disobedience, or "speaking up," can, in the long run, have greater effects than anticipated.

Causation can be attributed to field rather than particle effects (Bohm, 1980; Bohm and Peat, 1987). Borrowing from Bohm's insights concerning the *quantum potential* and the *enfolded order* where all is interconnected rather than focusing, as the modernists do, on particles, points and point events, all of which are narrowly, spatiotemporally defined (analogously, consider the subject in traditional positivistic sciences: an object, located socio-economically, who has engaged in some act at a particular time and place) the unit of analysis, for postmodernists, should be a field with its moments, duration, intensities, flows, and displacements of libidinal energy. Moments, unlike point events, have fluctuating time-space co-ordinates that defy precise measurement (Bohm, 1980: 207). Within this field heterogeneous intensities can affect movement, even if they are not immediately discernible or linear and/or local. Non-linear and non-local factors, therefore, even at a distance, can have a noticable effect (Bohm and Peat, 1987: 88–93, 182–83). Research awaits in drawing out the implications of moving from 3-D to 4-D space; that is, what is knotted in the former becomes unknotted in the latter (Rucker, 1984; Kaku, 1994; consider Lacan's borromean knot in 4-D space, Milovanovic, 1993a).

In the postmodern view, certainties that do appear are often the creation of subjects: Nietzsche has shown, for example, how a subject in need of "horizons" finds *semiotic fictions* that produce the appearance of a centered subject; Peirce, anticipating chaos, has shown how free will is often created after the event as the "facts" are rearranged to fit a deterministic model and individual authorship (1923: 47); legal realists, in the early part of this century, have shown that what creates order in legal decision-making is not syllogistic reasoning and a formally rational legal system, but *ex post facto* constructions; and so forth. For postmodernists, especially Nietzsche, Serres, and Foucault, it is the "fear of the chaotic and the unclassifiable" (Dews, 1987: 186) that accounts for the order we attribute to nature.

Social Change

Given an ongoing social system, how is it that social change may occur? What, in fact, provides stability? To what degree does history unfold in a linear way? How is oppression overcome? Modernist and postmodernists offer different answers.

Modernist Thought. Modernist thought often describes change in terms of evolutionary theory, in various versions of Darwinian dynamics, particularly in terms of some "invisible hand" (i.e., Adam Smith) at work, or some working out of a logic as in the Absolute Spirit of Hegel, or in forces of rationalization as in Weber, or in dialectical materialism as in Marx. What often underlies these approaches is some linear conception of historical change. Perhaps praxis is the upper limit of modernist thought.

In the most liberal modernist view, Hegel's master-slave dialectic is a key parable of change. It is premised on reaction-negation dynamics. The slave (the oppressed) only creates value by a double negation. The slave (i.e., the proletariat) is relegated to reacting to the master (i.e., bourgeoisie) and negating. Nothing new is offered. The limits of an alternative vision remain tied to the initial logic of the major premise of the master-slave dialectic that falls on the side of the master. At best we have the oppositional subject who finds her/himself in the discourse of the hysteric, sometimes slipping into nihilistic and fatalist stances—in neither case offering anything new; at worst, a subject that inadvertently recreates the dominant repressive order (hegemony).

Modernist thought that often takes the form of evolutionary theory of change attempts to account for three phenomena: variation, selection, and transmission (Sinclair, 1992: 95; Luhmann, 1985: 249; see also Sinclair's critique of evolutionary theory of law, 1987). Luhmann's analysis is instructive. He tells us that the continuous differentiation of society tends to produce an *excess of possibilities* (1985: 237; see also Manning's application to police bureaucracies and how diverse voices are channeled into "relevant" categories, 1988). Given this creation of excesses, law, Luhmann claims, functions to reduce complexity so that subjects may plan within certain discernible horizons which, in turn, produce predictability in social planning. Social change is therefore a linear affair with continuous adjustments of social institutions to continuous processes of differentiation.

Postmodernist Thought. Postmodernist thought focuses more on nonlinear conceptions of historical change, genealogical analysis, and transpraxis, a materialistically based politics that includes a language of critique and possibility (Freire, 1985; McLaren, 1994; Aronowitz and Giroux, 1985). Postmodernists are in general agreement that, in studying historical change, much room must be made for the contributions of contingency, irony, the spontaneous, and the marginal. Nietzsche, once again, is the dominant thinker (1980; see also Love, 1986; Deleuze, 1983).

Nietzsche's version of the master-slave dialectic is a key for postmodernists. Here, rather than reaction-negation dynamics as in Hegel, an inherently conservative approach, Nietzsche's position advocates active change. This includes deconstruction and reconstruction as inseparable elements. This has been captured by the idea of a transpraxis rather than a praxis (Henry and Milovanovic, 1991, 1993; Milovanovic, 1993a).

Most prominent in recent days are feminist postmodernist theorists who have built on various versions of Lacanian psychoanalytic semiotics as well as those who have developed a standpoint theory aided especially by numerous productive critiques. Accordingly, Cornell has identified the contributions of the imaginary and the rethinking of the myth (1991, 1993; Cixous, 1986; Arrigo, 1993); Cornell (1991: 147) and Grant (1993: 116) have noted that given ideologies "leave some critical space" or "slippage" (in this context Peirce's notion of *musement* or *Pure Play* is also relevant (1934: 313–16); Kristeva has focused on the idea that semiotic processes that are situated in the form of the *readerly text* of Barthes are faced with semiotic overflow at privileged moments specified as the subversive triad: "madness, holiness and poetry" (cited in Grosz, 1990: 153); Pecheux has focused on the notion of disidentification (1982); Irigaray on *mimeses* (1985; see also Cornell's commentary, 1991: 147–50); Lacan on the discourse of the analyst (1991; see also Bracher, 1993); Milovanovic on the revolutionary subject (composite of the hysteric and analyst, 1993b) and on knot-breaking (1993a).

Some current trends in postmodernist analysis draw out the implications for social change from Freire (1985), whose work lies between modernist and postmodernist analysis. The wherewithal of the revolutionary and social change may be fruitfully situated in the integration of Lacan's work on the discourse of the hysteric/analyst with Freire's notion of *conscientization* rooted in social struggles over signification. In this integration, structure and subjectivity, material conditions and ideology, the macro- and the micro-sociological, critique and visions for change, undecidability and decidability can be reconciled. The signifier can be rooted in the concrete, historical arena of struggles; it can attain provisional decidability and a *contingent universality* in producing utopian visions of what could be and contribute, by way of a dialogic pedagogy, to the subject-in-process (generally, see McLaren, 1994; Ebert, 1991; Zavarzadeh and Morton, 1990; Butler, 1992).

Postmodernists, too, are concerned with the possible negative and unintended effects of struggles against oppression and hierarchy. Reaction-negation dynamics may at times lead to what Nietzsche referred to as *ressentiment* as well as to new master discourses, forms of political correctness, exorcism (Milovanovic, 1991), and dogma. Transpraxis, however, has as a central element the privileging of reflexivity of thought and the specification of contingent and provisional foundational political positions for social change (i.e., contingent universalities can become the basis for political alliances and agendas for change; McLaren, 1994). In other words, political agendas can be constructed, alliances can be built; but agendas are always provisional and contingent, subject to further reflection, modification, deletion, and substitution.

Among ethical principles that may come into play, for the postmodernists, perhaps Lacan's idea of "assuming one's desire" will become a key one. Faced with the passivity of the *common man* (woman), Lacan advocates that the *hero* is the one who does not betray her/his desire; meaning s/he will act in conformity with it and not embrace the offerings of manipulative powers that offer an abundance of substitute materials, or what Lacan referred to as *objets petit(a)* (Lacan, 1992: 309, 319–21; Lacan, 1977: 275; Lee, 1990: 95–99, 168–70; Rajchman, 1991: 42–43). Here, the productive use of desire is advocated, not one based on lack, tension-reduction, and stasis. Thus, a socio-political system that maximizes the opportunities for avowing one's desire is a good one; conversely, hierarchical systems, whether under the name of capitalism or socialism, that systematically disavow subjects' desires are bad ones. Elsewhere, a postmodernist definition of crime/harm has been offered based on harm inflicted (Henry and Milovanovic, 1993, 1996).

Postmodernists faced with the question of variation, selection, and transmission opt for the development of the greatest variation, the most expansive form of retaining local sites of production, and the most optimal mechanisms for transmission. Accordingly, faced with an increasingly differentiating society with "excesses in possibilities," and the modernists' call for ways of reducing complexity—the most extreme form being in pastiche (Jameson, 1984; Sarup, 1989: 133, 145), an imitation of dead styles as models for action—the central challenge of the postmodernist alternative is to create new cultural styles that privilege chance, spontaneity, irony, intensity, and so on, while still providing some dissipative horizons within which the subject may situate her/himself.

CONCLUSION

This chapter has presented some of the salient differences between modernist and postmodernist thought. Contrary to modernist critics, a new paradigm is upon us. And it is neither fatalistic or nihilistic; nor is it without visions of what could be. We were especially concerned with the possibilities of a new transpraxis and the development of replacement discourses. It might be argued that the postmodernist paradigm may take on the form of a *normal science* and tend toward closure. But, unlike the modernist enterprise, there are intrinsic forces that militate against closure and stasis.

NOTE

This chapter is a revised version of D. Milovanovic, "Dueling Paradigms: Modernist versus Postmodernist Thought," *Humanity and Society* 19(1) (1995): 19–44.

REFERENCES

Althusser, L. 1971. *Lenin and Philosophy*. New York: Monthly Review Press.

Aronowitz, S. and H.A. Giroux. 1985. *Education under Siege*. South Hadley, MA: Bergin and Garvey.

Arrigo, B. 1992. "An Experientally-Informed Feminist Jurisprudence: Rape and the Move toward Praxis." *Humanity and Society* 17(1): 28–47.

———. 1993. *Madness, Language and the Law*. Albany, NY: Harrow and Heston.

Baker, P. 1993. "Chaos, Order, and Sociological Theory." *Sociological Inquiry* 63(2): 123–49.

Balkan, J.M. 1987. "Deconstructive Practice and Legal Theory." *Yale Law Journal* 96(4): 743–86.

Banchoff, T. 1990. *Beyond the Third Dimension*. New York: Scientific American Library.

Barthes, R. 1974. *S/Z*. New York: Hill and Wang.

Bartlett, K. 1991. "Feminist Legal Methods." Pp. 333–50 in K. Bartlett and R. Kennedy (eds.), *Feminist Legal Theory*. Oxford: Westview Press.

Baudrillard, J. 1981. *For a Critique of the Political Economy of the Sign*. St. Louis: Telos Press.

Bohm, D. 1980. *Wholeness and the Implicate Order*. New York: ARK Publisher.

Bohm, D. and F.D. Peat. 1987. *Science, Order, and Creativity*. New York: Bantam Books.

Bracher, M. 1988. "Lacan's Theory of the Four Discourses." *Prose Studies* 11: 32–49.

———. 1993. *Lacan, Discourse, and Social Change*. Ithaca, NY: Cornell University Press.

Brennan, T. 1993. *History after Lacan*. New York: Routledge.

Briggs, J. and F.D. Peat. 1989. *Turbulent Mirror: An Illustrated Guide to Chaos Theory and the Science of Wholeness*. New York: Harper and Row.

Brion, D. 1991. "The Chaotic Law of Tort: Legal Formalism and the Problem of Indeterminacy." Pp. 45–77 in R. Kevelson (ed.), *Peirce and Law*. New York: Peter Lang.

Butler, J. 1992. "Contingent Foundations: Feminism and the Question of 'Postmodernism.' " Pp. 3–21 in J. Butler and J.W. Scott (eds.), *Feminists Theorize the Political*. London: Routledge.

Butz, M.R. 1991. "Fractal Dimensionality and Paradigms." *The Social Dynamicist* 2(4): 4–7.

———. 1992a. "The Fractal Nature of the Development of the Self." *Psychological Reports* 71: 1043–63.

———. 1992b. "Systematic Family Therapy and Symbolic Chaos." *Humanity and Society* 17(2): 200–222.

Cixous, H. 1986. *The Newly Born Woman*. Minneapolis: University of Minnesota Press.

Cornell, D. 1991. *Beyond Accommodation: Ethical Feminism, Deconstruction and the Law*. New York: Routledge.

———. 1993. *Transformations: Recollective Imagination and Sexual Difference*. New York: Routledge.

Deleuze, G. 1983. *Nietzsche and Philosophy*. New York: Columbia University Press.

Deleuze, G. and F. Guattari. 1986. *Kafka: Toward a Minor Literature*. Minneapolis: University of Minnesota Press.

———. 1987. *A Thousand Plateaus*. Minneapolis: University of Minnesota Press.

Dews, P. 1987. *Logics of Disintegration: Post-Structuralist Thought and the Claims of Critical Theory*. New York: Verso.

Derrida, J. 1973. *Of Grammatology*. Baltimore: Johns Hopkins Press.

Ebert, T. 1991. "Writing in the Political: Resistance (Post)Modernism." *Legal Studies Forum* 15(4): 291–303.

Feigenbaum, M. 1980. "Universal Behavior in Nonlinear Systems." *Los Alamos Science* 1: 4–27.

Foucault, M. 1973. *The Order of Things*. New York: Vintage Books.

———. 1977. *Discipline and Punish*. New York: Pantheon.

Freire, P. 1985. *The Politics of Education*. South Hadley, MA: Bergin and Garvey.

Geertz, C. 1983. *Local Knowledge: Further Essays in Interpretive Anthropology*. New York: Basic Books.

Gibson, W. 1984. *Neuromancer*. New York: Ace.

Gleick, J. 1987. *Chaos: Making a New Science*. New York: Viking.

Godel, K. 1962. "On Formally Undecidable Propositions." Pp. 173–98 in R.B. Braitewaite (ed.), *"Principia Mathematica" and Related Systems*. New York: Basic Books.

Granon-Lafont, J. 1985. *La Topologie Ordinaire De Jacques Lacan*. Paris: Point Hors Ligne.

———. 1990. *Topologie Lacanienne et Clinique Analytique*. Paris: Point Hors Ligne.

Grant, J. 1993. *Fundamental Feminism: Contesting the Core Concepts of Feminist Theory*. New York: Routledge.

Greimas, A. 1990. *The Social Sciences: A Semiotic View*. Minneapolis: University of Minnesota Press.

Grosz, E. 1990. *Jacques Lacan: A Feminist Introduction*. New York: Routledge.

Habermas, J. 1987. *The Theory of Communicative Action*. Vol. 2. Boston: Beacon Press.

Haraway, D. 1991. "Situated Knowledges." Pp. 183–201 in D. Haraway, *Simians, Cyborgs and Women*. New York: Routledge.

Harris, A. 1991. "Race and Essentialism in Feminist Legal Theory." Pp. 235–62 in K. Bartlett and R. Kennedy (eds.), *Feminist Legal Theory*. Oxford: Westview Press.

Hayles, K. 1990. *Chaos Bound*. New York: Cornell University Press.

——— (ed.). 1991. *Chaos and Order: Complex Dynamics in Literature and Science*. Chicago: University of Chicago Press.

Henderson, L. 1983. *The Fourth Dimension and Non-Euclidean Geometry in Modern Art*. Princeton, NJ: Princeton University Press.

Henry, S. and D. Milovanovic. 1991. "Constitutive Criminology." *Criminology* 29(2): 293–316.

———. 1993. "Back to Basics: A Postmodern Redefinition of Crime." *The Critical Criminologist* 5(2/3): 1–2, 6, 12.

———. 1996. *Constitutive Criminology*. London: Sage.

Hilbert, D. and S. Cohn-Vossen. 1952. *Geometry and the Imagination*. New York: Chelsea Publishing Company.

Hunt, A. 1993. *Explorations in Law and Society: Toward a Constitutive Theory of Law*. New York: Routledge.

Irigaray, L. 1985. *Speculum of the Other Woman*. Ithaca, NY: Cornell University Press.

Jackson, B. 1988. *Law, Fact and Narrative Coherence*. Merseyside, UK: Deborah Charles.

Jameson, F. 1984. "Postmodernism, or the Cultural Logic of Capital." *New Left Review* 146(26): 143–149.

JanMohammed, A.R. 1993. "Some Implications of Paulo Freire's Border Pedagogy." *Cultural Studies* 7(1): 107–17.

Jessop, B. 1990. *State Theory: Putting the Capitalist State in Its Place*. Cambridge, England: Polity Press.

Kaku, M. 1994. *Hyperspace*. New York: Oxford University Press.

Kerruish, V. 1991. *Jurisprudence as Ideology*. New York: Routledge.

Knoespel, K. 1985. *Medieval Ovidian Commentary: Narcissus and the Invention of Personal History*. New York: Garland.

Lacan, J. 1975. *Encore*. Paris: Editions du Seuil.

———. 1977. *Ecrits*. New York: Norton.

———. 1985. *Feminine Sexuality*. New York: W.W. Norton and Pantheon Books.

———. 1987. "Joyce le Symptome 1." Pp. 21–29 in J. Aubert (ed.), *Joyce Avec Lacan*. Paris: Navarin.

———. 1991. *L'Envers de la Psychanalyse*. Paris: Editions du Seuil.

———. 1992. *The Ethics of Pyschoanalysis*. New York: Norton.

Landowski, E. 1991. "A Note on Meaning, Interaction and Narrativity." *International Journal of the Semiotics of Law* 11: 151–61.

Lecercle, J.J. 1985. *Philosophy Through the Looking Glass: Language, Nonsense, Desire*. London: Hutchinson.

———. 1990. *The Violence of Language*. New York: Routledge.

Lee, S.L. 1990. *Jacques Lacan*. Amherst: University of Massachusetts Press.

Leifer, R. 1989. "Understanding Organizational Transformation Using a Dissipative Structure Model." *Human Relations* 42: 899–916.

Lem, S. 1984. *Microworlds*. San Diego: Harcourt Brace Jovanovich.

Love, N. 1986. *Marx, Nietzsche, and Modernity*. New York: Columbia University Press.

Luhmann, N.A. 1985. *Sociological Theory of Law*. Boston: Routledge and Kegan Paul.

———. 1992. "Operational Closure and Structural Coupling: The Differentiation of the Legal System." *Cardozza Law Review* 13(5): 1419–41.

Lyotard, J-F. 1984. *The Postmodern Condition: A Report on Knowledge*. Minneapolis: University of Minnesota Press.

McLaren, P. 1994. "Postmodernism and the Death of Politics: A Brazilian Reprieve." Pp. 193–215 in P. McLaren and C. Lankshear (eds.), *Politics of Liberation: Paths from Freire*. New York: Routledge.

Mandelbrot, B. 1983. *The Fractal Geometry of Nature*. New York: W.H. Freeman.

Manning, P. 1988. *Symbolic Communication*. Cambridge, MA: The MIT Press.

Matsuda, M. 1989. "When the First Quail Calls: Multiple Consciousness as Ju-
    risprudential Method." *Women's Rights Law Reporter* 11: 7, 9.
Milovanovic, D. 1988. "Jailhouse Lawyers and Jailhouse Lawyering." *Interna-
    tional Journal of the Sociology of Law* 16: 455–75.
———. 1991. "Schmarxism, Exorcism and Transpraxis." *The Critical Criminologist*
    3(4): 5–6, 11–12.
———. 1992a. *Postmodern Law and Disorder: Psychoanalytic Semiotics, Chaos and
    Juridic Exegeses.* Liverpool, England: Deborah Charles Publications.
———. 1992b. "Re-Thinking Subjectivity in Law and Ideology: A Semiotic Per-
    spective." *Journal of Human Justice* 4(1): 31–54.
———. 1993a. "Borromean Knots and the Constitution of Sense in Juridico-
    Discursive Production." *Legal Studies Forum* 17(2): 171–92.
———. 1993b. "Lacan's Four Discourses." *Studies in Psychoanalytic Theory* 2(1):
    3–23.
———. 1994a. "The Decentered Subject in Law: Contributions of Topology, Psy-
    choanalytic Semiotics and Chaos Theory." *Studies in Psychoanalytic Theory*
    3(1): 93–127.
———. 1994b. "Postmodern Law and Subjectivity: Lacan and the Linguistic
    Turn." In D. Caudill and S. Gould (eds.), *Radical Philosophy of Law.* New
    York: Humanities Press.
———. 1994c. "The Postmodern Turn: Lacan, Psychoanalytic Semiotics, and the
    Construction of Subjectivity in Law." *Emory International Law Review* 8(1):
    67–98.
———. 1994d. *Sociology of Law.* 2d ed. Albany, NY: Harrow and Heston.
———. 1996. "Postmodern Criminology." *Justice Quarterly* 13(4): 567–609.
———. 1997. *Postmodern Criminology.* New York: Garland.
Nietzsche, F. 1980. *On the Advantage and Disadvantage of History for Life.* Cam-
    bridge, MA: Hackett Publishing Company, Inc.
Peat, D. 1989. *Superstrings and the Search for the Theory of Everything.* Chicago:
    Contemporary Books.
Pecheux, M. 1982. *Language, Semantics and Ideology.* New York: St. Martin's Press.
Peirce, C.S. 1923. *Chance, Love, and Logic.* New York: Goerge Braziller, Inc.
———. 1934. *Pragmatism and Pragmaticism.* Cambridge, MA: Harvard University
    Press.
———. 1940. *The Philosophy of Peirce: Selected Writings.* J. Buchler (ed.). London:
    Routledge and Kegan Paul.
Penrose, R. 1989. *The Emperor's New Mind.* New York: Oxford University Press.
Pepinsky, H. 1991. *The Geometry of Violence and Democracy.* Bloomington: Indiana
    University Press.
Pitkin, H. 1971. *Wittgenstein and Justice.* Berkeley: University of California Press.
Pribram, K. 1977. *Languages of the Brain.* Englewood Cliffs, NJ: Prentice-Hall.
Prigogine, I. and I. Stengers. 1984. *Order Out of Chaos.* New York: Bantam.
Rajchman, J. 1991. *Truth and Eros: Foucault, Lacan, and the Question of Ethics.* New
    York: Routledge.
Rucker, R. 1984. *The Fourth Dimension.* Boston: Houghton Mifflin Company.
Russell, F. 1956. *Foundations of Geometry.* New York: Dover Publications.
Sarup, M. 1989. *Post-Structuralism and Postmodernism.* Athens: University of Geor-
    gia Press.

Schwartz, M. and D.O. Friedrichs. 1994. "Postmodern Thought and Criminolog-
  ical Discontent: New Metaphors for Understanding Violence." *Criminology*
  32(2): 221–46.
Sellers, S. 1991. *Language and Sexual Difference: Feminist Writings in France*. New
  York: St. Martin's Press.
Serres, M. 1982a. *Hermes: Literature, Science, Philosophy*. Baltimore: Johns Hopkins
  University Press.
———. 1982b. *The Parasite*. Baltimore: Johns Hopkins University Press.
Shaw, R. 1981. "Strange Attractors, Chaotic Behavior, and Information Flow."
  Zeitschrift fur Naturforschung 36: 79–112.
Silverman, K. 1983. *The Subject of Semiotics*. New York: Oxford University Press.
Sinclair, M.B.W. 1987. "The Use of Evolution Theory in Law." *University of De-
  troit Law Review* 64: 451.
———. 1992. "Autopoiesis: Who Needs It?" *Legal Studies Forum* 16(1): 81–102.
Stewart, I. 1989. *Does God Play Dice?* New York: Basil Blackwell.
Talbot, M. 1991. *The Holographic Universe*. New York: HarperCollins.
Thom, R. 1975. *Structural Stability and Morphogenesis: An Outline of a General The-
  ory of Models*. Reading, MA: W.A. Benjamin.
Unger, R. 1987. *False Necessity*. New York: Cambridge University Press.
Vappereau, J.M. 1988. *Etoffe: Les Surfaces Topologiques Intrinsiques*. Paris: Topolo-
  gie En Extension.
Volosinov, V. 1986. *Marxism and the Philosophy of Language*. Cambridge, MA: Har-
  vard University Press.
Weeks, J. 1985. *The Shape of Space*. New York: Marcel Dekker.
Williams, J. 1991. "Deconstructing Gender." Pp. 95–123 in K. Barlett and R. Ken-
  nedy (eds.), *Feminist Legal Theory*. Oxford: Westview Press.
Williams, R. 1987. "Taking Rights Aggressively: The Perils and Promise of Critical Legal Theory for Peoples of Color." *Law and Inequality* 5: 103.
Whorf, B. 1956. *Language, Thought, and Reality*. J. Carrol (ed.). New York: John
  Wiley and Sons.
Young, T.R. 1991a. "Change and Chaos Theory." *Social Science* 28(3): 59–82.
———. 1991b. "Chaos and Crime: Nonlinear and Fractal Forms of Crime." *Critical Criminologist* 3(4): 3–4, 10–11.
———. 1992. "Chaos Theory and Human Agency: Humanist Sociology in a Postmodern Era." *Humanity and Society* 16(4): 441–60.
———. 1994. Personal correspondence, November 29.
Zavarzadeh, M. and D. Morton. 1990. "Signs of Knowledge in the Contemporary
  Academy." *American Journal of Semiotics* 7(4): 149–60.

CHAPTER 2

Challenges: For a Postmodern Criminology

T.R. Young

INTRODUCTION

In the past 40 years, a new set of ideas has emerged to describe the behavior of complex dynamical systems. It is called chaos theory.[1] There are several challenges which chaos theory offers, but perhaps the most important is the effort to reconceptualize both the forms and magnitudes of crime in terms of these new insights. That is the aim of this chapter. There are other corollary challenges, some of which I shall mention briefly in the last section.

The first and more general lesson chaos theory has to offer is that new forms of crime emerge as one of many economic or political adaptations people make in order to fit themselves within the larger, changing dynamical environment. The solution to crime in chaos theory becomes, thus, an effort to modulate those key parameters such that people have other ways to adapt themselves to the political and economic realities in which, perforce, they must live out their lives.

In this chapter, I will explicate a set of terms with which to grasp the basic ideas of chaos theory as they help enrich our understanding of the complexity of crime. With the tools of chaos data analysis just now being developed for non-linear social dynamics, we may well be able to sort out the changing sources of crime, distinguish between prosocial and anti-social innovations, offer guidelines for social policy and, thus, augment human agency to some limited extent. All these possibilities play off and against modernist approaches to criminology which promise quicker and more tidy answers to questions of crime and justice but which freeze such correlates into a theoretical model unalterable by time or social policy.

A BRIEF TUTORIAL

Chaos theory is a science which deals with the complex harmonies and disharmonies exhibited by natural and social systems. It involves the study of the changing ratio of order and disorder in an outcome field. Chaos theory focuses upon states with multiple periods or without predictable periodicity. Chaos research is designed to study the transitions between linear and non-linear states of such dynamical systems.[2]

The single most encompassing thing one might say about non-linear social dynamics in terms of social policy is that only chaos can cope with chaos. That means that certainty, predictability, sameness, and standardization do not always serve our interest in either equity or justice. But, more than that, only chaotic dynamics can give us those great leaps, jumps, twists, and turns in human activity that mark invention, evolution, mystery, and miracle. Indeed, the self-fulfilling process in the constitution of social reality requires faith, trust, and belief such that people together can make that transcendent leap between what is not yet real and what can be realized.[3] One is not to fear disorder in the heart of human institutions but rather to understand it and include it as the source of whatever progress in human affairs awaits the human project in the twenty-first century.

Basic Concepts of Chaos Theory

The first step in this journey to new understanding is an understanding of the new geometry of non-linear process and fractal structures revealed by this perspective: the attractor. There are three to five generic kinds of attractors, depending on how one counts; I use five since, for human purpose, the differences between the torus and the butterfly attractor are of great interest; more so than to mathematicians who count three. The five I use begin with the *point* and the *limit attractor*. I promptly set these first two attractors aside as irrelevant to actually existing dynamics. The *torus*, the *butterfly attractor*, and a fifth dynamical state, called here *deep chaos*, are the regions of non-linear dynamics in which human societies rise or fall; in which human beings live or die; in which peace and justice mix inextricably with crime and inequity.

Attractor: A region in phase-space to which the dynamics of a system tends to take it. If there is enough similarity from iteration to iteration in the dynamics of a system, we can speak of structure even if it is a very loose and fuzzy structure.

Figure 2.1
Four Well-Ordered Attractors

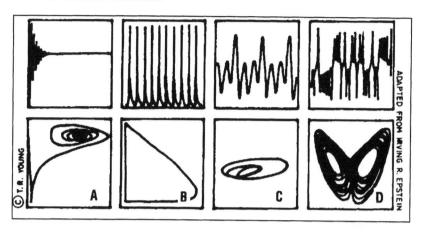

Strange Attractors

The first two attractors, point and limit attractors, are familiar; they fit the assumptions of modern science nicely. If we know the initial conditions, we can predict where a system will be at any given time in phase space. Simple systems are predictable; complex systems are not. This is very strange to the research of a modern scientist; they simply don't behave in the neat and tidy fashion that Bacon, Newton, Descartes, and Laplace assumed held true for all systems in nature and society. A strange attractor does not have neat edges, smooth surfaces, compact content, or clear boundaries between it and the next attractor. Indeed, some attractors are so open that one or more other attractors, entirely different, can occupy the same time-space dimensions. This will become important when we think of how to honor diversity in ethnic, racial, gender, and religious systems.

One can "see" two views of four of the five attractors in Figure 2.1. Beyond these, there is a region of deep chaos of which I will speak later. Social dynamics seldom produce the well-ordered structures found in the first two boxes of Figure 2.1. Indeed, much of criminal law is grounded on the futile attempt to force order into an inherently flexible, adaptable, changeable system. And, much to the dismay of those oriented to order and sameness, change and adaptability are requisite for all social life, for all living creatures that live in complex environments. A postmodern criminology must forge a legal philosophy which permits of variety, difference, change, and trans-rationality in both legal specifications and in legal practices.

The time-series in the first three boxes of Figure 2.1 are neat and or-

Figure 2.2
Progression of Attractors from Order to Disorder

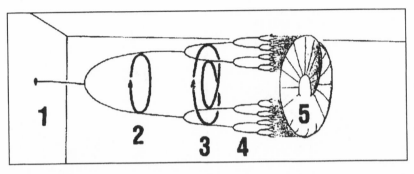

derly enough for us to see the patterns in them without great difficulty. Looking at the fourth attractor, Box D, we see that the time-series is so complex it is hard to imagine any kind of order in it; when we turn to analytic geometry, the picture resolves itself into a very definite shape. Looking at a chart of its ups and downs, ins and outs, turns and twists does not help much for us to see its overall behavior. These dynamics become even more jumbled up as we approach deep chaos.

The remarkable finding in chaos theory is that these dynamical states exhibit an elegant and well-ordered progression from certainty to uncertainty. Figure 2.2 offers a connected view of how these attractors fit together in a very orderly transformation from order to disorder. That progression is called a *bifurcation map* since, at each bifurcation, new outcome states emerge and uncertainty increases by orders of magnitude. Yet even in deep chaos there is order and thus possibility of useful social policy.

In Figure 2.2, one can see the point attractor in Region 1; the limit attractor in Region 2; the torus in Region 3; and the butterfly attractor in Region 4. Region 5 is the region in phase space in which dynamics are very chaotic. As one moves from Region 1 to Region 5, order decreases and disorder increases. Later on, we will find that, in deterministic chaos, there are very specific points at which these bifurcations occur to alter the ratio of order and disorder in any given dynamical regime. These bifurcation points are very important to the possibility of social policy in keeping or changing a given dynamical state.

Orders of Change

There are three orders of change found in a bifurcation map. The torus represents first-order change since the system always takes a similar but not precisely the same pathway in the same time-space. *Self-similarity* replaces sameness. The attractor in Box D embodies second-order change. It is called a butterfly attractor since there are two distinct "wings" or patterns it could make. In social dynamics, two very differing fates may await the child, the family, the business, the church, the school, *even when they begin in the same initial circumstances!* In non-linear dynamics, the same set of variables can produce two, four, eight, and far more outcome basins. Third-order change is found in the creative ferment of deep chaos.

Cascading Attractors

It is one of the most interesting features of this science of complexity that it is possible to have more than one pattern which describes the behavior of any system or set of systems. This does not seem to be paradigm-shaking until one realizes that, in normal science and given the same factors, there is one and only one "natural" or "normal" pattern to which a system is "attracted." What makes this new science complex is that there is a sequence (cascade) of the dynamical patterns a system with exactly the same set of parameters could take; that sequence takes us from very ordered social dynamics to very disordered dynamics. Think of it: instead of being able to predict the outcome or fate of a person, firm, group, or society by knowing in precise detail all the parameters that shape its behavior, there are three kinds of dynamics in which this is not possible. Prediction fades and fails at the edge of chaos.

The important thing for criminologists to think about is, thus, when and why do ordinary people move from one way of behaving to another way; that is to say, when and why do new attractors arise in a causal field with the same variables. Why do some people move from a peaceable style of behavior in dealing with people to another, more violent way. It turns out that, given a slight increase in a common ordinary parameter/variable, entirely new ways of behavior arise; some of which we may call crime.

If we can find these patterns, then we can experiment to see how and when small changes produce such bifurcations in human behavior since the size and shape of any strange attractor depend, sensitively, upon key parameters. And, although there are limits to human agency in such situations, still there are moments when very small adjustments might prevent or stimulate the kind of attractors which benefit individuals and societies alike. In this limited intrusion into the dynamics of strange attractors is the possibility of social intervention not possible in the fixed and certain worlds of modern science.

In the case of fish, bird, and insect populations, weather and competition for food are key parameters which shape and preshape attractors; which drive a population from one dynamical state to another, more complex state. In the case of the burglar, a wide variety of parameters merge to give rough and uncertain similarity to the behavior of our thief. The range of needs and desires for resources, the number of potential victims, the kinds of goods found inside a house, as well as policing patterns are key variables and take, themselves, the shape of a fuzzy attractor.

So, instead of one kind of behavior produced by a given set of variables, there may be up to five generic attractor states with which to describe the pattern of behavior of any complex system from a pendulum to a bird, a star, a person, or a whole society. The first two attractors in Figure 2.1 are not ordinarily observed in nature or society; they can be found if one controls all but one or two variables in a dynamical regime but in the doing, much of interest escapes human understanding. It is the last three attractors which are of great interest to criminology; indeed to every social scientist. We will cover these in more depth later but, right now, it is important to get a basic idea of each kind of attractor and tie it more closely with human behavior generally and crime in particular.

Challenges

For the criminologist, there are three most interesting research questions lurking in such structures; (1) how to find these attractors hidden in raw and very complex data; (2) how to identify the key parameters which produce those attractors; and (3) how to find the bifurcation points which alter the ratio between certainty and uncertainty. Given those nonlinear attractors, the parameters which produce them, and especially, the bifurcation points, we then have the beginnings of social policy informed by postmodern science.

A subsidiary interest for the criminologist involves the ways in which contrary behaviors occupy the same regions of phase space. It turns out that more than one attractor can occupy the same regions in time-space. In complex systems, as in specific human beings, prosocial behavior may be found in every region in which anti-social behavior is observed; anti-social behavior in every region in which prosocial behavior is observed. It is the changing mix of such behaviors within and between attractors toward which this new science points us. It does not serve to "throw people in prison and throw away the key." It better serves to alter the ratio between the uncertainties and necessities of life such as to forestall behaviors we care not to experience in our daily lives.

Finally, chaos and complexity are sciences of the whole. While the individual person is always responsible for his or her anti-social behavior, still there are non-linear macro-structures in complex societies for which s/he is not responsible; to which s/he must perforce adapt. It is these whole-system variables which must be found and must be altered if we want a more peaceable society. The challenge is how to provide for autonomy, change, flexibility, creativity and, in the same moment, prosocial behavior. Again, these new sciences offer the postmodern criminologist the beginnings of a solution in the forms of non-linear feedback we make to social problems. In a word, linear feedback tends to drive a system to deep chaos; non-linear feedback tends to maintain a delicate ultra-stability in which both order and variety are found.

Non-linear Social Dynamics

When one leaves the well-ordered realm of point and limit attractors, one enters into the surprising world of non-linear transformations; leaps, twists, reverses, turns, and knots which cannot be followed by rational numbering systems or by formal logic. We approach the edge of this strangely ordered world of non-linearity when we follow the dynamics of simple systems. The first such attractor is a torus. The torus becomes of more interest to the criminologist since, on the one hand, causality becomes fuzzy and uncertainty sets in as partner to predictability. Measures of correlation which require and look for a tight connection between cause and effect lose epistemological utility in sorting out the dynamics of crime, reward, and punishment.

Attractor, Torus: An attractor created by the dynamics of a simple system driven by two variables and exhibiting one and only one degree of uncertainty.

Figure 2.3 gives a better view of the torus itself. It is shaped a bit like a doughnut. A non-linear system such as the torus is driven by two interacting key parameters (defined here by angles $\bar{\theta}_1$ and $\bar{\theta}_2$) which interact and feed back to drive the system in a loose and limited pattern. One cannot say just where the system will be found at any given time; all one can say is that it will be somewhere on a pathway produced by two variable and interacting parameters. Such systems thus can be found anywhere on or in the cylinder of the torus but cannot be found far outside the region occupied by the torus.

In the case of medical malpractice, the two interacting variables might be (1) some uncertainties in income and expenditures and (2) changes in opportunities for generating additional funds by the physician which are limited by time and specialty. Figure 2.4 shows fluctuating behavior with three distinct periods in the complete cycle. In the case at hand, such an attractor might arise if a doctor were to have a seasonal ebb and flow of cases. Cases of unnecessary operations, of fraudulent billing of insurance carriers, or of hasty and poor diagnoses may arise when these two sets of variables interact in non-linear ways. For example, in winter, opera-

Figure 2.3
A Torus

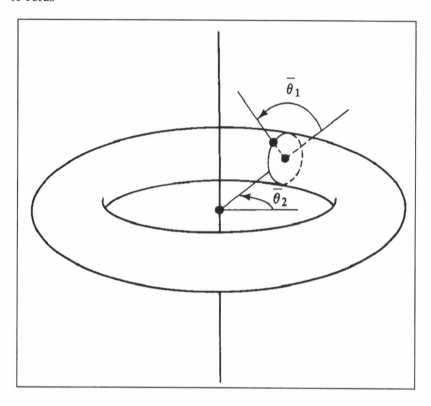

tions might be few since weather and holidays converge to divert doctors, staff, and patients; in early spring, when doctors buy new cars, when income taxes for self-employed professionals have to be paid, when one must buy an IRA and other self-managed tax-exempt annuities before April 15, such operations might increase. In summer, real estate purchases, vacations, and social rounds require extra funds and may drive another round of criminal malpractice. In the fall, when children are off to expensive colleges and universities, demands on income increase; revenue has to be generated from a patient population.

The same shift in ratio between income and expenses can arise from fall in income as well as increase in expenditures. Divorce, stock market crises, and accidents occur to alter the ratio between income and outgo. These attractors/patterns/rhythms might well be hidden in the more complex data of medical practice and, in the searching of such data with statistical tools which assume linearity, might escape attention, since the connections between income and expenditure are so loose that standard

Figure 2.4
Uncertain Pathways in Phase Space

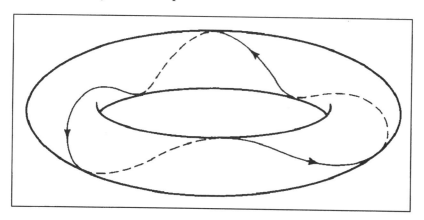

techniques push them aside as "not significant." Using new techniques for finding such attractors in data sets, we might find a torus which tells us that, far from being insignificant, there is a non-linear but underlying structured pattern which could be modulated.

The torus thus can be used as a research tool for any number of simple forms of crime. However, the torus is of limited value for most forms of crime, since they take place in a very complex social matrix. In order to understand the number, geometry, and transformations of most forms of street crime, white-collar crime, corporate crime, and political crime, we need to move closer to the edge of chaos and notice that the same set of variables can produce two or more outcome *basins*.

Basin: The region(s) in a larger field of outcomes toward which a set of initial conditions patterns, i.e. "causes," a system or set of similar systems to move.

Imagine a saucer inside which spins a marble. The actual path of the marble is the attractor; the whole saucer is the outcome field in which the attractor is confined. Yet the marble could go anywhere inside the saucer as long as it is moving. If the path is a non-linear function of two key parameters, say, gravity and friction, the marble never takes quite the same path twice. Gravity may act linearly but tiny variations in the surface produce uncertainty in predicting the future state of the marble.

Depending upon scale of observation, much or little space is visited by the marble but never does the marble visit each and every point on the surface of the saucer; therefore, that area can be considered a *fractal* causal basin; the marble visits only a fraction of the space available to it in the saucer. Even if we could keep the marble spinning forever, there would still be points on the surface of the saucer not visited . . . the un-visited regions would get smaller and smaller as a portion of the total space inside the saucer but never completely disappear.

This fractal character of an outcome basin is most trenchant to a theory of truth. In modern science, truth statements are valid if and only if they are absolutely true. In this new science of complexity, truth statements themselves become fractal since the field upon which truth claims depend is fractal. In modern science, one seeks a "strong" correlation upon which to ground social policy on, say, low-level radiation, on cigarette smoking, on toxins in food and water supply, on television and preteen violence, or any number of factors which are said to do harm to body and spirit. In such a science, the very notion of crime is changed from an absolutistic concept to a more nuanced one with infinite shades of grey. Verdicts of guilty and not guilty are far too binary and mutually exclusive to capture the complexity of crime in this postmodern criminology which is aborning.

Complex Causal Basins

The butterfly attractor exhibits not only non-linear dynamics but, rather than one and only one outcome, we find two outcome basins resulting from the same initial settings. This binary outcome basin is strange indeed in terms of modern philosophy of science in which all similarly situated cases end up in one and only one region of an outcome basin. In chaotic regimes, the same variables can produce two very dissimilar patterns of behavior. More about this later; right now, let us look at the structure of this attractor.

Attractor, Butterfly: A butterfly attractor has two outcome basins in which a system might be found. The butterfly attractor can be thought of as two connected tori; at a given setting of a key parameter, an individual system could wind up in either wing (torus) of the butterfly.

The butterfly attractor in Figure 2.5 is most interesting to the criminologist, indeed to every behavioral scientist, for a very practical reason. The implications for social policy are profound; for example, rather than reducing criminal behavior, chaos theory suggests there may be a point at which punishment increases crime rates. Moreover, for the first time in the philosophy of science, we see empirical grounds for a theory of normal/deviant behavior which accepts that there are two outcome basins in the larger outcome field which are equally natural to the behavior of a system in a given environment. I will pick up on the plurality of quite ordinary variations within a given causal complex in a postmodern theory of deviancy in another discussion, but for now, let us focus on

Figure 2.5
Twinned but Different Outcome Basins

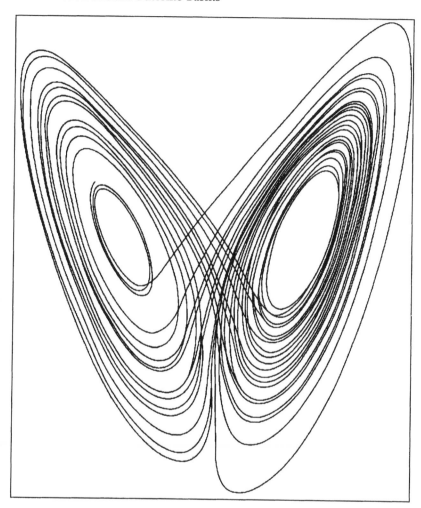

the meaning of the bifurcation (forking) of an attractor for the genesis of criminal behavior itself.

If we draw a Cartesian map in which prosocial behavior is charted on the left wing of the butterfly while behavior on the right wing is anti-social, then, in logging of the unit acts of a given individual over time we can see that the same individual, with the same socialization and with the same set of circumstances, may fluctuate between very helpful behavior and very harmful behavior. The point of most uncertainty occurs just at the juncture between the two wings; in terms of our interest in criminology, at such points it is uncertain whether a person exhibits criminal or more prosocial behavior. At that point is room for a whole theory of human agency.[4] I have given preliminary thought to such a theory in another place but for criminology and for the social control of crime, it is of great importance to understand the dynamics by which a torus depicting prosocial behavior is transformed into a butterfly attractor; one in which there is both pro- as well as anti-social behavior.

The butterfly attractor brings two outcome basins to an outcome field. Given a small increase in a critical variable, a set of persons, businesses, churches, or sets of societies might take a qualitatively different pathway in response to the same set of initial conditions. I have mentioned some of the more arresting implications of this twinned but different outcome field for philosophy of science. For criminology it means that more of the same can force completely different ways of behaving. A slight increase in taxation can make corporate officers consider criminal actions that would be unthinkable in a "more favorable" investment climate. A slight increase in unemployment may produce a huge increase in the frequency of battering by spouses. A slight change, in short, increases the ratio between order and disorder in the whole outcome field. A person, corporation, or social group can no longer be depended upon to act in habitual ways.

The geometric ratio between a wing depicting anti-social behavior on the one side and prosocial behavior on the other can vary. It varies by virtue of the objective circumstances of the person, the firm, the group, or the nation in the larger social order. Thus, the science of complexity is a science of the whole rather than of the parts. One cannot sort out the origins of most criminal behavior by focusing upon genetics, psychology, or body chemistry. And if people are mad when they kill spouses, presidents, or popes, the prior question is why this madness resides in this attractor rather than in more harmless basins.

Robin Hood banditry offers this kind of bifurcated dynamics. The same individual(s) acts kindly and offers support for some persons while cheating, stealing, and robbing others. Thus, a kidnapping in Italy may redistribute wealth from wealthy landlords in Rome to poor villagers in Sicily. A prostitute may be cheating clients, dealing in drugs, or shoplifting during the day while supporting his/her children and other kin at other times. A pharmaceutical firm may add to the infant mortality rate in Puerto Rico by its polluting practices yet may dramatically lower the death rate for cancer patients in Oklahoma by importing drugs at a cost low enough to satisfy stock investors. The geometry of good and evil is not simple in the postmodern paradigm informed by chaos theory.

Chaos theory would lead us to expect to find that, at quite specific points, defined by the Feigenbaum values discussed below, persons and groups may make a qualitative transformation from prosocial behavior at time one to both prosocial and anti-social behavior in the same time-space continuum at time two. For banditry, the feudal system might produce deference and subservience at one setting in the transfer of wealth from serf to master but, with a small increase in such transfer, evoke resistance and rebellion; two quite different behaviors in the same causal matrix modeled by the non-linear transformation between one outcome basin of the butterfly attractor and the other basin.

The appearance of new outcome basins in an outcome field is explored, in the science of complexity, by bifurcation theory. Why and when do these slight changes trigger large transformations. The when is well-known; the Feigenbaum points discussed below identify the onset of bifurcation(s). The "why" is known in mathematics and in thermo-dynamics; it is not known in social phenomena. In that profound ignorance is the challenge of the next generation of criminologists in particular and all behavioral scientists in general.

Bifurcation Theory

The concept of bifurcation is most important to the criminologist in that it sensitizes one to expect the emergence of alternative ways to do business, family, religion, or perchance, crime. You have seen the bifurcation map in Figure 2.2 and appreciate that there is a variable number of such basins/attractors, depending on how many bifurcations have occurred. This is where the criminology informed by chaos theory departs most dramatically from that informed by the Newtonian paradigm. In non-linear dynamics, it is possible that the same variables involving the same systems produce two or more very different outcome basins with no change in the physical, chemical, or biological character of the systems concerned. There will be considerable psychological and socio-logical change for living forms, of course, but these are adjustments to the changes in the larger, bifurcating dynamics of key variables in the environment of the living system. Bifurcation points are most important to any effort to build social theory or any effort to set social policy.

Bifurcation: A doubling in the pattern of behavior of a system. With each doubling, there is distinct change from one behavioral regime to new pattern(s) for all systems. Small changes in one or more key parameters produce that doubling. After the third bifurcation in key parameter(s), the system tends to move in ways which fill the space available to it in an outcome basin. This latter state is a far-from-stable chaotic state.

Butterfly attractors may be considered as two linked tori. Each wing of a butterfly attractor may bifurcate and thus produce 2n, 4n, 8n or even more complex non-linear social dynamics. Indeed, it is rare when a so-

Figure 2.6
Anatomy of a Torus

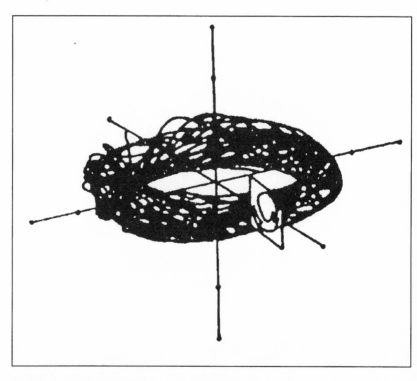

ciety offers only two or four meanings of a word, only two or four divisions of labor, only two or four ways of doing gender. Social life is far
more complex than either language or philosophy permit. Let us now
look at the process by which outcome basins proliferate and expand both
the outcome field and increase complexity of social life.

The Birth of Complexity

In order to see the beginning of a butterfly attractor just before a bifurcation of a torus, we will take a cross-section of the torus in Figure
2.6. This cross-section shows a two-dimensional portrait of the points
through which a physical or social system travels on its non-linear pathway. If we take the cross-section at just the right time, we can catch the
birth of complexity. A second, entirely different region of phase space
begins to open up and, in the case of social forms, offers an entirely new
way to do gender, marriage, politics, business, or in this case, crime.

In Figure 2.7, one can see more closely that tongue which marks the
advent of a new outcome basin. That tongue may or may not grow to

Figure 2.7
Poincaré Section of a Torus

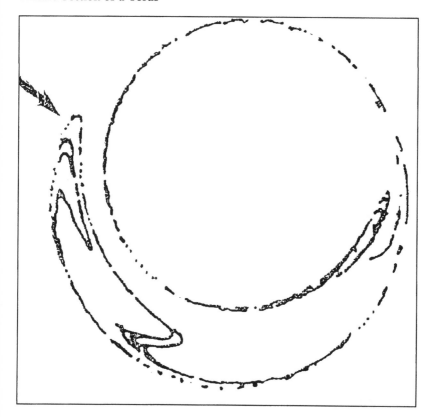

create new regions in an outcome field; however, some key parameter is near a critical change point; a bit more food, a bit more heat, a bit more competition, a slight increase in taxation, a slight change in the frequency of police brutality or in the ratio of class inequality may trigger an entirely new behavioral field for an insect population, for a water crystal, for a whole industry, for racial violence, or for organized rebellion in a Third World country.

Feigenbaum Points

Identification of the points at which murder, theft, malpractice, embezzlement, or warfare emerge offer some of the greatest challenges to postmodern criminologists.[5] The particular content of the behavior found in those new fields is explained by larger social and cultural factors. The new attractors may be shaped by religious compassion; they may be influenced by the ugliest ethnic loyalties; they may arise out of the sheer genius of an author, poet, politician, or labor leader. In a word, new behaviors may be prosocial and work to the common good or may be narrowly limited to private gain and survival. Chaos theory does not instruct us about the nature of the field except to say that, here, at the edge of chaos, resides the possibility for human agency. For weal or for woe, there are, in the options awaiting, some options amenable to human understanding and action.

Deep Chaos

It is a curiosity of chaos theory that even in deep chaos with such progressive, non-linear increases in uncertainty, there is so much order and, with order, science is still possible; prediction of a sort is possible, truth statements become fractally valid, and for human purpose, some small control and planning are still possible.

The criminologist would do well to conceptualize theft, prostitution, conversion of property, price-fixing, genocide, or fee-splitting as outcome basins to which people and firms move as a consequence of small changes in external variables; constraints and opportunities interacting, perhaps, with internalized needs or desires.[6] Given such a view, the multitude of parallel economic activities, some of which are prosocial, some anti-social, can be seen to be adjustments people, firms, and societies make to small changes in the larger whole in which they are found. Given such a view, recourse to violence, self-destructive behavior, or hate crimes can be seen to be adjustments permitted/obstructed by the larger structures in which a person or a group find themselves. Thus, one need not have a theory of crime per se, in order to understand why new but anti-human behavioral patterns arise; one needs a theory of the interactions between needs, wants, goals, and cultural imperatives on the one side, and constraints on the number and accessibility to given basins on the other side. A theory of crime is thus also a theory of alternatives in a changing mix of order and disorder. In such a view, crime and its dynamics are relocated from the separate person to changes in constraints within the larger environment.

Genes, drives, physiology, and psychology of the acting individual are essential to all behavior. Labeling and societal reaction are essential to all human behavior. Differential association is essential to all behavior; both social and harmful. Controls are essential to all behavior from talking to warfare. Habit, addiction, passion, and desire are common to all forms of human behavior. When we speak of crime, we speak of patterned behavior. When we speak of patterned behavior, we speak of the parameters which limit and facilitate that behavior. Those parameters are the proper concern of postmodern criminology and, indeed, all behavioral science. The interesting question becomes, what are the points on those key parameters beyond which anger, violence, oppression, and exploitation are directed at innocent others? For social policy, the complementary question becomes, what are the settings of key parameters which maximize prosocial behavior and minimize behavior hurtful to others in a socio-cultural complex?

Whatever constancy and predictability obtain within a causal field is found in a changing range of causal basins produced by those non-linear transformations; not in any unchanging connectedness between dependent and independent variables, as presumed in modern science. Thus, poverty could produce sharing and helping at one setting of another variable and, with a slightly differing setting, degenerate into theft and violence. Causality opens, closes, and transforms in this paradigm. Contradictory findings; inconsistent findings and changing correlations are commonplace as bifurcations ensue. The relationship between variables changes as one samples different regions in an outcome field. In some basins, causality is fairly tight and positive; in other basins, it is fairly tight and negative; in the regions between basins of a butterfly attractor certainty yields to surprise, creativity, and wonderment.

Control Theory: Each attractor has its own characteristic set of complex cycles. This is called a *dynamical key*. If one can identify that key and match it with countervailing input, then it is possible to affect the behavior of the system (Hübler, 1992:18). In theory, chaos is manageable.

Far from being unmanageable, chaos is in fact manageable (Hübler, 1992). Hübler says that, in the management of chaos, the more unstable the causal field, the gentler must be the touch in trying to control the dynamics of the phenomena in question. Heavy-handed control tactics might work with point, limit, and in torus attractors; such tactics might work even in regions of a butterfly basin but, for causal fields with four, eight, or sixteen attractors, control efforts lose efficacy.

In criminology, if we are able to identify the key parameters which drive a system and match the complex cycles of those parameters with unwanted non-linear response, it is possible to maintain an uncertain stability, even in deep chaos. More feasible for postmodern criminology is the insight that perhaps social justice is preferable to criminal justice. It may well be the case that small change in cultural and economic parameters can increase or decrease theft or violence. It may be the case that building of great prisons and introduction of ever more efficient policing technology only add to the population of those engaged in criminal behavior. It is far better to prevent rape, burglary, theft, murder, pollution, embezzlement, or warfare than to watch everyone ever more closely or to put ever larger segments of the population in prison. The research capacity needed to provide information about such dynamical keys is a matter of national and international importance and should take priority over super-colliders, nuclear weaponry, arms production, or military ventures in the Third World.

Feedback: When a system acts in such a way to affect other systems in a causal field, and when those systems, in turn, affect the behavior of the first system, a feedback process occurs. There are three kinds of feedback of considerable interest to behavioral science and criminology; positive feedback, negative feedback, and non-linear feedback.

The kind of feedback between the system and its environment has great import for a postmodern criminology. Linear feedback tends to result in either death or deep chaos. Negative feedback produces death; positive feedback produces great disorder. It is a curious feature of chaos theory that non-linear feedback produces stability. This last form of feedback has most interesting meaning for both the management of chaos and for social policy of any society that wants to maintain enough disorder to permit adjustment to a disorderly environment and enough order to permit prediction and control.

For the criminologist as for the public, the most interesting challenge one can take up in aid of domestic tranquility is, what kind of feedback is effective in creating a low crime society? In brief, non-linear feedback is preferable to either positive or negative linear feedback. In brief, social justice is preferable to criminal justice since social justice is based upon such non-linear social processes such as mercy, compassion, forgiveness, and transformation, while criminal justice, as it has developed, is based upon certainty, sameness, routine, or rational application of either pain or pleasure. Criminal justice focuses upon the single, acting person; social justice focuses upon the conditions of life in the whole society.

Compiling Stress

Every non-linear attractor has a fractal value. Attractors with low values occupy but a portion of the space available to them; those with high values occupy all the space available to them. A point attractor has a higher fractal value than a limit attractor, even though a limit attractor occupies a larger volume of space, since the limit attractor uses a smaller portion of what space it does occupy. The higher the fractal value of an attractor, the less uncertainty, the more predictability, and the greater the possibility of control.[7] If one looks at the portion of space available in an outcome field with four or more attractors, there are many places where one could find a given system at a given moment and few regions where one actually finds that system. The problem of prediction arises due to the fact that one cannot be sure just where, within that region bounded by the geometry of the complex fractal, that system will be found. With each additional bifurcation, uncertainty increases for the persons concerned. Uncertainties on the job may join with uncertainties in family dynamics, uncertainties in school, or in health. Stress may compile such that entirely new forms of behavior may emerge for some unknowable number of those affected.

For example, in terms of domestic violence there might not be much domestic violence at low levels of unemployment, in which case perhaps psychological variables would be most helpful in sorting out as between those who do beat a spouse or a child and those who do not. At higher levels of unemployment, domestic violence might well explode; the possibility of predicting who will be violent and who not fades and fails.

The sources of stress are many. Problems of life become stressful in that there is greater uncertainty in how to deal with budget problems, health problems, marriage problems, or problems at work. It is not the number of problems that produce stress but the uncertainty about how to deal with them. A criminologist might do well to consider the ways in which uncertainty-cum-stress contributes to crime. In the life space of a firm or a person, uncertainty in one key parameter might not push one into criminal activity; a person might be able to manage two interacting uncertainties but, if a third uncertainty occurs, a person or a firm may opt to move to a more certain line of activity; some of which may be criminal. In general, if there are solutions, then problems are manageable and thus routine.[8] The operative point here is that, if we want to keep crime stable and thus controllable, we must consider policy for the kinds of uncertainties with which students, spouses, doctors, brokers, prostitutes, and priests must deal.

Ultra-stable Structures

One of the more puzzling, challenging, and promising findings in chaos research is that of the soliton. It has profound implications for the only kind of ultra-stability in complex dynamical regimes. Briggs and Peat (1989) have a very accessible discussion of the soliton from which the following definition comes.

Soliton: A soliton is a fractal which is able to keep its form through non-linear feedback with other fractal structures through which it passes. Briggs and Peat use the example of a wave which is able to keep its form over thousands of miles of ocean.

In human affairs, the ability of the Amish to survive in Pennsylvania and the ability of a small shopkeeper to survive near a Wal-Mart, K-

Mart, Target, or other discount stores serve as everyday examples. In similar fashion, two very different economic systems are able to coexist in the same ecosystem provided that the feedback loops between them are non-linear.

There are many implications of this concept to criminology. In the first instance, economic, religious, or political integrity is possible for indigenous cultures if there are non-linear (i.e., irrational) feedback loops between the religious, economic, and political institutions of colonial masters. This means that there have to be different and incompatible legal systems coexisting side-by-side if the cultural richness of ethnic groups is to be retained by a society. We see these forms of self-contained legal systems in American Indian enclaves; in professional peer group processes; in the differing administrative policies of large corporations as well as in schools and universities. The integrity of social solitons can be sustained through and only through a larger irrationality in which rationality itself is contained and limited to the internal operations of the social soliton.

The rational, rigorous application of legal norms set in Europe to Native American marriage forms, water rights, child-rearing practices, or communal pastures destroys the integrity of the indigenous culture. More than that, it may well destroy a system well adapted to the climate and soil conditions at hand. And, to be sure, it destroys cultural variety in a region. On the other hand, when most of the incompatible religious, familial, political, or economic activities of an indigenous peoples are routinely excepted from law and enforcement, differentiation without integration or stratification can occur.

The concept of the soliton, when applied to the different patterns of unit acts of a doctor or a priest or a policeman, can be useful in sorting out the "criminality" of such persons. Some police officers will take small bribes to overlook some small crimes, but will not take bribes to overlook *some* crimes large or small. With non-linear feedback, small-time graft can continue for years inside a police department without compromising its overall functioning. Too close a policing of such graft amplifies the problem in many ways, largely by sending it underground and thus allowing it to be unconstrained. If one conceives of the set of unit acts oriented to bribery as a soliton, one can see that such a "structure" can coexist in the totality of unit acts of the same police officer which serve the law as writ excellently well.

The soliton gives lie to the domino theory: there are no mechanical connections; more precisely, there need be no mechanical connection between one kind of crime and another kind. There is no necessary progression from one kind of drug use to another. There is no necessary progression from low-level police brutality to the formation of a neo-Nazi police state. Conservatives and liberals who use mechanical cau-

ality to predict outcomes will find themselves sorely tested by the
olitons found in the data of criminality.

FUTURE CHALLENGES

The concepts above are available as tools with which to grasp the great
complexity of social life in its more helpful as well as its more harmful
embodiments. These concepts join together to form a set of ideas, less
than theorems but more than poetry, with which to ground a postmodern social science in general and a postmodern criminology in particular.
There are more challenges which await the criminologist who works
within the logics of chaos theory.

There is, as well, its promise for a much-improved knowledge process.
The effort it takes to learn and to use the concepts and ideas which have
been revolutionary in the physical, the natural and, to a lesser extent in
psychology and economics, is well worth the time. And it is simply a
matter of time until chaos theory works its way through to unite and
inform the knowledge process for the twenty-first century.

Among those I have not mentioned here are ideas which help ground
a constitutive theory of justice. Then too, chaos theory, with its manifold
attractor basins, forever changes our ideas about deviancy. There well
may be grounds for claims of necessary repression; however, chaos theory and complex social dynamics set aside claims of one and only one
way to do gender, marriage, family, schooling, or art. So much of our
social philosophies now built upon modernist, linear models of nature
and society will perforce be replaced by a much more open, much more
nuanced, and much more complex philosophy of science and philosophies of life.

The whole structure of social control and its attendant psychologies of
stimulus and response, of operant conditioning, of learning theory, and
of pain and pleasure are modified greatly by chaos theory and the non-
linear dynamics from which it comes. If causality fades and fails with
each successive bifurcation, then efforts at linearity in social control, efforts to apply neat and tidy regimes of reward and punishment also fade
and fail. As social dynamics become ever more non-linear and complex,
then non-linearity itself becomes the point of departure for a theory of
social control. In brief, one must turn to the sort of non-linear feedback
mentioned above.

Part of that knowledge process will depend upon a new mathematics
I have not yet mentioned. It is very different from the linear, rational
mathematics of Newton and Einstein but yet elegant enough in its own
way. John Briggs and F. David Peat have a most engaging and accessible
treatment of that math in their *Turbulent Mirror: An Illustrated Guide to
Chaos Theory and the Science of Wholeness*. Indeed, their treatment of many

of the concepts presented here is a fine place to begin to flesh out the content of chaos theory.

That math can give one a very close approximation of the fractal geometry of the structures of crime in a society. It can predict with pinpoint accuracy when one of the three great transformations in system dynamics will happen. It can find the hidden attractors buried deep in a data set which looks random and unpatterned. It can separate noise from order and it can help us gently and inexpensively design social policy that is more amenable to human dignity and human agency than is now the case. And that is the lesson which chaos theory offers criminology; the best solution to crime is not a bigger and better criminal justice system but rather a good and gentle society in which the ratio of order to disorder serves the human need for constancy on the one side and creative response to new conditions on the other. We are now challenged to abandon the quest for order and certainty in order to move to a more stable but variegated social life world.

NOTES

1. Application of chaos theory to complex social dynamics is centered, at present, in the Santa Fe Institute.

2. The word comes from the Latin, *chaos*, meaning abyss; from which our word *chasm* also comes. In mythology, chaos was the original state of the cosmos before the gods gave it shape and form.

3. *Warning*: In most of the literature on chaos theory, authors presume what is called *deterministic chaos*. Deterministic chaos emerges from very specific algorithms. Human behavior, on the other hand, emerges from socially conventional algorithms. They are not at all deterministic in the technical sense presumed by mathematicians, physicists, and chemists. One should note and beware of the danger of presuming deterministic chaos in most social dynamics. Indeed, much of what is set forth here well may be adjusted when better research findings are available.

4. What is necessary (and not found in the logics of "superb" theories of modern science) for human choice is a situation with uncertainty in local regions and certainty in macro-structures. The local uncertainty permits latitude while the larger certainty permits planning and achievement of plan. This combination is found for the first time in the first-order change observed in the torus. We have a look at second-order change in the butterfly attractor. First-order change permits creativity within a universe of behavior; second-order change permits qualitative change from one universe of behavior to another.

5. It is important to note that complex systems often absorb even large changes. It is at the bifurcation points, often called Feigenbaum points after Mitchell Feigenbaum (1978), who first identified them.

6. I want to stress that part of the non-linear dynamics in the constitutive criminology used here views those internalized needs and desires as themselves created through socialization and, later, advertising. Most of the "needs" which

drive street crime, white-collar crime, corporate crime, and political crime are themselves the product of intensive symbolic interaction. Survival needs are more than adequately met for most people in the United States; it is the layers of desires fostered by advertising in all its forms which create the high crime rates in affluent societies.

7. See Nicolis and Prigogine (1989: 113) for a discussion of the fractal.

8. In the philosophy of science, if a solution exists for an exigency, then one has a problem; if no solution exists, then one has an issue . . . the issue of which, among alternate ways to handle an exigency, one should chose. As you might guess, in chaos theory, that question is made more complex by the changing efficacy of given solutions.

REFERENCES

Ashby, H.R. 1968. "Variety, Constraint, and the Law of Requisite Variety." Pp. 135–47 in W. Buckley, ed., *Modern Systems Research for the Behavioral Scientist.* Chicago: Aldine.

Barnsley, M. 1988. *Fractals Everywhere.* San Diego: Academic Press.

Briggs, J. and F.D. Peat. 1989. *Turbulent Mirror: An Illustrated Guide to Chaos Theory and the Science of Wholeness.* New York: Harper and Row.

Feigenbaum, M. 1978. "Quantitative Universality for a Class of Nonlinear Transformations." *Journal of Statistical Physics* 19: 25–52. Cited in Gleick, p. 157.

Glass, L. and M. Mackey. 1988. *From Clocks to Chaos.* Princeton, NJ: Princeton University Press.

Gleick, J. 1987. *Chaos: Making a New Science.* New York: Penguin Books.

Holden, A. 1986. *Chaos.* Princeton, NJ: Princeton University Press.

Hübler, A. 1992. "Modeling and Control of Complex Systems: Paradigms and Applications." In L. Lam, ed., *Modeling Complex Phenomena.* New York: Springer.

Mandelbrot, B. 1977 (rev. 1983). *The Fractal Geometry of Nature.* New York: Freeman.

Nicolis, G. and I. Prigogine. 1989. *Exploring Complexity.* New York: Freeman and Company.

Penrose, R. 1989. *The Emperor's New Mind.* Oxford: Oxford University Press.

Pepinsky, H. 1988. "Societal Rhythms in the Chaos of Violence." Paper presented at the Meetings of the American Society of Criminology, Chicago.

Prigogine, I. and I. Stengers. 1984. *Order out of Chaos: Man's New Dialogue with Nature.* New York: Bantam Books.

Young, T.R. 1991a. "Chaos Theory and Symbolic Interaction: Nonlinear Social Dynamics." *Symbolic Interaction* 14(3).

———. 1991b. "Change and Chaos Theory: Metaphysics of the Postmodern." *Social Science Journal* 28(3): 59–82.

———. 1991c. "Part I. Crime and Chaos." In *The Critical Criminologist* 3(2): 3–4, 13–14.

———. 1992. "Chaos Theory and Human Agency." *Humanity and Society* 16(4): 441–60.

PART II

Chaos, Criminology, and Law: Critical Applications

CHAPTER 3

Chaos and Modeling Crime: Quinney's *Class, State and Crime*

Allison Forker

INTRODUCTION

The theory of chaos introduces implications which result in a fundamental shift of how we understand and respond to the natural and social worlds. We will explore the restrictions placed on the construction of reality under modernist thought and science, within the postmodernist framework. The basic terminology and concepts of chaos theory as a "hard science" will be discussed. I will demonstrate how the science of chaos can be applied to the social sciences. This will be accomplished by visually applying chaos theory to Richard Quinney's theory of "crime in the development of capitalism" (1980). With the utilization of chaos theory in the social sciences we will witness the transformation of the criminal justice system to a system built on social justice.

What is reality? Anything which can be touched, witnessed, or perceived by the human physical senses as true? Or could there be more to it than that? Is there an essence to reality that this definition has ignored? Could reality consist of multiple dimensions which fold and wrap around each other in such a way that perception of these dimensions becomes undetectable to the human senses? The reality chaos theory uncovers certainly allows for such possibilities to exist. However, the door to this reality has been locked and barricaded by modernist thought and the limits it places on the construction of reality. To unlock the barriers which have enshrouded these mysterious notions, we are required to adopt a framework of thought that will allow such chaotic realities to exist. The key is postmodernist thought.

Postmodernist thinking encourages a shift to be made away from traditional quantitative science. The focus is on the qualitative nature of the subject being studied. Realized is the inadequacy of studying the individual unit in order to gain an understanding of the whole. The focus is on examining systems in terms of their correspondence across micro and macro scales. It is no wonder chaos has found a niche within the postmodernist framework. Our notions of reality are constructed based on scientific understanding of the world. Chaos theory has put into question firmly held scientific "facts." If traditional science has been unsuccessful in revealing truth, our whole notion of reality is shattered. The implications are indeed extensive for how this assertion will frame our understanding of the natural world and our social relations.

THE SCIENCE OF CHAOS, A GUIDE TO UNCERTAINTY

Before we completely dive into the realm of exploring chaos, it is important to grasp certain traits which chaotic structures exhibit. The unit of study within chaos is the system. In order for a system to be capable of exhibiting chaotic behavior, the system must be iterative (Smith, 1995: 22). This simply means that the system has the ability to refer back to itself. Self-similarity is also a characteristic the chaotic system displays. In self-similarity, a small portion of the system is representative of the whole. In other words, the system is repeated at descending scales (Wegner and Tyler, 1993: 18; Series, 1992: 147). Mandelbrot related these characteristics of chaotic behavior to a form of geometry which is far more representative of nature than traditional Euclidean geometry (Hayles, 1990: 164; Wegner and Tyler, 1993:16). Fractal geometry measures the degree of complexity of an object. The measurement of a subject is dependent on the initial unit of measure utilized. As the unit of measure decreases in size, the object or space being measured increases. Fractal geometry unleashes fractal dimensions and fractals, which display a pattern of self-similarity at descending scales (Wegner and Tyler, 1993: 16; Series, 1992: 139). The outcome state of the system is dependent then on the systems' initial conditions (the numbers iterated into the equation).

With these tidbits of information in mind, here we go; we are about to enter the turbulent world of chaos. As mentioned before, chaos examines units called systems. A characteristic of a system is that it is open, meaning forces outside the system have an effect on the system's functioning. Each system contains a number of values that can be modified, referred to as parameters (Stewart, 1992: 56). Variables taken into account constitute the system's initial conditions. The system is extremely sensitive to the slightest change in these initial conditions. The most infinitesimal input and iteration can lead to a disproportionate outcome, culminating in potential chaos.

Phase Space Maps

A system's complexity and movement can be observed on what is known as a phase space map. Phase space maps have the unique ability to expose the peculiar existence of otherwise hidden complexities of the system's movement (Briggs and Peat, 1989: 32). The ability to achieve this is made possible by phase space consisting of as many variables or dimensions (fractal dimensions) as are needed to portray the system's movement. Representing the system's history of movement through phase space is the trajectory of the system, a line. An orbit, or trajectory, is a map of the system's behavior over cycles. The shapes that appear on a phase space map reveal how the system has changed over time (Hayles, 1990: 148). A system does not usually explore the entire phase space; instead it is drawn to magnetic regions known as attractors (Briggs and Peat, 1989: 36; Hayles, 1990: 147; Stewart, 1992: 46).

Attractors

The attractor can be either a point, limit, torus, or strange. The attractor to which a system is drawn is dependent largely on changes in the system's key parameters and degrees of freedom a system contains (Briggs and Peat, 1989: 33–37). The degree of freedom is simply the number of ways a system has the ability to move. A point attractor is a system that is moving toward a particular point. The movement of a pendulum can help us visualize this attractor (Briggs and Peat, 1989; Hayles, 1990). A pendulum with only one degree of freedom is limited in its range of motion. It can swing in only one direction, back and forth. The system's movement is mapped by recording the pendulum's movement in terms of speed and position at a given time. The movement of the pendulum, left on its own, will eventually arrive at a final resting point where all motion has ended. On a phase space map this can be represented by a spiral that will eventually reach a point.

However, if a mechanical motor is used to drive the motion of the pendulum the attractor type changes. We now have a limit cycle attractor. This system contains one degree of freedom, as does the pendulum in the point attractor (Briggs and Peat, 1989: 34). We are still mapping the movement of the pendulum in terms of velocity and position at a given time; however, when driven by a motor the pendulum will consistently return to an initial position with each oscillation. This system is represented by a cyclical path in phase space. This system occurs within well-defined boundaries in which restraint of variations per orbit is exemplified. For a more illustrative view of how this system in this type of attractor functions, the predator-prey cycle can be examined. This system is resistant to change through coupling and feedback. Coupling is the movement of information between the structure and the environment (Milovanovic, 1995a). Positive and negative feedback are aspects of a system's self-regulation. Negative feedback loops regulate the system's initial conditions. Positive feedback amplifies the system's initial conditions. These loops are interconnected so the system can regulate itself to meet demands placed on it by its environment and its ability to incorporate these changes into the system's functioning (Briggs and Peat, 1989: 153).

When two independent limit cycles interact, a higher dimension in phase space is needed to represent this occurrence. As one system follows the other, variables greatly increase as well as the degrees of freedom. The shape this system resembles in phase space is that of a doughnut; this is called a torus attractor. The coupled motion of the interacting systems wrap themselves around the surface of the torus. The periodic torus represents coupled systems that are in direct ratios with one another, meaning they will at some point hook up with one another. Their periodic relationship can be expressed by a rational number ratio form (1:2, 2:3, etc.). A torus in which the period cycle cannot be represented by rational numbers is quasi-periodic. What this means is that the frequency of a cycle is represented by irrational numbers. There is a certain amount of predictability in this combined system. It will wrap around the torus; however, it will never hook up with itself. This means each oscillation will have a unique position in time, never exactly repeating itself. The interacting systems, with their combined degrees of freedom and dimension, leave the door wide open for uncertainty to enter. The combined systems open to unpredictability, interact with other systems which can cause perturbations in the initial conditions, magnifying key parameters. If a key parameter reaches a critical value of three times its previous iteration, the torus will fragment into a state of complete unpredictability; we now have a strange attractor (Briggs and Peat, 1989: 46).

The strange attractor can easily be recognized as turbulence (Briggs and Peat, 1989: 45). A strange attractor, known as the Lorenz, may be called strange because it has a fractional dimension of 2.06. This fractional dimension is trapped between a plane (two-dimensional) and a solid (three-dimensional) (Briggs and Peat, 1989: 51; Palmer, 1992: 73). The butterfly attractor, as it is also called, was developed by Edward Lorenz at the Massachusetts Institute of Technology in 1963. He constructed three non-linear differential equations that represented the system (Hayles, 1990: 146; Palmer, 1992: 75). Resulting from his discovery was the portrayal of a system that contained so many degrees of freedom that the trajectories oscillated in a completely random fashion with no predictability as to the system's position at any given time. Points of this system that begin close together lose contact with each other in this inerwoven mesh of systems. The system loses its ability to regulate itself through "communication" with the breakdown of self-regulatory feedback, due to increased sensitivity to the system's initial conditions and increased sensitivity to environmental factors (Briggs and Peat, 1989: 143). With the onset of this occurrence, uncertainty prevails. The number of a system's potential outcomes increases and chaos ensues.

Bifurcations, Outcome Basins, and Uncertainty

A basin outcome is the number of potential prospects a system has to choose from, stemming from a change in a key parameter (Young, 1991: 3). The point at which these choices arise is referred to as bifurcation (Butz, 1992: 1050). Through the iterative process of a system, a minute change in the system's initial conditions can result in a splitting (bifurcation) of paths (Briggs and Peat, 1989: 143). When a system bifurcates, one path is chosen and the other is forgone, and so, too, are the future potentials that accompanied that path. At this point the system is in a state of transition. With each bifurcation there is a doubling of outcome basins available to that system. For example, in a point attractor there is the possibility of two outcome basins (see Young, chapter 2, figure 3; chapter 4, figure 2). The system is said to be in homeostasis or equilibrium, meaning it can regulate itself through positive and negative feedback. A critical point is reached stemming from a change in a key parameter, and the system moves toward a limit attractor in which the outcome basins have been doubled. There are now four potential choices for the system to select. Subsequent changes in the parameters can result in the system moving into a state of far-from-equilibrium conditions. This means the system's ability to maintain itself through coupling and feedback is greatly diminished. The trajectory at this point reveals eight possible outcome basins of the torus attractor. If the system completely loses its ability to regulate itself through "communication," the torus will fragment into a strange attractor. At this point there are sixteen attractor basins pulling at the system; chaos has been reached. As the system reels toward this chaotic state, it increasingly becomes sensitive to the initial conditions (parameters). The most infinitesimal changes or fluctuations can have substantial effects. The linkage between cause and effect can no longer be determined; the system is completely interconnected to other systems and therefore is subjected to the whim of its environment (Young, 1991: 3; Briggs and Peat, 1989: 52). The critical point where an infinite number of possibilities lurk is exemplified by the Reynolds number. When a system enters a chaotic dimension, the system contains so many degrees of freedom that it is impossible for an accurate prediction or description of the system (Briggs and Peat, 1989: 49). From this state

Ilya Prigogine has proclaimed a transformation to a new order can occur (Hayles, 1990: 9; Briggs and Peat, 1989: 135; Young, 1992: 455).

This state of chaotic turbulence is interspersed with periods of serenity, known as intermittency (Briggs and Peat, 1989: 62). This is a period of stability within the random fluctuations of chaos, which cannot be defined as order or disorder (Hayles, 1990: 17). The system during this time remains open and extremely sensitive to its environment. One tiny fluctuation could initiate the system to once again enter a chaotic state (Briggs and Peat, 1989: 62). The other possibility that arises from this fluctuation is that the system somehow incorporates the change into its being. Is it possible intermittency reveals the system's ability to self-organize?

The Reemergence of Order

Prigogine made the distinction between two separate forms of chaos. He recognizes "Equilibrium thermal chaos" and "far-from-equilibrium chaos." The system experiencing "equilibrium thermal chaos" will eventually dissipate due to the conditions of maximum entropy (Briggs and Peat, 1989: 136). This means that the system has reached a static state of equilibrium and is releasing its energy as a non-usable waste product into the environment (Butz, 1992: 1050). The system is not renewed with new forms of energy; it experiences "heat death" (Briggs and Peat, 1989: 139), it is isolated (Butz, 1992:1050). In "far-from-equilibrium turbulent chaos" the system remains open; this is the factor that enables the potential of an evolutionary system to arise. In this type of chaos, as the system dissipates, it releases its energy in the form of waste, entropy. Simultaneously, the system is incorporating environmental conditions, including other systems' entropy, into its structure (Baker, 1993: 129; Briggs and Peat, 1989: 139). This system is referred to as a dissipative structure. The dissipative structure implies somewhat of a contradiction in terms. Dissipative, meaning the disintegration of the system and structure, implies a stable entity. It is through this contradiction in terms that the system has the spontaneous ability to preserve its being through self-organization (Butz, 1992: 1050). The dissipative structure remains open to its environment, incorporating environmental fluctuations and entropy into its being through feedback and iteration (Briggs and Peat, 1989: 139). Feedback and iteration are in this sense tools used to manipulate the system's initial conditions. As a result, the system evolves constantly to adjust to environmental changes while maintaining its unique history and identity. A new form of order within the system is achieved: order out of chaos.

With this realization it becomes evident that the systems existing in this universe, including humans, are not independent and separate from each other. In fact, they are intimately bound through a web of positive and negative feedback loops (Baker, 1993: 128; Briggs and Peat, 1989: 148).

Autopoetic Paradox

Human beings are open systems existing in the natural world. We are not separate from our environment as we have been conditioned to believe. The natural world, of which humans are a part, is constantly subject to fluctuations of forces that are beyond measurement. Nature is bombarded with constant flux of gravity, electricity, and temperature (Briggs and Peat, 1989: 148). Humans are embedded in their environments; therefore so, too, are social relations that arise through human interaction. We as humans are victims of the autopoetic paradox. Humans maintain that they are independent individuals in control of their own destinies. The autopoetic paradox claims that by this we masquerade ourselves as autonomous individuals; however, the more autonomy a system has the greater number of feedback loops the system needs in order to maintain itself. The increased number of feedback loops thus opens avenues for external systems to enter (Briggs and Peat, 1989: 165). As a result we, as humans, are not quite as determining as we think.

We have creatively explained our perceptions of the natural and social world in terms of reason based on linear systems. Science and reason are socially constructed. Do not reason and science then have the ability to change? Chaos theory presents a framework of understanding that embraces change and new thought. Acknowledged is uncertainty of what appears to be reality. There have been models developed which help us to envision the unfolding of unpredictable behaviors. To gain further insight into the functioning of chaotic social systems, let us explore the utilizations of such tools.

CHAOS AND THE MODELING OF CRIMINAL BEHAVIOR

At this point, I will utilize a model from an established theory of criminal behavior in order to construct visual models that illustrate the dynamics of a system moving toward chaos and how order can arise from such situations. The model presented in this application is the bifurcation diagram, which illustrates the system's movement from order to disorder. The theory which I will be applying to the model is adapted from Richard Quinney's work regarding "Crime and the Development of Capitalism" in *Class, State and Crime* (1980).

Brief Presentation of Quinney's Theory

According to Quinney, in order to understand crime in our society, we must critically examine criminal activity within the capitalist mode of production (Quinney, 1980: 39). Inherent in the nature of capitalism are the alienation, inequality, and unemployment of a large portion of the population (Quinney, 1980: 39). As a result, tension arises between the owners of production (i.e., the dominant class) and the workers (i.e., the subordinate class). Capitalism's intrinsic qualities ultimately result in the system's own demise through the increasing tension derived from the ever-widening gulf between the "haves" and the "have nots" (Quinney, 1980: 47). In order for the capitalist economy to continue, the state protects the interests of the capitalist class; the political economy of capitalism is developed (Quinney, 1980: 41). The owners of the means of production thus have the ability to define acts as criminal in order to control the marginalized, working class. Criminal action can then be understood as a response, conscious or unconscious, to the conditions capitalism manifests. The type of criminal activity evolves as does the perpetrator's consciousness of his or her activity (Quinney, 1980: 64). Quinney explains,

Crimes . . . range from unconscious reactions to exploitation, to conscious acts of survival within the capitalist system, to politically conscious acts of rebellion. These criminal actions, moreover, not only cover a range of meaning but actually *evolve* or progress from unconscious reaction to political rebellion. (1980: 65; emphasis added)

It is within this light that the goal of criminal activity is an expression of rebellion by the working classes to bring about societal transformation.

Quinney makes the distinction between "crimes of accommodation," defined as personal or predatory crimes, and "crimes of resistance," defined as conscious political acts of rebellion. With the contradictions that arise from the political economy of capitalism, the working class is further exploited (Quinney, 1980: 47). "Crimes of accommodation" can be further defined as an unconscious *reaction* to the alienation one suffers. These crimes can also be conscious acts of survival, since within capitalism one's survival is not necessarily guaranteed. An individual may have to resort to deviant behavior in order to exist (Quinney, 1980: 64). "Crimes of resistance" can be understood as an appropriate *response* to the oppression and alienation one suffers within the capitalist society. Those constituting the "disposable industrial reserve," as Marx has termed the expendable labor force, are under constant tension and pressure for maintaining a position of gainful employment. According to Quinney, not only is mental distress a reaction to these conditions, but so, too, are acts of personal violence and societal destruction (Quinney, 1980: 64). Crime can either be a reaction or a response to the capitalist order; it represents the class struggle in an attempt to create a new society (Quinney, 1980: 60). With this in mind, we can begin the process of application of criminal behavior to chaos.

Parameters, Variables, Vectors, and State Space

To observe this evolution of criminal behavior we must choose the critical aspects necessary to do so. This process of simplification is referred to as "dimensional reduction" (Abraham, 1992: 111–26). The starting point is to pick a control parameter which the variables can be measured against. In this case, the particular stage of capitalism functions nicely as our control parameter. The control parameter, stage of capitalism, ranges from early stages in development, movement to the left, to advanced stages of development, movement to the right (see Figure 3.1). The variables chosen represent forces that contribute to the maintenance of status quo relations during a particular stage of capitalist political economy. In this case we will use the individual's alienation from participation in the dominant capitalist forces, the degree of alienation. The extent to which the state can manipulate an individual is achieved through the implementation of various strategies exemplifying domination/repression, which will serve as our other variable. Both variables range in degree from low to high. The variables chosen, alienation and domination/repression, represent what Quinney asserts to be unavoidable effects of the capitalist economy (Quinney, 1980: 41). The dimensions chosen constitute the state space of the system. The state space of the system relays the phase portrait, which is the change in the control parameter, in this case, the significance of the occurrence of criminal activity during various stages of capitalism.

The variables chosen are not solely responsible for influencing the system. This notion introduces the transition of a state space to a vector field. The vector field of state space is filled with forces, or vectors as we call them. Vectors, in our case, could be an individual's attributes (i.e., class, race, sex, and age), law, current definitions of crime, media, social policies, employment rate, peers, and so on. The list could continue; it literally is endless. Each variable is then coupled, or influenced by the other with the aid of vector points (Abraham, 1992: 111–27). When there is a change in the variables, vectors push and pull the system around, influencing what type of behavior the individual will commit during a particular stage of capitalism. This constitutes the system's trajectory. In order to now show the transformation of the system in movement, we need to add a third dimension to our variables. For our purposes, the third variable introduced is the individual's political consciousness. This

Figure 3.1
Chaotic Attractor

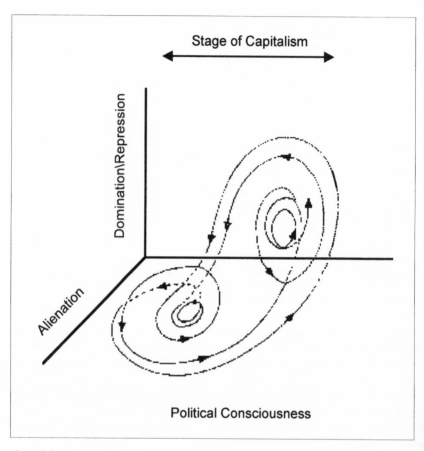

Adapted from Abraham, 1992.

variable interacts with the previously mentioned variables (alienation, domination/repression). With this addition, not only will the degrees of freedom the system contains increase, but also more than one vector field is available for any combination of the variables. The significance here is that more than one vector can influence the movement of the system (Abraham, 1992: 111–32). There is now the possibility for two regions to attract the system. These regions represent the nature of the crime committed, which will be either a "crime of accommodation" or a "crime of resistance" (see Figure 3.2). We will now have the opportunity to witness the capitalist system's movement toward chaos and the reemergence of a new order.

Figure 3.2
Bifurcation Sequence

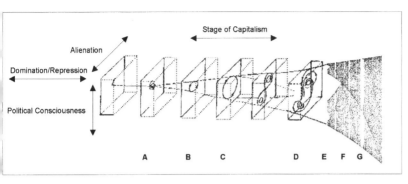

Adapted from Abraham, 1992; Cislo, 1996; Fractint software provided by Wegner and Tyler, 1993.

Disorder to Order: The Transformation of Criminal Action

We are ready to apply the theory to a bifurcation diagram to understand how order can emerge from the occurrence of criminal actions, which range from unconscious actions to conscious acts of rebellion. The goal of the capitalist state, according to Quinney, is to secure the capitalist order (1980: 51). Criminal law has been enacted in order to serve as a form of legal repression, so as to control the working class (Quinney, 1980: 53). Not only does criminal law play a major role in securing the position of the dominant class, but so, too, does the manipulation of the exploited class's consciousness. This is essential to conceal the reality of one's alienation and domination/repression (Quinney, 1980: 51). According to Alan Wolfe, "The most important reproductive mechanism which does not involve the use of state violence is consciousness manipulation" (cited in Quinney, 1980: 54). In this sense it becomes a priority of the state to create automatons or the "crippled monstrosities," to use a phrase coined by Marx. The individual suffering these conditions is unaware of his or her alienation and experiences of domination/repression (s/he has a very low political consciousness). The individual displaying these qualities is represented by the spiral point of Figure 3.2-A. The individual may intuitively feel his or her level of alienation and domination/repression; however s/he cannot define it. The state is completely successful in manipulating the consciousness of this individual so that it remains low. As the levels of alienation and repression increase, the individual may react deviantly to particular situations s/he may find him/herself in. The crimes committed by the individual in this low state of consciousness are "crimes of accommodation." According to Quinney: "Much criminal activity in the course of accommodation is an expression of false consciousness, an individualistic reaction to the forces of capitalist production" (1980: 60). "Crimes of accommodation" can be personal or predatory in their nature. Personal crimes are an unconscious reaction to the individual's alienation and low political consciousness. These crimes are interpersonal in nature, such as rape, murder, assault, and family abuse. The perpetrators of crimes of this nature are acting out of an undefinable frustration, an unconscious reaction to the exploitation and alienation they suffer (Quinney, 1980: 65). The individual may lash out toward another in a violent manner. "Crimes of accommodation" can also be predatory in nature. Perhaps an individual who has lost his or her job cannot find work. He or she may engage in predatory crimes (Quinney, 1980: 61). These crimes are acts of survival, such as burglary, theft, and drug dealing. In these cases the individual acts to self-correct the inequalities of the capitalist system at a particular stage. According to Quinney, "The class that does not own or control the means of production must *adapt* to the conditions of capitalism" (emphasis added, 1980: 60). That is precisely what these individuals are accomplishing. Through the acts committed, be they senseless acts of frustration or acts of survival, the capitalist state is reconstituted. These outlets and avenues of behavior enable the individual to return to a homeostatic position, maintaining capitalist conditions. The spiral point of Figure 3.2-A is representative of this state. The trajectory of the system is tightly confined, not straying far from its point of origin, and returning quickly when it does deviate, thus limiting the potential for new avenues of behavior to emerge.

As already mentioned, Quinney observes that the goal of the capitalist system is to reproduce itself (1980: 51). As the stages of capitalism advance (as we move from left to right in Figure 3.2), more policies are needed to regulate the population's consciousness of inequities. It becomes necessary to implement social welfare programs, including the development and utilization of the criminal justice system, in order to achieve this goal (Quinney, 1980: 51–52). For the individual who is not responsive, the system directs, through the implementation of criminal law and social policy. The goal of law and social policy is to force the individual to return to a position of homeostasis. What this actually results in is an increase in the degrees of freedom the individual is subject to. The amplitude of the trajectory is dampened, each oscillation is delayed. This in turn increases the potential of erratic behavior to enter into the open system.

As long as the variables, alienation, domination/repression, and political consciousness are kept in check, maintaining the current capitalist conditions, the system will return to a state of "normalcy" or homeostasis. However, when there is a change in the control parameter, the stage of capitalism advances, the variables fluctuate. For example, the individual may become more aware of the degree of governmental control and may become consciously aware of the alienation s/he suffers as well as the domination and repression s/he experiences. The amplitude of the system's trajectory begins to increase and the time it takes for the system to return to a state of normalcy is increased, thus opening up the potential for other behaviors to become visible; here, alternatives emerge (Abraham, 1992: 111–28). This marks the first bifurcation (Figure 3.2-B). Not completely able to define it consistently, or accurately, s/he acts in a manner that at times allows an awareness of the nature of their actions. At this point "crimes of resistance" are introduced (Quinney, 1980: 63).

"Crimes of resistance" are a conscious act of rebellion (Quinney, 1980: 65). As individuals begin to realize the plight that they face within a capitalist system, they may engage in concrete political action, such as civil rights or a labor movement, while simultaneously reacting to the conditions by utilizing "crimes of accommodation." There are two attractors influencing the system (Figure 3.2-B). Said differently, we have two outcome basins. The second bifurcation occurs and the individual oscillates between the two attractors (Figure 3.2-C). At each bifurcation point, the trajectories' amplitude increases, bringing about further changes in the levels of the system's parameters. The actor's consciousness may be raised to a political level, but may not remain consistently so. Regulatory systems of the state, such as the criminal justice system, continue to have the ability to influence an individual's consciousness by utilizing its repressive functions. This situation is represented by the strange attractor (Figure 3.2-D); one wing represents what Quinney calls conscious acts of rebellion, or "crimes of resistance" (Quinney, 1980: 65); the other wing represents "crimes of accommodation." At this point, it doesn't take much for the system to undergo the third bifurcation (Figure 3.2-E). As the stage of capitalism increases, there is an increased disproportional responsiveness to initial conditions, including environmental factors, represented by vector points; for example, a high unemployment rate. The individual's consciousness is raised and the state loses the ability to manipulate consciousness. The effectiveness of coercive forces begins to dissipate, coupling and feedback completely fail, due to the increased amplitude, or variability in behavior. A state of chaos has been reached (Figure 3.2-F). The individual revolts against the capitalist order consciously, against high levels of alienation and repression with high levels of political consciousness. The reality of the capitalist system has been revealed to the now conscious actor.

When people become conscious of the extent to which they are dehumanized under the capitalist mode of production, when people realize the source and nature of their alienation, they become active in a movement to build a new society. (Quinney, 1980: 66)

It is at the first bifurcation point that Quinney's theory loses its usefulness in regard to the occurrence of a non-linear transformation of society. The linear design of Quinney's theory allows for only one possible course of action at a time, meaning both crimes of accommodation and crimes of resistance cannot exist simultaneously. The actor within this framework is predicted to evolve from point A, "crimes of accommodation," to point B, "crimes of resistance." Chaos theory allows for both "wings" of the attractor to exist at the same time, allowing for unpredictable, non-linear behavior. Thus, criminal behavior, as it evolves, can lead to a transformation in consciousness of actions. The actors are no longer willing to play the previous game; a new one is created. Within this light crime can be viewed as a force in development (Quinney, 1980: 68). As Quinney has noted, "Conditions are created for the *transformation* and abolition of capitalism brought about by class struggle" (emphasis added, 1980: 47). The point of intermittency signifies the restructuring of society. Represented in Figure 3.2-G, the white band region, is the emergence of a new society, order out of disorder.

NON-LINEAR REALITY AND SOCIAL JUSTICE

It has been suggested that we shape our social world around our conceptions of reality. As Milovanovic has stated, "Our reality is imprisoned by the paradigms of our time" (Milovanovic, 1995a: 65). Our scientific notions of natural law as a result have determined the nature of our social policy. The application of chaos theory to social structures thus provides a new perspective from which social behavior and social policy can be conceptualized. Young observes, "Chaos theory . . . suggests that social policy can be formed which satisfies our interest in stability and continuity on the one hand together with creativity, spontaneity and flexibility on the other" (1992: 458). With this in mind we can examine the implications that previous policy based on modernist science has employed. We will then be able to explore the policy implications that the acceptance of chaos theory has in social policy regarding the criminal justice system.

Modern Understanding of Social Policy

Previous science has been focused on discovering the foundations of reality and thus attempting to control the natural and social world. By examining and categorizing only observed behaviors, contained within a rational Newtonian linear framework, we have limited our social response to prescribing corrective policies that are aimed at rectifying what is thought to be the isolated cause of social unrest. Policies that have been developed are retroactive in their nature. As a result, social policies based on linear scientific notions are unable to deal with the complexities of the ever-changing social systems. Notions of reality based on modern science have been quite ineffective in determining the causes of crime. The result is the construction of futile policies aimed at curtailing deviant behavior.

The science of chaos argues that in the real world systems do not progress linearly, they change unpredictably (Allen, 1994: 583). When applying linear policies to non-linear systems, such as the criminal justice system, what results is the magnification of inequalities existent in the social system (Young, 1992: 457). The acceptance of the scientific notions of chaos into our construction of reality may result in the development of a flexible, responsive social system based on non-linear dynamics, which may smooth out these apparent inequalities of current social relations (Young, 1992: 457). The transformation from a society which magnifies inequalities, stemming from linear social policy, to one of social justice becomes a feasible reality. This is perhaps why Milovanovic has suggested that "We in the social sciences need new visions of conceptualizing space, time, subjectivity and social action" (Milovanovic, 1995a: 74). The science of chaos provides a paradigm which encompasses all of these things.

Reconceptualization of Space and Time

At first glance, the ramifications that the acceptance of fractal geometry would have on the social world may seem unrelated to social policy development. However, when we run out the notion of a reality based on fractal geometry as opposed to Euclidean geometry, the non-linearity of the natural and social world is revealed. When we begin to construct a reality based on the notion of fractal geometry we begin to witness something magical happening: space is actually opened up. Within this newfound space is the existence of multiple dimensions beyond human perception. There are literally an infinite number of points which fractal geometry can explore due to fractal dimensions. With the acceptance of this reality into the social world, the magic is furthered. Our whole perception of truth is altered. Fractal geometry opens up space for a continuum of non-linear truth values to exist; truth is acknowledged as fractal (Milovanovic, 1995b: 268).

It has been suggested that under the current hierarchical structure of society, the linear search for truth ultimately becomes a quest for power and control (Young, 1992: 445). Refer back to Quinney's argument that the inevitable result of a capitalist society is the exclusion and inequality of the working class, and that the goal of the proprietorial class is to maintain its position of dominance in society (Quinney, 1980: 51). Laws, therefore, are constructed to reflect the interests of the privileged, discarding the interests of the marginalized as invalid (Milovanovic, 1994: 14). This notion is currently hidden by the existence of the principle of formal equality within the functioning of the law, which claims that under the Fourteenth Amendment, those equally situated are equally treated (Milovanovic, 1994: 59). In a body of law which at the onset is developed to favor the proprietorial class, is this actually possible? Milovanovic argues that "If we begin with a concrete situation of inequality, followed by an application of an equal scale . . . we reinforce systemic inequalities" (1994: 74). Thus, contained in the structure and function of law is the primacy of one group over another. The marginalized, oppressed voices and truths are denied expression and consideration within a linear function of truth. The recognition of non-linear truth enables power to actually be distributed more proportionally. Perhaps law would function to recognize the individual's unique placement within a particular situation and thus be able to apply policy appropriate for the individual, so as to recognize the uniqueness of him or her.

Chaos encourages areas of study that have been previously overlooked or dismissed as bad research. Prigogine's discovery of the irreversibility of time is an example of this. Intrigued by how little information there was to be found on the subject, Prigogine moved on (Briggs and Peat, 1989: 135). Within Prigogine's argument for the irreversibility of time is the notion that time is a form of "symmetry breaking" (Briggs and Peat, 1989: 147). Basically, this notion challenges linear notions of time that enable us to return to the past and construct the future. It is with this notion that Briggs and Peat observe that:

It is an illusion to speak of isolating a single interaction between two particles and claim that this interaction can go backward in time. Any interaction takes place in the larger system and the system as a whole is constantly changing, bifurcating, iterating. So the system and all its "parts" have a direction in time. (1989: 148)

The implications of this in the realm of social policy cannot be underestimated. As was mentioned before, current social policy is retroactive, relying on previous observations in order to create policy to correct current behavior of the local and global system. The irreversibility of time, which can be envisioned by the bifurcation diagram, implies that there is a constant progression of behavior; in other words, it is impossible to return to the point of "breakage" in order to "fix" the system.

Thus, what is encouraged is the recognition and examination of the system's key parameters in order to maintain near-to-stable social dynamics (Young, 1992: 456). Because of the system's high sensitivity to initial conditions a small change in a key parameter could result in unanticipated behavior. Careful modification of the parameters is required to avoid the system's cycling past the Feigenbaum point of chaos (Young, 1992: 456).

To outline the importance of this in the realm of social policy, let us employ the parameters of the bifurcation diagram utilized earlier. Recall the key parameters as the individual's alienation, political consciousness, and domination/repression. Implied in the Feigenbaum numbers is the existence of a ratio of key parameters which an evolving society must not exceed (Young, 1992: 456). Also possible is a ratio of these key parameters which a stable society does not exceed. Chaos theory implies that the manipulation of consciousness through coercive state policy, such as law, serves a particular group of individuals in order to maintain linear, status quo relations. The group holding more power implements social policy which, when carried through in the public and private sectors, reflects its own interests. Those alienated from access to these particular benefits actively create new outcome basins (Young, 1991: 4), thereby creating the possibility for a new system to emerge. The acceptance of such a realization would clearly have a profound effect within the realm of social policy. Policy would be directed toward dealing with the present situation. In other words, it would be understood that there could be no return to the good old days where only the voices of a privileged group are heard. This would result in limiting the repressive function that is currently embedded in the law to maintain the status quo of the privileged group. A non-linear system of social justice may be more flexible to recognize and meet ever-changing needs of a just society. Rational social policy based on linear dynamics tends to be destabilizing, producing chaos; social justice in its "irrationality" tends, ironically, to be stabilizing (Young, 1992: 456).

There is, however, a possible problem with regard to determining social policy in a non-linear framework. As the past cannot be reconstructed, the future cannot be told. Prigogine stated, "There is no short cut to learning the fate of a complex system, the future is told only in the moment-by-moment unraveling of the present" (Briggs and Peat, 1989: 180). The onset of chaos cannot be determined with precision; therefore, we will never know precisely what to expect from the implementation of certain policies. Policy based according to the benefits that would ensue from present conditions may be catastrophic in the long run or implementation may not be continued long enough to determine if the policy would result in just relations. The creation of social policy serves only as a temporary function. In other words, the policy enacted may not be allotted adequate time to attain its potential before it is replaced with a new program. In addition to this, there may be individuals or systems that continually succeed in making short-term decisions which are successful in the long run (Allen, 1994: 584). Thus, power may be distributed into their hands and the cycle of privilege begins again.

Subjectivity and Social Action

"One can never know the episteme in which one lives, we do not live in any single epistemology, but in a complex space characterized by innumerable fissures" (Hayles, 1990: 220). The science of chaos encourages the exploration of these fissures, through the use of fractal geometry. We, as iterative beings, take form. Chaos provides us with the ability to acknowledge this and incorporate it into a new conceptualization of how we perceive and understand ourselves and our social world. In other words, we iterate our surroundings and experiences into our body of knowledge. We are embedded in an environment from which we gain knowledge. Thus, we develop rich critical views of ourselves and our social systems precisely because we are able to take into consideration the individual and social iterative processes.

Chaos theory questions sure and certain knowledge (Young, 1992: 441). The existence of fractal dimensions exemplifies this. Fractal geometry is also responsible for solidifying the notion that the point and measure from which observation is taking place vary greatly. The scale-dependent quality of fractal geometry maintains that the placement and length of measurement employed in observation may result in a variety of possible conclusions. In other words, conclusions are subject to alterations simply by implementing different measurements and views. Hayles has stated that "When the object has a complex internal structure consisting of distinct local levels, the length of the scale is critical because different portions of the structure move at different speeds (Hayles, 1990: 210). This is an essential point to realize in regard to social policy. We can refer back to the implications of the prior arguments of reconceptualizing space and time to reveal the importance of this notion within social policy, law, and crime. Currently, the construction and implementation of law in defining deviant behavior depend on the position of those who hold positions of power, privileging their truths and excluding others; this reality would be recognized because the point of observation is recognized within the framework of non-linear dynamics.

This may perhaps be one of the most clearly defined ways that the acceptance of social policy based on non-linear dynamics can affect social relations and policy. Simply put, individually and societally, the nature of our "minor" actions, or for that matter, inaction, can have a profound effect in the formation of social policy. The non-linearity of cause and effect with disproportional outcomes then asserts that social action, or inaction, must be dismissed as being infinitesimal to make a difference.

Unfortunately, within the current construction of reality, based on prediction and control, there are negative aspects within the notion of unpredictable outcomes. Prigogine has observed that "this is also a threat, since in our universe the security of the stable, permanent rules seem to be gone forever. We are living in a dangerous and uncertain world that inspires no blind confidence" (Briggs and Peat, 1989: 151). It is with this notion, as current society is based on hierarchical relations, that danger lurks. Let us return briefly to Quinney's assertion that one of the main goals of the capitalist system is to reproduce itself through manipulation of consciousness. Who within this society can be trusted to have transcended this consciousness manipulation in order to promote social policy based on morality, ethics, and freedom? In addition to this, when implementing social policy, do we hold individuals responsible for their actions which unintentionally result in catastrophic events? If so, to what point do we trace accountability back? And furthermore, who decides?

Conceptualization: Chaos Leading to Social Justice

Chaos is a holistic science, unlike the previous linear science of our time; it requires the examination of non-linear global and local systems. The overall system is understood as the global which can be defined as any system or theory that subsumes certain phenomena into a universal explanation (Hayles, 1990: 209). The individual can be conceptualized as the local. Chaos does not give primacy to local or global; rather, it focuses on the intermingling of the two. This can be envisioned by returning to previous models utilized. Attractors, for example, enable us to view a global pattern while recognizing local variation and indeterminacy (Milovanovic, 1995: 268). The torus attractor clearly exemplifies this. As we view each oscillation within the torus, we note that there are infinite variations contained in the system as a whole.

Chaos recognizes this microscopic diversity; totalizing entities do not exist, behavior of the parts is contributing meaning and direction (Young, 1992: 443). Prigogine has beckoned a call to the scientific community to recognize that nature "does not suppose any fundamental mode of description; each level of description is implied by another and implies the other. We need a multiplicity of levels that are all connected, none of which may claim to have preeminence" (Briggs and Peat, 1989: 149). The same call needs to be voiced in regard to our social systems: "totalizing entities should be discredited because they are associated with oppressive political structures" (Hayles, 1990: 209). The science of chaos encourages the breakdown of oppressive bureaucratic structures, which employ the utilization of social policy to oppress the consciousness of the alienated individuals and groups. "Microscopic diversity maintained at the level of individual experience can help to constantly question and modify existing structures and organization so that they may adapt to changing circumstances" (Allen, 1994: 594).

The local can also be globalized. The existence of the Feigenbaum universals is suggestive of this notion (Hayles, 1990: 216). Inequalities experienced at the local level, such as discrimination and unemployment, can, in effect, through the individual's action, result in a transformation of the global system.

With the interplay between the local and global levels it can be suggested that the local and global are mirror images of each other (Young, 1992). The implications this would have regarding policy in the criminal justice system would be tremendous. As it stands now, and for the most part in the past, criminality is thought to be caused by individual deviancy. With the acceptance of chaos the personal characteristics and behavior of the individual would, as a result, not be viewed as defective or deviant in and of themselves, but the actions engaged in would be understood as an overall reflection of society as a whole; perhaps, as Quinney has suggested, a reaction to the nature of the capitalist mode of production. Henry and Milovanovic suggest that "integrating the micro- with the macro-level of analysis . . . would not fall within the modernist paradigm metaphysics and would not constitute macro and micro as discrete unitary constructs, abstracted from the infinite range of their continuous possibilities" (1995: 170). The ability to recognize the distribution of ideology and power across micro and macro scales leads to the realization of the necessity of a non-linear reality for the transformation to social justice.

The non-linear, iterative reality chaos provides would have a profound effect within the realm of our social policy and criminal justice system. Our reality would be shaped by a new paradigm that questions sure and certain knowledge, and embraces the creative nature of the individual and society. A social policy based on chaos theory would serve as an equalizer in social relations, constantly recognizing individual variance while attempting to balance the scales of society creatively. According to Young:

Given the unresponsive institutionalization of social practices which amplify inequalities, full blown chaos with its destructive/creative dialects may serve to unfreeze existing power/class configurations while producing innovations, some of which may be most congenial to the human project. (1992: 458)

CONCLUSION

Resulting from chaos theory is the emergence of a reality which is fundamentally at odds with the reality created by modern science. The "hard" science of chaos provides useful tools, such as the strange attractor, which exemplify the existence of uncertainty. When situated within a postmodernist framework, the acceptance of chaos theory enables us to envision an alternative understanding of the world in which we live; an understanding that acknowledges the fractal nature of the natural and social world. We can only speculate about the implications; however, we can certainly predict the alteration of our conception of reality.

REFERENCES

Abraham, F. 1992. *Visual Introduction to Dynamical Systems Theory for Psychology.* Santa Cruz, Calif.: Aerial Press.

Allen, P. 1994. "Coherence, Chaos and Evolution in the Social Context." *Futures* 26(6): 583–97.

Baker, P. 1993. "Chaos, Order, and Sociological Theory." *Sociological Inquiry* 63(2): 124–44.

Briggs, J. and F.D. Peat. 1989. *Turbulent Mirror: An Illustrated Guide to Chaos Theory and the Science of Wholeness.* New York: Harper and Row.

Butz, M. 1992. "The Fractal Nature of the Development of the Self." *Psychological Reports* 71: 1043–63.

———. 1993. "Systemic Family Therapy and Symbolic Chaos." *Humanity and Society* 17(2): 200–223.

Cislo, A. 1996. "Order out of Disorder: A Vision of Heraclitus." *Humanity and Society* 20(1): 19–41.

Hayles, K. 1990. *Chaos Bound.* New York: Cornell University Press.

Henry, S. and D. Milovanovic. 1995. *Constitutive Criminology: Beyond Postmodernism.* London: Sage.

Milovanovic, D. 1994. *A Primer in the Sociology of Law: Second Edition.* New York: Harrow and Heston.

———. 1995a. "Dueling Paradigms: Modernist versus Postmodernist Thought." *Humanity and Society* 19(1): 19–41.

———. 1995b. "Inscribing the Body with a Sign: Semiotics and Punishment." In R. Janikowski and D. Milovanovic (eds.), *Legality and Illegality, Semiotics, Postmodernism and Law.* New York: Lang.

———. 1995c. "Moral Philosophy, Social Justice and the Question of Punishment in a Just Society." In R. Janikowski and D. Milovanovic (eds.), *Legality and Illegality, Semiotics, Postmodernism and Law.* New York: Lang.

Palmer, T. 1992. "A Weather Eye on Unpredictability." Pp. 69–80 in N. Hall (ed.), *Exploring Chaos.* New York: W.W. Norton.

Quinney, R. 1980. *Class, State and Crime.* New York: Longman.

Series, C. 1992. "Fractals, Reflections and Distortions." Pp. 138–46 in N. Hall (ed.), *Exploring Chaos.* New York: W.W. Norton.

Smith, D. 1995. "The Inapplicability Principle: What Chaos Means for Social Science." *Behavioral Sciences* 40: 22–39.

Stewart, I. 1992. "Portraits of Chaos." Pp. 44–57 in N. Hall (ed.), *Exploring Chaos.* New York: W.W. Norton.

Wegner, T. and B. Tyler. 1993. *Fractal Creations.* Corte Madera, Calif.: The Waite Group.

Young, T.R. 1991. "Chaos and Crime Part II: The ABC of Crime: Attractors, Bifurcations, Basins and Chaos." *Critical Criminologist* 3(4): 3–4, 13–14.
———. 1992. "Chaos Theory and Human Agency: Humanist Sociology in a Postmodernist Era." *Humanity and Society* 16(4): 441–459.
———. 1994. "Postmodern Religion and the Global World Order: Postmodern
Theology and Social Justice." *Humanity and Society* 18(3): 2–22.

CHAPTER 4

The ABCs of Crime:
Attractors, Bifurcations,
and Chaotic Dynamics

T.R. Young

INTRODUCTION

In this chapter, I want to offer the reader a view of crime from the perspective of non-linear dynamics. Non-linear regimes produce fuzzy, fractal structures of social behavior called *attractors*; non-linear dynamics also
produce three orders of change in the geometry of these attractors at
very specific bifurcation points.[1] First-order change, a change from sameness to self-similarity, is met in the *torus*. Second-order change comes
with the butterfly attractor, while third-order change is found in deep
chaos. Together, the concepts and the insights offered by this new science
will help redirect attention to the sources and solutions to criminal behavior as we enter the twenty-first century.

Second- and third-order change come when key parameters *bifurcate*,
producing two (or more) basins of attraction to which a molecule, an
animal population, a person, or a firm could move. In order to grasp
this idea, think of a leaking water faucet. Without any transformation of
the structure of a water molecule, a slight change in a key parameter
(temperature, for instance) will offer two basins of attraction between
which a water molecule could move, where before there was but one
pattern. The same is true of a wide range of complex systems; viruses,
moth populations, fish populations, economic activity, psychological
states and, perchance, crime.

ATTRACTORS

In the literature on chaos, a strange attractor is simply the pattern, in
visual form, produced by graphing the behavior of a system in phase

space.[2] Since a non-linear attractor tends to have discernible geometric shape, a person, firm, or group of systems is said to be attracted to that shape. Since it does not fit the neat and tidy dynamics of Newtonian physics, it is said to be strange. Strange attractors are messy; they take up but a fraction of the space available to them in any given set of dimensions. Thus, they are said to have fractal geometry rather than Euclidean.

For our purposes, we will think about five such dynamic patterns. Of the five, one attractor has one point toward which it moves. A second has two points which mark the limits of time-space in which it is found. The first two are found in very simple mechanical systems. They embody the dynamics which fit Newtonian physics and exhibit Euclidean geometries. Aristotelean logic and rational numbering scales are suitable epistemological tools for the study of their dynamics. Not so for more complex attractors. Three attractors are strange, they display non-linear dynamics; these are called the torus, the butterfly, and deep chaos.

The Torus

The simplest strange attractor is the torus. The word *torus* comes from the Latin, which means, literally, a swelling. In geometry, a torus is a doughnut-shaped structure in which the pathways of a system expand to encompass more of the time-space available to it.

Self-similarity. The key feature of the torus is that sameness is replaced by *self-similarity*. In terms of ordinary workplace behavior, self-similarity means that a worker might arrive at the factory every morning within the same ten- to fifteen-minute span; sometimes two minutes late, sometimes five minutes early, but with regularity sufficient as a ratio of the time available such that great predictability and reliability of her/his work schedule are possible. In the case of criminal behavior, doctors might include fraudulent billings to Medicare in the millions of billings which they send out each year. It would take a special research design and special research tools to find the hidden attractors in such complex data.

The torus also carries within its dynamics a resolution of the polemics about process and structure. One can see, in Figure 4.1, that structure emerges out of process. The tracing of the behavior of one system over time yields sufficient regularity such that other systems might adjust to it; it then has the features of a social structure in that it sets the limits or shapes the behavior of other systems. If a doctor bills $4,000 for a given procedure and that cannot be negotiated by his/her patients, then such billing practices "structure" the economic behavior of the patients. If all doctors in a region bill the same way for the same procedure, then the predictability and certainty of the billing process produce a structure

Figure 4.1
Process Becomes Structure

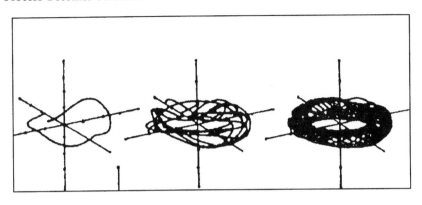

which provides a great deal of order—at least for the doctor; at least for the short term.

The Butterfly Attractor

The butterfly attractor emerges when a small change in one or more of the key parameters exceeds a critical limit. This change point is called a Feigenbaum point, after the mathematician Mitchell Feigenbaum (1978), who discovered a set of four such points as well as the elegant regularity with which they appeared. A remarkable surprise comes with the butterfly attractor. The same set of systems (persons, firms, groups, or societies) can behave in two (or more) entirely different ways. Modern science, modeled after the regularities of Newtonian physics, permits one and only one outcome basin/attractor for the same set of systems. Chaos theory grounds a postmodern philosophy of science in which very different outcomes can await very similar systems.

The butterfly attractor (Figure 4.2) can be understood as two linked tori, each of which has limited uncertainty. A second-order (and much more unpredictable) change resides at the points of connection between tori. In terms of non-linear social dynamics, a person, firm, or group might, at such a juncture, go to either attractor. Under the kinds of demand for income mentioned just below, it would be impossible to predict just which (e.g., in any given set of doctors, lawyers, or brokers) would jump from a prosocial practice of medicine, law, or finance to a decidedly parasitic practice.

Cascading Uncertainties. Chaos theory suggests that, while most people can cope with one or two uncertainties, the interactive effects of three or more uncertainties drive people to look for new ways of dealing with

Figure 4.2
A 2n Outcome Basin: The Butterfly Attractor

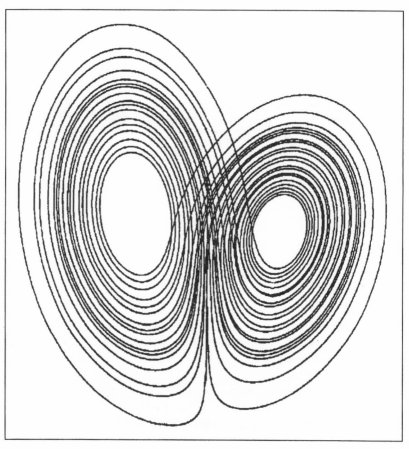

these exigencies. Among the new ways, some are most congenial to the human project; others inimicable. Among these latter are, for the example of white-collar employees and professionals, all sorts of illegal and unethical behavior which help the doctor or the lawyer cope with uncertainties in his or her life, but put added stress on patients, clients, and employees who have to participate in such fraud or corrupt activities. Order is obtained for the white-collar criminal by increasing disorder in the lives of patients, clients, customers, or competitors.

Concern with uncertainty and the emergence of new strange attractors in a basin of outcomes is, thus, a central contribution which chaos theory can make to a postmodern philosophy of science in general and a postmodern criminology in particular. But concern with uncertainty should not be confused with the concept of normlessness, for several reasons. First, it is the normative structure itself which is often the source of non-linear change. Small changes in tax law, small changes in labor law, small changes in market dynamics, or small changes in size of classes may trigger large changes in bankruptcy, strikes, disemployment, or vandalism. Second, in marriage, crime, and business, try as one might, one cannot embody the norms as given; small changes in other parameters call forth other patterns of behavior. Third, the interaction of norms in two or more realms of life may produce great uncertainty.

BIFURCATIONS

All complex natural and physical systems so far studied begin to bifurcate when a key parameter exceeds three times its value at a semi-stable dynamical regime. And if the ratio exceeds 3.44, still another bifurcation occurs such that four outcome basins develop. Eight attractors develop at the critical value of 3.56 while 16 such fuzzy patterns appear when a key parameter reaches a value of 3.569. After four such bifurcations, the period between them decreases precipitously such that the pattern of such bifurcations is said to "cascade" toward deep chaotic regimes in which pattern and predictability are very seldom observed.

This elegant and stately dance toward deep chaos is a constant source of wonderment in complexity theory. It is a feature of deterministic chaos in which a constant and a random variation combine to produce elaborate patterns of uncertainty. As yet, there is no empirical evidence that the march toward uncertainty in social life displays the same precision in bifurcations as do physical and biological systems. Indeed, the non-linearity in symbolic interaction, in social change, and in human agency may be considerably less precise and thus more difficult to manage. But the changing mix of order and disorder is there in every form of social life. New uncertainties emerge as non-linear feedback among interdependent systems works through an ecosystem.

A bifurcation is a forking or splitting of a parameter. Figure 4.3 shows the map of a bifurcation process in which a stable parameter, Y, explodes to fill the space available to it after it has undergone three doublings of its cycles. In natural or social systems, there are moments when a very small change in a parameter can explode to open up a new track for a system. If the system bifurcates again, then a torus develops (Region B). First-order uncertainty creeps in after the second bifurcation. Sameness is replaced by self-similarity.

It is these bifurcation points which one can use for a theory of exploding crime rates. For some few and unpredictable number of young people, professionals, corporations, or societies, crime may be a way to reconcile the otherwise intractable parameters of life. Property crime,

Figure 4.3
From Order to Disorder

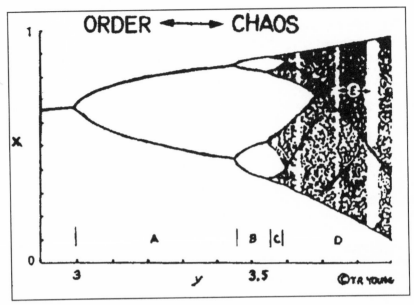

ORDER ←——→ CHAOS

violent crime, and political crime may surge non-linearily when critical social parameters bifurcate. In all complex systems, one finds people who skirt the borders of criminal behavior now and again. When uncertainty increases qualitatively, a new basin of attraction opens up; some may involve prosocial behavior; some anti-social. Well-socialized, employed, church-going, and otherwise solid citizens begin to find crime a way to restore order and ambition in their own lives.

Bifurcations and Crime

In a basin with two attractors (each of which can be viewed as a torus loosely connected to each other), the geometry of behavior becomes ever more uncertain; one may move between anti-social and prosocial behavior; one may be involved in both criminal and prosocial behavior at the same time. Indeed, the one act may be criminal while the next unpredictable run of acts is prosocial. The concept of "the criminal" becomes very fuzzy while the geometry of crime becomes very complex.

In order to cope with these exigencies, a person would have to lower desire or increase income to regain the semi-stable pattern marked by the torus. If neither is changed, or if either variable, desire, or income changes in the wrong direction, a second economic activity with which

to augment income might be attractive which, only yesterday, was unthinkable. There are about 800,000 doctors in the United States. Suppose
their incomes are stable while insurance rates double for certain medical
procedures. Chaos theory suggests that even with a doubling of insurance rates, doctors would be able to adjust other expenses and remain
within the constraints of law and ethics. Suppose insurance corporations
triple insurance costs to cover a great increase in claims and/or jury
awards. If so, they would have created the first Feigenbaum point. A
number of doctors might begin to move to a form of low-risk practice
in which insurance rates are lower because damage claims are lower,
while others might hang on, making adjustments in other expenditures
rather than make the qualitative break to illegal practices.

At the same time, a number might move to a strategy in which they
use the trust within the patient/doctor relationship to increase the number of unnecessary operations, while other doctors in the same circumstances might lower lifestyle ambition. If illegal billing procedures are
adopted, a new attractor is born. While new attractors emerge with
astonishing predictability, the remarkable thing is that it is impossible to
predict which subset of physicians, out of all physicians similarly situated, might move to the new attractor comprised of illegal behavior.

Attractor Basins

In the chaos paradigm, systems tumble from one dynamic state to
another in a very complex pattern of behavior, as bifurcations follow one
another. In so doing, they produce a fractal basin of outcomes with any
number of attractors. There may be two, four, eight, sixteen, or many,
many more states (attractors) to which they are attracted. If we were to
translate the complexity of such a basin to corporate crime, given income
or cost problems, a corporation might generate several loose fractals in
which they generate incomes both in legal and illegal ways. In such a
field, returns from sales would be the dominant attractor in an outcome
basin. In other regions of the basin we might find small and loose basins
of income generated by federal grants and subsidies. In other, less visible
mappings, corporations might defraud customers or plunder retirement
funds in order to increase the size and stability of a given attractor. And
in order to lower costs, some corporations may well endanger workers,
violate minimum wage laws, or dump dangerous toxins in rivers, earth
fills, or the atmosphere. At times, the basin of attractors for corporate
crime might explode to fill the space available; in times of prosperity,
such fractals may well be very small and very loose; so loose that conventional analytic techniques could not find them hidden in even careful
mappings of income categories. The operative question for a theory of
corporate crime centers around those parameters which drive a system

into ever more strange behavior with ever more attractors in a causal basin.

The Geometry of Crime

The size of the basin of outcomes and its geometry are central to a theory of crime based upon chaos theory. In a society with non-linear economic processes (Berry, 1991) and with two sets of compelling parameters—D^1 = parameters of desire, need, obligation, or affiliation, and D^2 = parameters of income and resources—given persons or groups may be attracted to more than one behavioral state. Thus, a professional person might depend upon salary, fees, embezzled funds, insurance fraud, and income tax fraud as well as fraudulent billings in order to expand the geometries of income to match the geometries of lifestyle expense. If one is disemployed, one might steal a little, accept state welfare illegally, prostitute oneself occasionally, and borrow from friends and family in order to reduce the uncertainties in desire and demand.

Given compelling need, desire, or obligation along with income uncertainty, a person or a group may seek new ways to meet the contingencies and exigencies of life. Some of these pathways may be harmful to the human project. The challenge to criminology, indeed to all social science, is to understand why stable systems bifurcate.

Feedback and Bifurcations

The question becomes, what kicks a system into far-from-stable dynamics? The answer is that a small change produced by feedback loops may produce large changes at key points. Generally, linear feedback amplifies variation while non-linear feedback tends to promote stability. Negative feedback extinguishes activity while non-linear behavior often stabilizes it; a precept in chaos theory is that only chaos can cope with chaos. More about this in the last section on social control.

In social terms, the question becomes, what is it that makes crime an "attractive," that is, normative pattern for some subset of all persons or firms in a society; for some subset of societies in a globalized economy? The answer has not yet been uncovered. In general terms, feedback loops in key social parameters may trigger the search for a new way to deal with uncertainties by otherwise ordinary human beings. We can speculate on some of these.

Key Parameters in Criminal Behavior

I tend to think that when differences in class, status, or power bifurcate without restraint, both property crime and violence pops open in a fractal basin of social dynamics.[3] We can begin to pursue the idea with crime in rural societies. The question then becomes, how great can inequalities be before they trigger harmful behaviors? A great deal of research is required to pursue such questions. We gain a feel for such inequalities for their meaning for crime in peasant societies.

Rural Crime

In the case of peasant society, most people engage in peaceful agriculture as their main source of income. Small changes in class, power, or status might force some off the farm and into a city to seek a living or to supplement income. Buyers from rich countries might offer prices double, triple, and quadruple that of a yearly wage for the land. The commodification of land creates great uncertainties for the children of peasants. Many will migrate to the city; others will stay and try to supplement income by wage labor if possible; by theft and prostitution if necessary, to reunite desire and demand.

Interest rates for those left in a farming community might increase, weather conditions might exceed crucial limits, food imports might increase, tax on farm land might exceed a critical value; any one of a dozen factors might change slightly and produce the need for different sources of income. Adoption of two (or more) forms of behavior which yield income takes the form of a butterfly attractor, Region C in Figure 4.3, with uncertain pathways within and between them. If wage labor is not available or help from kin or state welfare, some small set of farmers may turn to crime to cope with the uncertainty in the income they do have.

Banditry, rustling, kidnapping, and highway robbery developed in rural areas in Europe with the advent of industrial capitalism, which introduced great uncertainties in crops and cash for agrarian peoples. In the United States, Jesse James, Billy the Kid, Pretty Boy Floyd, John Dillinger, and Bonnie and Clyde, among others were folk heroes to populist sentiment from the 1870s to the 1930s as they "robbed from the rich and gave to the poor." In some societies, kidnappers are seen to be heroes, since they extort money from the rich.

In his excellent study of banditry, Pat O'Malley of LaTrobe University in Australia found that:

• bandits were supported by their rural community;

• bandits tended to rob class enemies: merchants and squatters;

• banditry tended to redistribute wealth downward; and

• bandits are symbols of resistance against the ruling class.

More to the question of control versus prevention of political crime, O'Malley (1979a; 1979b) confirmed Hobsbawm's thesis that banditry disappears when the state ceases to act on behalf of class elites. Hobsbawm held that unorganized class conflict is the natural terrain for banditry. O'Malley added that when the urban and rural poor are able to organize for political relief of uncertainty inflicted by class and ethnic stratifications in farm and village, such crime declines.

Third-Order Change

After the fourth bifurcation in one or more key parameters, uncertainty increases greatly. In technical terms, a system tends to fill the space available to it rather than settle down to a point or to fluctuate between two, four, or eight basins of attraction.[4] But note that there are regions of order even in deep chaos, Region E (Figure 4.3). These regions of order constitute third-order change. Here we might see revolutions in which one economic formation replaces another; great migrations in which cultures change and disappear. Great changes in the number and kinds of jobs in which one marriage form replaces another, as well as underground structures in which one sexual modality is replaced or supplemented. Of all the emergent orderlines in deep chaos, some may be congenial to the human project and some most hostile. All will be called sin, crime, deviancy, pathology, evil, or some such pejorative phrase which privileges more traditional ways of doing economics, politics, religion, or kinship (Young, 1996).

Property Crime

For our purposes, the unit of analysis involved in street crime may be a particular person or a set of persons. Since property crime is an economic activity, if one wanted the full portrait (in phase space) of the economic attractor(s) for that person, one would have to track the amount of income a person obtained from several sources, say, from wage labor, from private charity including friendship and kinship charity; from state welfare as well as from other unearned income sources such as rents, interest, and profits.

In Figure 4.4, each box gives two ways of displaying dynamic regimes; the first two are linear. The second two depict non-linear dynamics. For social life, Box A might depict the income pattern of a person as s/he grows older; high in the middle years and tapering off to a steady state at retirement. Box B could depict the income pattern of a seasonal worker; high in summer and low in winter with upper limits set by wage agreements between employers and lower limits set by welfare payments by the state. Box C represents the income pattern of, say, a real estate

Figure 4.4
Income Portraits

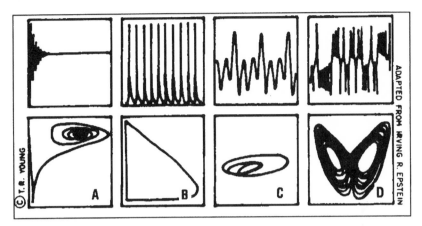

sales person over four or five months; four or five years; it grows and declines but keeps within limits set by a combination of market dynamics, pricing agreements on commissions by brokers, and individual effort. It is Box D that is interesting to a theory of crime.

One can see two distinct periods or patterns of income in Box D. One wing of the butterfly might be income that is generated by wage labor. If our subject turned to state welfare, borrowed money, begged from parents, or provided illicit services, the fractal would have two, three, four, five, or more wings in the total field of attractors. If our person or business invented a new form of crime, still another region would be constructed in a basin of outcomes.

For property crime the question arises, what forces the bifurcation from one source of income to two, three, four, or more? Young people, as they move into adulthood, undergo a lifestyle change. Desire for cars, separate lodging, fashionable clothing, concert tickets, jewelry, or other items special to youth culture may well exceed by some order of magnitude the income available. Allowances and part-time work might not suffice. Charity and welfare are closed options. Most are too young to have unearned income from property. But organized crime gives some low-income young people a chance for high incomes; the sale of drugs, prostitution, hijacking, auto theft, and arson constitute income opportunities for those whose desires and demands far outstrip the resources of family and/or minimum wage jobs.

I want to suggest that bifurcations in the magnitude of the ratio between desire for consumer goods and services on one side, and legal sources of income on the other, may well destabilize the economic life of a young person and open up, non-linearly, the possibility of property crime as an economic attractor. One must expand one's basin of income options if one is to participate fully in youth culture in a consumer society.

For some, mismatch between income and desire for goods might be resolved by dropping out of school and working full-time. For others, it might mean doing without and forgoing participation in youth culture. Some young people turn to petty theft as a way to match desire and income. Young men and women may shoplift in order to reconcile disparities between income and desire for commodities and services. Some steal from friends and family.

These are the lucky ones; in most American cities and in many towns, organized crime offers opportunity and income with which to reduce the uncertainties of desire and demand. The presence of organized crime circles which require illicit labor and offer relatively large wages in return makes crime as an economic endeavor even more attractive. Organized crime offers several manageable alternatives to open up (bifurcate) a basin of economic attractors for young people. One can steal and supply the demand for fenced auto parts. One can find work in the drug trade or in the policy rackets. One can find work in prostitution or pornography with which to reconcile desire and income. A young person would find it difficult to reconcile other parameters, however. Demand on time might be a problem.

For such a person, part-time work, social demands of friends, family problems, and street crime activity all make conflicting demands on time. If we were to map out such attempts to juggle the uncertainties of school, family, social life, and theft in phase space, we would find two, four, eight, or more attractors each demanding time.

Managing Uncertainties

There are several forms of power available with which one can manage uncertainties. I want to focus on four: physical power, economic power, social power, and moral power. The case I make here is that each form of power is an attractor. If we track the life of any given person or group, we would be able to map out use of each of these attractors. And each form of crime, indeed, each form of all human behavior, entails the exercise of some combination of the forms of power. Most of us use social power to shape the behavior of known others. Some of us use other forms of power to shape the behaviors of unknown others.

Social power arises from social relationships: family, work, church, recreation, and community. Those who are disemployed and who are embedded in a strong and supportive network of friends, neighbors, and family often rely greatly upon social power to meet the contingencies and exigencies of life. Symbolic interactions are the media of social power. Social power is usually deployed in prosocial activities, but both white-collar crime and corporate crime exploit social power, sometimes ruthlessly.

Economic power can be used to shape the behavior of unknown others: indeed it is bad form to use money to shape the behavior of friends and family, but clerks, doctors, lawyers, consultants, and tradespersons respond to money quickly enough. Given a regular and adequate income, given levels of desire manageable by either social power or economic power, and physical violence is not likely to be used. Social bonds and legal tenders are the media of power but sometimes direct force is used.

Given uncertainties in resolving discrepancies between needs and resources; given limited resources available within social networks; given limited job opportunity; given incremental debt burden; given continuing and increasing desire for housing, food, transport, entertainment, and clothing; and given demands by friends or family, one might well use violence to take what cannot be bought or borrowed. One scarcely need mention that it is minority youth who are most often closed out of social power and economic power by class and race. But do note: it is racism rather than race which is the key parameter at hand. One's genetic structure is stable over one's life; racism is variable and is located in the larger social order in which class, status, and power ebb and flow.

Moral power arises from shared values. Those values are often embedded in a religious tradition, but can be secular. Professional ethics is a source of moral power as are laws and civil rights. Moral power can be a constraint on the use of social, economic, and physical power in the pursuit of desire. Bifurcations in social life tend to dilute moral power. Generally, social justice is preferable to criminal justice as a solution to crime. I need not mention that social justice is founded upon morality, while criminal justice is grounded upon the use of physical force.

Gender Violence

There are several values found in American culture which tend to promote violence against women and men. Men are taught assiduously from childhood that violence is a solution to the determination of status and dispute. One fights with fists, knives, or guns at home until a certain stable hierarchy is known, until a given goal is met. Given small change in the structure of social power, economic power, or physical power, violence may explode.

Patriarchy sets the larger stage for violence against women. It demands that females defer to male demands and desires. By itself, patriarchy might not produce high levels of gender violence, but, when coupled with the use of physical power as a cultural and technical solution to uncertainty, it produces dangerous instabilities. Low-level violence is normative for some families. When a male has a dispute with a female, he often uses physical power to supplement social and economic power inside the household. Small changes in the number of people employed may trigger large changes in domestic violence if non-linearity is found to be a feature of economic life. Small changes in the number of women entering the work force alter the structure of economic power in the family. Small changes in education, in feminist activities, or in the number of children in a household all alter the mix and measures of power in gender relations. Within patriarchy, these small changes in larger social life may trigger explosions in domestic violence, divorce, child abuse, suicide, and/or refusal to commit to a marriage.

If empirical research reveals non-linear dynamics in gender violence, one cannot predict when a given person in a time of unemployment and/or inflation will move from supportive gender relations to abusive; nor can one ascertain the precise mix of violence and caring. All one can say within the chaos paradigm is that women should be on guard when uncertainty enters the life space of males socialized to the use of physical power.

Racial Violence

Given a racist social order, discrimination against minorities becomes acceptable. As in the case of gender violence, uncertainties in the lives of a majority may trigger qualitative increase in crimes against those without economic, social, physical, or moral power. One might expect declassed males, declassed workers, or declassed ethnic groups to use violence in their existential terror over jobs, housing, status, and local politics. Given the covert backing of institutional racism, moral constraints on majority violence are reduced.

Organized Crime

The essential thing about most goods and services offered by organized crime is that these were/are solidarity supplies used as pathways to the Holy in premodern societies. Massification of markets, schools, and churches, as well as their bureaucratization together with industrialization, has reduced both the realm and the reach of the Holy. Privatized use of drugs, sex, gaming, erotic literature, and other psychogens as a way to manage uncertainty, combined with the market economy, tends to increase demand for such supplies. Organized crime involves the production, distribution, and profanation of sacred supplies. Use of such goods and services for private or for commercial purposes is defined as a profanation in a sacred society and prohibited by both legal and social norms. The commodification of sex, gaming, drugs, violence, and other such services continues to grow and thrive in a market economy. Many legitimate income attractor states are more or less saturated. Small business is very competitive. Large business organizes market monopolies. Professions require credentials. For those closed out of such occupations, illicit markets attract both workers and entrepreneurs. If police and courts do not complicate things too much, if markets are stable, if supply is available, then organized crime is an attractive alternative to income uncertainties. For persons excluded from legitimate economic life, organized crime offers jobs, income, and a certain status not otherwise available.

Given high levels of interpersonal insecurity and given the definition of such commodities as solidarity supplies, one learns to reach for them when the problematics of life grow intractable. When authentic intimacy, sensuality, and love are unavailable, commodity love and intimacy offer short-term satisfaction. When wages are uncertain, gambling becomes a magical way to reunite desire and need. When truly religious spirituality is lost to the rationalization and formalization of the church, a certain privatized spirituality is available through the use of alcohol or other drugs.

Corporate Crime

Corporations thrive in a rational environment. If labor is reliable, if demand is dependable, if taxes are low and stable, if competitors are cooperative, if retail outlets are captive, and if governments are friendly, one would not expect corporations to commit crime. In safe and dependable environments, desire for profits could be met. Small changes in such parameters could destabilize a whole economy and trigger great increases in corporate crime.

Changes in other parameters could affect corporate income. Labor costs, management perks, taxes, capital equipment, raw materials, licenses, bribes, campaign contributions, association dues are among the parameters which can force a bifurcation. Several can change at once and force a firm to look for other ways to generate order. As H. Ross Ashby (1968) put it in his Law of Requisite Variety, only variety can cope with variety to generate order. Crime offers several such options for reinstituting rationality and predictability.

The picture one gets from applying chaos theory to corporate crime is that, in order to forestall bankruptcy, to attract capital investment, to satisfy ownership and otherwise function as a corporate entity, corporate officers find crime an attractive alternative economic tactic. If workers are weak and/or legislatures friendly, labor can be exploited. If customers are unorganized and legislators indifferent, fraud and defective goods offer possibilities for reconciling desire for profits and expenditures. If legislators are carefully preselected and low-income neighborhoods vulnerable, toxic wastes can be dumped.[5]

Chaos theory teaches us that a corporation might live with two or three unmanageable parameters but when a fourth, fifth, or sixth parameter explodes to fill the space available to it, then crime becomes a quick and easy solution. One either eliminates the effects of the parameter or one turns to another parameter to generate order. If only one of these parameters is intractable, say, labor supply, then it can be managed by increasing wages. If two are unpredictable, say, labor supply and competition, then the corporate officer could reconcile desire for profits by increasing prices and seeking government subsidy. Disorder is transferred to customers or to the state. Chaos theory suggests that corporate officers might begin to consider criminal action as three or more attractors become fractal, that is, worker supply, competitor activity, or, say, customers become inpredictable and there are fewer alternatives from which to seek and obtain order for the system.

If governments become intractable, firms can exploit dealerships, franchises, captive-retail outlets, and thus transfer disorder to small businesses. If governments become too intractable, passing pollution laws, labor laws, consumer protection laws, and such, they close off the options for reconciling profits, costs, and income. If laws are passed and if corporations cannot count upon benign neglect, or if policing laws even become uncertain, the rational thing to do may be to move to, say, Mexico, Korea, or Malaysia. The uncertainties left behind become less important in the short run.

White-Collar Crime

White-collar crime involves deception and subversion of the social trust invested in doctors, politicians, lawyers, bankers, professors, and real estate brokers, not to mention small businesses which depend upon the social power of community, fellowship, and friendship with which to compete with big business.

If we use chaos theory as an intellectual tool with which to sort out white-collar crime, we would look for small changes in income or in lifestyle to trigger large changes in white-collar crime. Expenses might increase. Divorce is a particularly expensive process; it forces a sharing of income between two households, both of which have lifestyle needs. Lifestyle demands can be very high. Houses cost hundreds of thousands of dollars; furnishings and maintenance tens of thousands more. Country club memberships, cultural affairs, vacation plans, and community benefits demand thousands more each year. Add to that the costs of college for the children of the professional classes, tax burdens as well as insurance costs, and one has a demand for high and steady income sources.

If we put ourselves in the life of, say, a physician who has an income of $200,000 a year and expenses of roughly the same, then one has a steady state that might vary even less than the fractal in Box C. A small change in any one of their parameters might destabilize the economic state of a white-collar family. While the data suggest that income drops more for wives, curiously, it is white-collar males who tend to turn to crime; it is they who have positions of trust to exploit.

Generally, professionals have three sources of income: fee for service, rent from property, and investment portfolios. Income might drop. Investment portfolios might fail in a savings and loan crisis. Property income might fail if a major corporation moved from a city. Government may alter third-party health care schemes and curtail sources of income. Patients may default on bills as wages decline or jobs disappear. A doctor might be able to handle one, two, or three such losses, but four or more might drive her/him to crime.

The possibilities for violation of trust are many for doctors. They can prescribe unnecessary and expensive medical procedures. They can bill Medicare and Medicaid for services not rendered. They can massify and mechanize the clinic substituting interpersonal therapies with drug therapy. They can bill patients at $40 to $100 dollars a visit when most of that time is taken up with low-paid nurses and technicians. Doctors can exploit the labor of employees, promising retirement plans, profit sharing, and wage increases—then dismiss the nurse or technician without so doing.

Again, one must wonder why it is possible for good people to commit crime and to escape guilt and shame. In the case of a physician, third-party payment dilutes the moral onus of fraud. The putative "victim" becomes the abstract state or the remote insurance company. One has less compunction about robbing them than patients directly. But doctors do overprescribe drugs and operations for known, trusting patients. They tend to do so for persons of low status. People receiving state aid are degraded in our health care system much more so than in Canada or Europe. Women are the victims of choice for unnecessary operations in a sexist society. Elderly persons are the victims of choice for overprescription of drugs.

Those forms of crime which can be done by remote or diluted agency are preferable for those professionals who are well socialized and who have good images of themselves. There is less onus for harming nonpersons than persons with full social standing. The same doctor who exploits the government can be very compassionate for friends or for charity patients of his own. The more bifurcations of responsibility, the more attractive becomes the crime. The same is true of corporate officers or political criminals.

Causality and Control

As the dynamics of social life become more and more complex, causality fades and fails; uncertainty increases and predictability is lost. Yet there is enough order in even deep chaos to ground a knowledge process. This new, postmodern knowledge process is much more modest, much less devoted to control and command than that philosophy of science which came out of the study of simple systems in the 1700s. When complexity increases, social control becomes ever more difficult. However, a certain light and timely control is possible. To control the march toward disorder or to increase the variety in an outcome field, one must find the attractors in very complex data sets and identify the parameters which drive them. Then one must locate the Feigenbaum points at which non-linearity increases qualitatively, and regulate them very gently and in timely fashion.[6]

In the United States, criminal behavior is policed by a series of parallel control institutions. Street crime is policed by the Criminal Justice System; white-collar crime is policed by Peer Review Committees; corporate crime is policed by Regulatory Agencies, while political crime is seldom policed. These and other social control institutions such as religion, medicine, and private agencies give the appearance of rationality and equality before the law, since self-similarity of outcome may be found within any given wing of a complex set of attractors but, when one looks at each control institution as part of a whole, the vast differences in policing and punishment serve to reproduce great inequalities in class, status, and power.

CONCLUSION

This new science of complexity awaits the next generation of criminologists and, indeed, all social scientists. It is grounded upon a postmodern philosophy of science in which certainty and finality are replaced by variability and contingency. This new science requires a whole new set of research tools not yet developed and a whole new kind of research design which is oriented to the quest for change rather than for precision. The old tests of the validity of research claims must be discarded: replication, falsification, tight-knit correlations, as well as formal, axiomatic deduction based upon Aristotlean logic—all of these lose their epistemological value as uncertainty increases with each bifurcation.

But the more nihilistic views of postmodern critics are equally inappropriate. A well-tempered knowledge process is possible. It is, to be sure, much more modest and much less ambitious in the control of nature and society, but it does offer several tasks well worth the time and energy invested by a society. In general, the mission of postmodern research is to identify the key parameters which produce ever more uncertainty in the lives of animals, peoples, and whole societies. In postmodern criminology, the quest is:

1. To locate the attractors hidden in complex data sets.
2. To determine how many attractors exist in that data set.
3. To find the change point(s) at which new attractors are produced.

And for purposes of social control,

4. To identify the key parameters which drive the system into ever more uncertainty.

And for purposes of social policy,

5. To determine which setting of those key parameters is acceptable to the whole society.

When the regularities between cause and effect, between sanction and behavior, between plans and successes fail, a society must then consider other approaches to deal with the problem of crime. For the postmodern criminologists, chaos theory suggests that, rather than punishment and a narrow deterrence focused upon and only upon individuals, the better, more useful approach is to identify the key parameters driving these hidden attractors and, then, institute social policy which enables individual persons and whole social categories to cope with life on terms amenable to the larger concerns of social justice.

NOTES

1. It is very important to note that in the transformation to disorder, there is an elegant order at these transformation points which I call Feigenbaum points, after the mathematician who discovered them. It is also most important to know that these very specific transformation points are found in what is called *deterministic chaos*. We can grasp the incredible complexity of social life when we realize that some social processes are deterministic and some are not. Yet even the non-deterministic transformations have enough order in them to ground a new, postmodern science. This is discussed in Chapter 2.
2. Phase space is a method of analytic geometry developed by René Descartes in which the behavior of a system is tracked through time in two- or three-dimensional space. The display of a heartbeat on a cathode tube in a hospital is

a well-known example. One can "see" the geometry of the heartbeat registered as a changing curve with spikes and valleys, as the electronic impulses change in frequency and magnitude.

3. It well may be the case that some inequality is helpful to a society. Class inequalities of 2, 4, 8, or 16 times may be mediated by any number of sharing mechanisms and thus not distort economic or political processes. Some low-level income inequality may help motivation. High-level inequality may provide a surplus for investment and charity. Some small power inequality may be helpful to control those not yet socialized or those not well socialized. Great inequalities of power, as Lord Acton suggested, may corrupt both the strong and the weak. Corruption of the strong is registered in political crime; corruption of the weak in street crime, racism, drug use, and gender violence.

4. See John Briggs and F. David Peat (1989: 38) for a charming treatment of bifurcations. A more rigorous treatment is provided by Leon Glass and Michael Mackey (1988: 19–34). Glass and Mackey mention the feedback mechanisms which stabilize new patterns.

5. One might wonder why improvements in quality or reductions in price are not considered as options. They do work and work well in some conditions. But crime is often a source of profits while both improvement in quality and reduction in price deflate profits. When profit drives a system, other parameters must give way.

6. Hübler (1992), at the Beckman Institute at the University of Illinois, has shown that such control of non-linear regimes is possible.

REFERENCES

Ashby, H.R. 1968. "Variety, Constraint, and the Law of Requisite Variety." Pp 135–47 in W. Buckley, ed., *Modern Systems Research for the Behavioral Scientist*. Chicago: Aldine.

Berry, B.J.L. 1991. *Long-Wave Rhythms in Economic Development and Political Behavior*. Baltimore: Johns Hopkins University Press.

Briggs, J. and F.D. Peat. 1989. *Turbulent Mirror: An Illustrated Guide to Chaos Theory and the Science of Wholeness*. New York: Harper and Row.

Feigenbaum, M. 1978. "Quantitative Universality for a Class of Nonlinear Transformations." *Journal of Statistical Physics* 19: 25–52.

Glass, L. and M. Mackey. 1988. *From Clocks to Chaos*. Princeton: Princeton University Press.

Hübler A. 1992. "Modeling and Control of Complex Systems: Paradigms and Applications." In L. Lam (ed.), *Modeling Complex Phenomena*. New York: Springer.

Merton, R. 1957. *Social Theory and Social Structure*. New York: The Free Press.

O'Malley, P. 1979. "Social Bandits, Modern Capitalism and the Traditional Peasantry: A Critique of Hobsbawn." *Journal of Peasant Studies* 6:4.

Young, T.R. "1996 Chaos and Control Theory." Preprint available from the Red Feather Institute, 8085 Essex, Weidman, MI 48893.

CHAPTER 5

Geometric Forms of Violence

Hal Pepinsky

TWO WAYS OF RELATING

One might suppose that interaction would be highly chaotic in a culture in which a premium is placed on violence. In fact, scientists in the new field of chaos have discovered that order "strangely" emerges out of chaos throughout the physical and social world (summarized in Gleick, 1987). This chapter focuses on forms in which order emerges in attempts to use violence as an instrument of the state to control supposed social enemies of a supposedly law-abiding citizenry.

State power over others in the United States appears to be in the process of reaching unsurpassable limits, first in power to make war on foreign enemies, then in power to make war on domestic enemies. This leads state violence to become more concentrated. As it becomes more concentrated, it appears it is following the laws of chaos and dissolving into turbulence. In this turbulence, it will become increasingly difficult to separate enemies of violently imposed state order from defenders of that order. Optimistically, that turbulence would represent a transition from a culture of violence to a culture in which peacemaking is the prevalent social order.

We relate to one another, basically, in two ways. One I call "violence" (Pepinsky, 1991, particularly at pp. 8–33, and 85–98). I and others have used many terms for the other way of relating: responsiveness, democracy, love, compassion, mercy (Pepinsky, 1991), and ultimately, peacemaking (first with Richard Quinney in Pepinsky and Quinney, 1991; most recently in Pepinsky, 1995).

Violence to me means setting one's own goals and objectives and not changing them, regardless of the effects on others of trying to meet those goals and objectives. Violence is what repels us about what we call "crime." The scary part of rape is that one person is determined to make a particular use of another's body, regardless of the pain and fear that use causes in the other person. The scary part of theft is taking something from someone, regardless of the other's attachment to that thing. The scary part of addiction is being so focused on feeding one's habit that one tunes out one's sensitivity and responsiveness to others. However, "crime" is a politically and culturally arbitrary subset of violence. Some acts, some actors, get labeled criminal, while other equally violent acts may even be socially praised, as in war.

In any form, violence means subordinating concern for the effect of one's actions on others to one's determination to reach a goal. One may have to accommodate to others to reach the objective, but the measure of one's success is having the drive and the intelligence to stay focused on the objective and get there. I live in a culture, in the United States, in which violence is highly prized. Setting goals and achieving them is regarded as the most desirable quality for members of the culture to develop. Setting goals is commonly regarded as the first task of any group of people who would work together, and the evaluation of the quality of their group effort is how well and completely they have achieved those goals. If the meeting of one group's or person's goals conflicts with the meeting of another's, it is considered healthful to encourage the competition, and a net benefit to the society that those who have met their goals have had to struggle against and prevail over competitors. The winners' success implies that their knowledge is superior to the losers' and that we benefit by their free demonstration of their superiority. Laws are set and imposed to channel that competition while encouraging it, including allowing winners to protect the secrets of their success and to own the fruits of their own success.

In making peace, one continually reevaluates one's personal or group objectives in light of the effects on others of meeting one's objectives. The greatest threat to social order and, therefore, to one's own personal security is the overpowering of anyone's capacity to work toward what s/he honestly feels s/he needs and wants—the separation of members from one another's unguarded candor. Honesty and open sharing of personal feelings and inclinations are the most essential condition for bridging the separation; for maintaining trust and the foundation of community, wherein members' goals can be harmonized, wherein members can support one another's goal attainment rather than competing against it (Cordella, 1991). The next step beyond identifying one's own immediate interests to oneself and others is to reach out first to those who appear to be most separated from participation in community life, to listen hardest to those whose voices are least heard, to accommodate first to the most powerless, or weakest, or quietest, or most victimized members of the group. One's time and attention would be one's primary contribution to this social enterprise. Encouragement and support of that member's initiative would take precedence over one's own prior agenda, and one's own next direction or objective would be an interaction—a function—of one's own prior personal aims and those of the other. Together, they would confront those whose unilateral action was becoming most concerted, whose violence was most manifest, not to punish the violator, but to speak loudly and directly enough to bring the violator's effects on others to his or her attention, and to refuse to cooperate in the continuing of that course. The listening and validation are what Mohandas Gandhi called "ahimsa" or love, and "satyagraha" or holding onto truth, which Anderson (1991) describes as overcoming alienation from community life.

This way of relating amounts to resonance and harmony, which create their own social music. While chaos theorists study how power is transformed into order out of apparently chaotic exercises of force, peacemaking would be a transition into a state of "synergy" (Pepinsky, 1991: 86–91)—where a moment of interaction could sustain and build life with as much energy as unilateral effort exerted over a lifetime. It is what Eisler (1987) calls life in "partnership" rather than in "domination" and submission.

SOCIETAL RHYTHMS IN THE CHAOS OF VIOLENCE

In an essay actually written before the fall of the Soviet Union, I drew upon chaos theory to observe that state violence worldwide seemed to be oscillating between waves twelve to twenty-five years apart (Pepinsky, 1991: 34–61). This stable pattern of violence and its management now appears to be dissolving into turbulence. Following Eisler (1987), I hypothesize that the chaos in which we now find ourselves is a transition back to a preexisting global order, from 4.5 millennia in "dominator societies" to "partnership," as our violence becomes unsustainable.

Here is the pattern I saw: in one wave of state management of violence a new generation of political leadership assumed power. The new leaders were expected to make room for their own heirs to assume positions as high in the competitive world order as themselves by expanding their people's share of the global economic pie. Youth rebelled against the pressure, while their elders worried that the youth did not have what it took to take hold of their legacy. The elders saw a need for greater discipline of youth as well as a need to struggle against foreign competition. To win both struggles, the new generation of leaders was especially prone to mobilize the youth into military front lines to fight wars. When troops were mobilized in large numbers to fight, young men went to war instead of going to prison, and incarceration rates leveled off or dropped. The last such period in the United States was after John Kennedy succeeded Dwight Eisenhower as president, and eventually as many as a half million U.S. troops were sent to fight in Vietnam. As warfare and politics became globalized, these patterns tended to occur simultaneously across nations. One might characterize these waves as periods of explosive political conflict and change.

The second wave was a conservative backwash against the first. Once restless youth had now reached middle age; the haves among them had outgrown rebellion and wanted to be cared for by elder father figures, while aging leaders clung to incumbency. In this period the haves in each polity tended to turn their war inward against domestic enemies, in wars on crime. As the principal punishment for crime, incarceration rates climbed. In the United States, incarceration rates bottomed out in the mid-1970s and began their most dramatic climb in the 1980s, driven by renewed wars on drugs, as a senior father figure, Ronald Reagan, assumed the presidency (Beck and Gilliard, 1995; and Perkins et al., 1995).

A strange attractor is a pattern mysteriously formed and filled in by a line, generated by a non-linear equation, moving unpredictably from point to point, back and forth around itself. Together, the recurring waves of violence were like the two wings of the earliest "strange attractor" constructed in early chaos research in 1963 by Edward Lorenz (Gleick, 1987: 139–41). Tracing those cycles, I noted that over the past two centuries of incarceration in the United States, the swing back to wars against foreign enemies had periodically broken the upward climb in incarceration.

I saw that Mikhail Gorbachev heralded the onset of the next first wave of new leadership when he assumed direction of the Soviet Communist Party in 1985. I foresaw that as leadership in the United States changed to those not yet in adulthood in World War II, the Soviet and U.S. leadership would coalesce into the ends of a Northern European axis militarily mobilized against Southern leaders, predominantly against Muslim leaders. I was wrong. U.S. President George Bush managed to draw the Russian leadership into an alliance in his war against Iraq, but the Gulf War of 1991 signaled the end of the World War II generation of leadership in the United States. Military might had finally reached a point in the mightiest of superpowers of being potentially destructive beyond all political usefulness. A century ago, in 1897, Theodore Roosevelt could write a friend, "In strict confidence . . . I should welcome almost any war, for I think this country needs one," and help that wish become reality (Zinn, 1980: 290). Those days appear to have ended.

In the new generation, President Clinton and his administration have avoided mobilizing U.S. forces into combat, carefully engineering limited police roles instead. The young president aimed to continue the war on crime against underclass young men as though in deference to his elders' management of force and violence. Counts of juveniles and adults in custody in the United States come in bits and pieces, but all seem to be on the rise. The last report on those held under state and federal prison authority, for the year ending June 30, 1995, "was the largest one-year population increase the Department [of Justice] has recorded" (U.S. Department of Justice, 1995).

This is akin to pushing against the line in Lorenz's two-winged strange attractor as it verges on moving from one wing to the other, pushing the line back on itself. With successive pushes, the line bifurcates, bifurcates again, and soon moves back and forth erratically, "turbulently," on the side on which it is allowed to continue to move. More and more people are added to prison, but confusion can be expected to reign in the process of collecting criminals.

THE FLOW OF THE UNDISTURBED LEGAL PROCESS

Zinn (1980) applauds the genius of the design of the U.S. constitutional system as one providing a stable regime in which political and economic elites can operate without serious threat of revolution. The statutory law of the United States in each jurisdiction comes in several parts, which together operate to help ensure, as Reiman (1995) puts it, that "the rich get richer and the poor get prison." There is a civil law of LIABILITY. There is a law of government workers' ACCOUNTABILITY to the people they are supposed to serve. And there is a criminal law of RESPONSI-BILITY for private misbehavior. Preparing lectures during a period of study in Norway, I noticed that these three terms translate into one in Norwegian: "*ansvar*," which literally means "responsiveness." It was at this point that I recognized "responsiveness" to be the antithesis of violence and domination (Pepinsky, 1991:8–33).

I think it is significant that in English three different terms are used for parts of law which in turn generally are applied to different groups of people. The softest term is reserved for the law applied primarily to the business community. An important function of this law is to *limit* liability. One form of limitation now routinely granted major businesses to move into communities is on taxation—tax abatement. The other form is provision for incorporation, which literally serves to limit the liability of owners for corporate misdeeds to what they have already invested in the business. Adam Smith (1776) railed against provision for incorporation; Jesilow (1982) observes that, indeed, allowing investors to create businesses while limiting personal responsibility for harms done by the businesses has been an open invitation to white-collar crime. Meanwhile, too, civil courts are overwhelmingly used by large organizations rather than by individuals; even small claims courts have become corporate collection agencies to a great extent. At worst, the imposition of liability is less stigmatizing by far than a criminal conviction.

As someone with a legal background who has tried to help countless people appeal and aggrieve public actions or failures of action, I am accustomed to seeing complainants and grievants, myself included, being beaten down and back. In my experience, the first time an official says "no" to one's request, others to whom one appeals back the first official up as readily as iron filings snap in line with a magnet that is brought close to them. There are exceptions, of course, but generally speaking, it takes an insider to have another insider held accountable for wrongdoing. When it comes to politicians we elect or, like police, hire to improve the state of our social order, they tend to blame the weakest subjects of the order for social problems, attempting to mobilize support by getting tough on the subjects. As teachers like me are prone to blame our students for failures to master course material, so politicians tend to blame underclass or otherwise powerless young men and women for social problems, playing on stereotypes based on gender and race as well. Currently, across the United States, national and state politicians and candidates for office are vying to be tough on powerless figures like teenaged women who have children but not paid work (never mind whether they were raped by older men; never mind whether anyone is feeding or caring for the children while we force the women off welfare). They focus on use of drugs like crack cocaine, found most among poor young people of color, rather than on drugs of choice of middle-class white folks like powdered cocaine or the prescription drugs that kill users in the greatest numbers (Mauer, 1996; Morley, 1996). Incarceration rates continue to climb apace, fed by continuing political rhetoric that "the criminal element," including street gang members, is the biggest threat to the safety and security of us all; their confinement and punishment the highest priority for governmental action.

THE UNDERLYING FRACTAL REALITY OF VIOLENCE

Assuming that violence occurs like other phenomena observed by chaos theorists, the big official picture of violence repeats itself right down to the closest interpersonal level in our lives across social class and caste; violence occurs "fractally." One of the key chaos researchers, Benoit Mandelbrot, coined the term "fractals"—short for fractional dimensions—to describe a level of uniformity he saw in physical and social phenomena. First he noticed that although you could not predict the price of cotton in a market from one moment to the next, the curve-fitting fluctuations in price for each day matched the curve for monthly fluctuations. For coastlines, for wind, for clouds, Mandelbrot found that the patterns that formed at any level reappeared at other magnitudes of time and space, at varying scales. Reporting on this series of discoveries, Gleick (1987: 81–118) concludes that this "scaling" of phenomena in physics

led . . . to the discipline known as chaos. Even in distant fields, scientists were beginning to think in terms of hierarchies of scales, where it became clear that theory would have to recognize patterns of development in genes, in individual organisms, in species, and in families of species, all at once. (p. 116)

For one thing, small-time street crime is paralleled by big-time suite crime. By now there are numerous criminological studies reporting that property loss and damage, personal injury and death, and drug use and trafficking in violation of our criminal codes by persons of wealth and power in and out of government, including the military and law enforcement, vastly exceed that of street crime for which we customarily punish offenders. Examples include Chambliss (1988), Pepinsky and Jesilow (1992), and Reiman (1995). None of us is in a position to prove this proposition to those determined to believe that underclass young men are our most dangerous citizens. For that matter, a criminal conviction does not "prove" a defendant guilty of a crime. Although we throw the word "proof" around pretty liberally, tautology—being true by definition as in two plus two equaling four—is the only proof of anything. But it is awfully convenient to believe that crime happens most just where the police happen to be mobilized to look for it, and just where it is most politically acceptable for us to acknowledge it. Moreover, if the social theories we normally use to explain street criminality apply, then the more power our social position confers on us in relation to others, the more numerous and serious crimes we will commit, because we have more opportunity to do greater damage to others, and because we are less restrained by the watchfulness or threat of adverse response by others. Logically speaking, holding a position of power over others should be the primary social cause of misbehavior, including violent disregard of the harm, fear, or distress one causes in others. Notice how commonly this logic is applied across religious traditions to indicate that persons of wealth and high social position are particularly spiritually suspect. For wealth and high social position to retain legitimacy this logic has to remain politically denied and socially unacknowledged, but the fault does not lie in the logic itself. If, as I have here, one defines "violence" as power over others and the determination to have one's way with it, then to paraphrase Lord Acton, power causes violence; the greater one's power to have one's way with another person or group without effective resistance, the greater one's tendency toward violence.

If violence works fractally, as chaos scientists propose all the world works, the more intense the large-scale violence around us, the more intense and prevalent violence should become at the interpersonal level throughout the social system. Brock-Utne (1989) charts a range of levels of patriarchically generated violence from direct interpersonal to structural levels. Tifft and Markham (1991) have traced the connection between the propensity of home partners to batter women in the United States and the policy the United States has had of "battering Central Americans." If, as is now commonly supposed, adult women are commonly battered in all classes of homes in the United States and indeed elsewhere in the world too, then children should be even more violated, all the more so the younger they are and the more unquestionably entrusted unsupervised adults are with their care. Paradoxically, in a stable violent social order one would expect the violence to be more insistently denied by all concerned: (a) the more horrific and brutal the violence, (b) the higher the political and social standing of the violators, and (c) the closer and more sacrosanct the relationship between the adult and the child.

This is precisely the reality an increasing number of people see. By way of introduction, I particularly recommend Dziech and Schudson (1991) for a review of that reality as presented by children; Whitfield (1995) for an account of how survivors, unprompted, recover credible memories of the reality and heal from it; and Sakheim and Devine (1992) for a range of opinion, and DeCamp (1992) for the most copious published documentation of a case I know concerning the most gruesome and widely denied and dismissed reports of ritual abuse.

These past several years, I have become well acquainted with cases of alleged sexual assault of children and have gotten to know child complainants, their protective parents, adults reporting survival of child sexual assault, and therapists, activists, and investigators in these cases across the United States. This includes knowing several people who report that their socially prominent parents or grandparents in groups including other pillars of their communities have not only drugged and raped them repeatedly, but have tortured them and forced them to kill and eat others. One of these cases got as far as prosecution of sorts. A socially prominent father was under order of extradition for having raped his daughter several times when he died suddenly, of reported "natural causes" but without an autopsy. I have friends who have corroborated reports that named people were sacrificed with death certificates or by digging up a body (as DeCamp reports in one instance). I myself have stumbled onto one seeming grave (later dug up) in an elaborately constructed ritual site on private property, which the police say they lacked resources to investigate more than cursorily. As Whitfield reports, it is only since the 1960s that the sheer physical battering of children has been recognized to be more than an isolated occurrence.

Like Whitfield, I believe false reports to be few and far between; signs that memories might have been coached or implanted or concocted I believe are at best occasional, in a few notorious and oft-cited instances. If this part of the world, where it is generally agreed that a large proportion of women at some age are sexually assaulted by someone they know, and where we are alarmed at police reports that one person is apparently murdered for each ten thousand years of human life in our communities, the emerging picture of widespread, serious violence against children by adults we trust to take care of them makes fractal sense. It is also to be expected that this previously hidden violence would become less obscured by the spectacle of state violence and state-reported violence as that spectacle dissolved into turbulent activity.

THE PROSPECT OF TRANSITION TO A PEACEFUL ORDER

Making peace in the face of such pervasive, deeply seated violence requires putting validation of victims ahead of retaliation against offenders. Validation is the primary emphasis of therapists like Whitfield (1995) and Miller (1990), who are dedicated to helping survivors heal. The essence of healing lies in victims' discovery that they are persons of value—that the worthlessness, the shame, the initially nameless guilt they feel is not, to use Whitfield's term, their "true self." Memories of the most traumatic victimization, of the greatest betrayals of trust, are the last to return to a victim's consciousness, returning as the victim comes to feel safe, in control of interaction, not pressed to have to disclose anything for anyone else's benefit. Healing is essentially learning to trust that one can express one's true feelings without having them denied or losing control of what is done with one's expression. Remembering and sharing the things which hurt and threaten one most deeply grow with the opportunity to express what one truly feels and believes without being punished for it. Miller (1990) observes that all children begin with the inclination to be honest with others and to listen openly, attentively, and compassionately to what others feel and believe. Confusion, lying, and dissociation begin when we are forced to bury what we feel or believe in favor of expressing what others demand we feel or believe, on grounds it is "for your own good." Whitfield joins her in observing that we adapt to this pressure either by "acting in"—punishing ourselves, numbing ourselves, putting ourselves in abusers' hands to suppress the "bad" feelings we have—or by "acting out"—letting out our true suffering by inflicting the suffering on others. In case studies of a secret mass killer and of Adolf Hitler, Miller indicates that acting out can either be a horrible secret or become a public policy position.

Validation requires a safe opportunity to express one's anger and betrayal over victimization. Whitfield advises therapists working with survivors of child abuse to hold clients back from confronting their abusers so that this validation can occur. The greater the betrayal, the more horrific the abuse, the more likely the abuser is to deny all, to attack the victim for lying or being crazy or misled; and the more likely bystanders are to accept the denial and add to the pressure on the victim to recant or go silent. When it comes to parental sexual assault on children, as with any victimization, no healing is more magical than that which occurs where the victim confronts the offender, and the offender acknowledges the wrong, apologizes ("Why, why, why did I do it?") and offers to atone (as described by Gustafson, 1991). Unfortunately, this happy outcome is least likely in the severest cases of betrayal of personal trust, where the offender may even have repressed any memory of a prolonged series of assaults. Paradoxically, since violence itself is a product of victimization, it is when we feel least threatened by punishment and recrimination that we are most able to acknowledge the harm we have done others and assume responsibility for it. Our capacity to assume responsibility increases as the force of being "held responsible" diminishes. Our capacity to put victimization squarely in front of offenders where they cannot make it go away as they consider assuming responsibility rests on victims' gaining the strength of knowing they will be validated by bystanders, regardless of what we manage to get out of the offenders. We need to develop our capacity to validate victimization without regard to using it against offenders.

A climate of retribution forces us to bury victimization. It is rightly argued that no victim should be forced to confront an offender in a mediative setting. Confrontation for purposes of prosecution is worse. To begin with, especially in the intimate trauma of sexual assault, the imperative to gather physical evidence and statements takes precedence over simple care and comfort. Whether the victim has a real problem immediately becomes confounded with the issue of how unambiguously a prospective judge or jury can be expected to condemn the accused. What can be done for the victim becomes a matter of what the victim needs to do for law enforcement. An adversarial court process of confronting the accused and being subject to cross-examination is a license to attack the credibility and motives of the victim. Even if the accused pleads guilty, the victim sees the plea as a charade and never has a chance even to ask what s/he wants to know from the offender. We should not be surprised if victims do their best to ignore and forget what has been done to them rather than face this process.

Mediation processes like family group councils in New Zealand (Consedine, 1995) and victim–offender reconciliation programs (Zehr, 1990) are wonderful alternatives to prosecution in many cases, but they require that offenders acknowledge the victimization and volunteer to face those they already acknowledge to be their victims. All the evidence of child abuse that is rising to our social surface these days suggests that the deepest and most pervasive victimization suffered is only beginning to be acknowledged by victims, let alone by offenders.

The most poignant cases I have encountered are those of children who, in the midst of divorce and separation, return traumatized from visits with parents. When being with someone appears upsetting, especially in the midst of otherwise disruptive conditions, the most obvious response would be to allow some distance, as in having visits in neutral places or with third parties the children like. Instead, apparently in thousands of cases each year, courts deny such requests, and until criminal abuse is "proven," treat it as important to force the children into greater intimacy with the parents and to punish "protective" parents for resisting. This pressure tends to become greatest where corroborative evidence, as of damage to children's genitalia or anuses, is most dramatic, where the stakes in protecting parents' capacity to defend themselves against assault charges become highest because of the seriousness of the suspected abuse.

Even this evidence would not have come to light unless the parents had split up. All in all, there appears to be a need for children to have no-fault opportunities to get some distance from custodians when the children become upset, and generally to have access to a wide circle of adults, some of whom they can express themselves openly to, insofar as they feel victimized and trapped with others. The opportunity to choose to associate and disassociate with others unconditionally ought to be expanded at all ages, together with the expectation that we will spend more time sharing our sense of intimate victimization with one another, while suspending the presumption that we need to take out after one another's victimizers in the aftermath. In the process, we can nurture and rediscover honesty among ourselves, and become true selves who can respond to victimization at our own pace, on our own terms, instead of having law enforcers offer us the facade of protection by identifying and retaliating against offenders on their terms, on our behalf.

I see this as a part of the process of democratizing our lives, not only in how we respond to being violated, but in how we produce for and support one another (Pepinsky, 1991). It is a process of learning once again to live in partnership (Eisler, 1987). In chaos terms, "strange attraction" emerges in cross-sections of social life where people are allowed the opportunity to interact openly and unconditionally, and to negotiate and create their own ways out of problems gradually. Then social life becomes strong and stable like the chaos figure known as a "Menger Sponge," a block of holes surrounded by smaller holes surrounded by smaller holes ad infinitum in which the lines between holes add up to infinite length but occupy no volume. When instead we try to take over one another's problems and "solve" them by having some build structures for the rest to occupy, we force the strange attractors created by human trust to split apart again and again until community dissolves into turbulence, where the order rests more and more heavily on lies and (self-) deceit (summarized in Pepinsky, 1991: 44–61). We have reached the point in history at which building domination further defeats even the greatest dominators—first in foreign military conquest, then in exposing criminals without exposing their own criminality. We cannot correct this problem by exchanging dominators or leaders. Transition to life in partnership is the only way to gain the safety of community in the face of violence. Partnership begins by listening to one another's victimizations simply to acknowledge the true extent of the violence we face. In such relationships we enjoy safety from further victimization. To be able to attend to that task, to build true companionship into one another's lives, we have to let go of identifying, isolating, and subduing enemies on anyone else's behalf.

REFERENCES

Anderson, K. 1991. "Radical Criminology and the Overcoming of Suffering." Pp. 14–29 in H.E. Pepinsky and R. Quinney (eds.), *Criminology as Peacemaking*. Bloomington: Indiana University Press.

Beck, A.J. and D.K. Gilliard. 1995. "Prisoners in 1994." *Bureau of Justice Statistics Bulletin* NCJ-151654 (August).

Brock-Utne, B. 1989. *Feminist Perspectives on Peace and Peace Education*. New York: Pergamon.

Chambliss, W.J. 1988. *On the Take: From Petty Crooks to Presidents*, 2d ed. Bloomington: Indiana University Press.

Consedine, J. 1995. *Restorative Justice: Healing the Effects of Crime*. Lyttleton, New Zealand: Ploughshares Publications.

Cordella, J.P. 1991. "Reconciliation and the Mutualist Model of Community." Pp. 30–46 in H.E. Pepinsky and R. Quinney (eds.), *Criminology as Peacemaking*. Bloomington: Indiana University Press.

Dziech, B.W. and C.R. Schudson. 1991. *On Trial: America's Courts and Their Treatment of Sexually Abused Children*, 2d ed. Boston: Beacon Press.

Eisler, R. 1987. *The Chalice and the Blade: Our History, Our Future*. New York: HarperCollins.

DeCamp, J.W. 1992. *The Franklin Cover-Up: Child Abuse, Satanism, and Murder in Nebraska*. Lincoln, NE: AWT, Inc.

Gleick, J. 1987. *Chaos: The Making of a New Science*. New York: Viking Penguin Books.

Gustafson, D. 1991. "Incest: The Theft of Childhood, A Survivor's Story." *Interaction* (Spring): 12–13.

Jesilow, P. 1982. "Adam Smith and the Notion of White-Collar Crime: Some Research Themes." *Criminology* 20(4): 319–28.

Mauer, M. 1996. "The Drug War's Unequal Justice." *The Drug Policy Letter*, no. 28 (Winter): 10–13.

Miller, A. 1990. *For Your Own Good: Hidden Cruelty in Child-Rearing and the Roots of Violence*. New York: The Noonday Press.

Morley, J. 1996. "White Gram's Burden." *The Drug Policy Letter*, no. 28 (Winter): 17–19.

Pepinsky, H. 1995. "Peacemaking Primer." *Peace and Conflict Studies* 2(2): 32–53.

Pepinsky, H.E. 1991. *The Geometry of Violence and Democracy*. Bloomington: Indiana University Press.

Pepinsky, H.E. and P. Jesilow. 1992. *Myths That Cause Crime*, 3d ed. Washington, DC: Seven Locks Press.

Pepinsky, H.E. and R. Quinney (eds.). 1991. *Criminology as Peacemaking*. Bloomington: Indiana University Press.

Perkins, C.A., J.J. Stephen, and A.J. Beck. 1995. "Jails and Inmates, 1993–94." *Bureau of Justice Statistics Bulletin* NCJ-151651 (September).

Reiman, J. 1995. *The Rich Get Richer and the Poor Get Prison*, 4th ed. Boston: Allyn & Bacon.

Sakheim, D. and S.E. Devine. 1992. *Out of Darkness: Exploring Satanism and Ritual Abuse*. New York: Lexington Books/Maxwell Macmillan International.

Smith, A. 1937 (1776). *The Wealth of Nations*. New York: Modern Library.

Tifft, L. and L. Markham. 1991. "Battering Women and Battering Central Americans." Pp. 114–53 in H.E. Pepinsky and R. Quinney (eds.), *Criminology as Peacemaking*. Bloomington: Indiana University Press.

U.S. Department of Justice, Bureau of Justice Statistics. 1995. "State and Federal Prisons Report Record Growth During Last 12 Months." Press release (December 3).

Whitfield, C.L. 1995. *Memory and Abuse: Remembering and Healing the Effects of Trauma*. Deerfield Beach, FL: Health Communications, Inc.

Zehr, H. 1990. *Changing Lenses: A New Focus for Crime and Justice*. Scottsdale, PA: Herald Press.

Zinn, H. 1980. *A People's History of the United States*. New York: Harper Torchbooks.

CHAPTER 6

Law and Social Change: The Implications of Chaos Theory in Understanding the Role of the American Legal System

Glenna L. Simons
and William F. Stroup II

INTRODUCTION

Much has been written about the relationship between law and social change. According to functionalist views, the legal system is a component of a larger social system which is charged with maintaining order. Ideally, change comes about slowly and gradually, following a shift in the normative consensus. Functionalist perspectives, by emphasizing a linear model of change and a view of law as a mechanism of social control, leave something to be desired in the attempt to explain sudden or radical change and the role of law as instrument of this change. Conflict perspectives, on the other hand, view change as inevitable, as more "normal" than order. Many conflict theories conceptualize law as a method or tool of domination constructed by the privileged in order to exercise social control over those less powerful. While this view recognizes the potential of law as an instrument of change, the perspective can be criticized for oversimplifying the complex and dynamic relationship between the law and social change.

Kellert (1995) has suggested that a metaphorical extension of the concepts developed in chaos theory can provide a new resource which may be used by social scientists seeking to explain social phenomena in terms of non-linear dynamics. This chapter proposes that a chaos perspective be employed in a metaphorical sense to enhance our understanding of the relationship between law and social change by incorporating some of the ideas of both functionalist and conflict perspectives. The concepts of chaos theory, including attractors, recursive symmetry, and self-organization, can provide additional insights into this relationship which help to correct for deficiencies in earlier approaches. In so doing, this chapter helps to dispel two commonly held myths regarding the applicability of chaos theory in the social sciences, namely: (1) that either "order" or "conflict" is the "normal" state of a society, and (2) that the concepts of chaos theory are irrelevant to or incompatible with other social theories.

THE RELATIONSHIP BETWEEN LAW AND SOCIAL CHANGE

Functionalist Perspectives and the Problem of Order versus Change

Baker (1993) has discussed early approaches to the problem of order in society, and notes that when social scientists pursue a linear type of logic to study society, society itself becomes a "thing." The problem of explaining how order in society is possible becomes the "problem of integration and the intellectual perspective used to investigate it, functionalism" (p. 125). Baker points out that functionalist approaches to the study of society have largely concentrated upon the discernment and description of ordered relationships of institutions within society, but have neglected the relationship between society and its environment, positing that society itself is somehow *separated* from its environment. Baker also notes that there are methodological problems encountered by functionalists in trying to apply scientific methods to the study of society, since societies are, in fact, embedded in their environments and cannot be taken into a lab and studied as though in isolation. Talcott Parsons's work is cited by Baker as perhaps the most famous example of an attempt to understand our social world as an "integrated whole." In the 1960s and 1970s, of course, Parsonian functionalist sociology came under heavy attack by Marxists, critical theorists, and those who wished to place a greater emphasis upon the processes of conflict inherent in social systems (Turner, 1991). Because the functionalist perspective seemed to regard a system in equilibrium as the norm or the ideal, the functionalist perspective came to be seen as an inadequate conception of the processes of social change, and functionalism came to be seen as supportive of status quo.

Young (1993) remarks on the problem in assuming that order is given and preferable, and refers to this assumption as the "fatal flaw in modernistic legal codes." Because of the emphasis upon "order" as the natural or preferred state of a society, law in context of the functionalist perspective comes to be seen as a social control mechanism, and the legal system is seen as that element of a larger system which functions to maintain order in the system as a whole.

In discussing the role of law as a social control mechanism, Milovanovic (1994) identifies and discusses three functions of law as (1) repressive, involving the external threat of physical force to ensure compliance to a society's norms; (2) facilitative, as in "assuring predictability and certainty in behavioral expectations" (p. 9); and (3) ideological, a systematic embodiment of the values of a given group. He cites Luhmann (1985) as a more contemporary neofunctionalist writer who describes the function of law as "generalized expectations." According to Luhmann, law becomes a uniform reference point in modern complex societies which can no longer be integrated through a consensus of values. In this way, law functions to maintain order within a society by providing for structured expectations. Thus, whether we think of law as repressive, facilitative, or ideological, we see that a common theme in the functionalist perspective of law is the maintaining of societal order as a preferred goal, whether this order emanates from a full-fledged value consensus, or from mere generalized expectations. This view conceptualizes law as a sort of dependent variable, resulting from some type of societal "need" or "requisite," and fosters an impression of the disorder inherent in social change as somehow deviant and pathological.

To be sure, some sociologists (for example, Coser, 1956) have endeavored to correct for this bias by emphasizing the positive and adaptive functions of conflict in a changing society. The end result of this approach, however, is to see conflict as not only inevitable, but as fulfilling a functional need or requisite of a social whole which remains independent of its environment. To say that conflict ultimately fulfills an integrative function for society is to still emphasize the need for integration as the ideal or goal, implying some end point equilibrium.

Conflict Perspectives

Conflict perspectives to the study of society, on the other hand, do not see disruption or conflict as pathological, but rather as the moving force behind social changes needed to address injustices and inequities within society. In adopting a non-linear, non-equilibrium approach to social change, dialectical conflict theorists see a constant dialectical process of thesis and antithesis. While many conflict theorists would probably agree that law in society fulfills repressive, facilitative, and ideological functions, the question becomes, "functional for whom?" Many of these theorists would insist that the use of law as a social control mechanism functions only to maintain a given set of power relationships within the system. Instrumental Marxists, feminists, and critical theorists involved in the study of law and society have recognized that law constitutes a tool or method of domination through which those who have the power to do so can exercise social control over those less privileged. These perspectives have led to the debunking of the myth of law as objective, fair, and neutral, and have emphasized the role of power relationships and competition for resources within societies. These perspectives see instability or conflict within society as a "normal" component inherent in the dialectical process. While these perspectives recognize the potential of law as an instrument of social change, the function of law remains that of social control, as well as a basis of legitimation for those in power to maintain their relative positions. The social changes brought about by law are thus temporary, maintained for the benefit of a particular group. While law may not always be employed to restore order to a society, it may be the instrument which brings in a new order. The view that conflict is inevitable leads to a belief that the conflict within societies is somehow more "normal" than stability.

Although a dialectical conflict approach shares many of the characteristics of the chaos perspective, including an emphasis on process and non-linearity, the approach does not seem adequate to explain certain types of change. For example, if law is used as a tool of repression, then how can we explain the passage of the civil rights acts, which brought needed social change for the poor and disenfranchised classes of American society? To see the law as merely a method of exploitation would seem overly simplistic. The dialectical approach, by emphasizing the processes of conflict, ignores the fact that change does not *always* come as a result of conflict, but is, at times, gradual after all.

CHAOS THEORY AS A MORE ENCOMPASSING ALTERNATIVE WHICH EMBRACES THE INTERPLAY OF ORDER AND CHANGE

The chaos perspective in science is really the advent of a new paradigm which, when embraced by social scientists, can help us to reconcile the problem of order and change in a society. In describing the new perspective, Young (1991) states that "Instead of seeking universal laws that allow prediction, certainty, and stability of findings, it elevates variation, change, surprise and unpredictability to the center of the knowledge process" (p. 290). Chaos theory helps us to stop thinking in terms of "order" *versus* "conflict," by revealing that these are really two phases of the same phenomenon or process, rather than opposites which cannot be reconciled (Prigogine and Stengers, 1984). In this way, chaos theory can help to "free" us from thinking about either change or stability as being the "norm" in society, and can help us to see that it is really the *interplay* between change and stability, order and conflict, which becomes the norm. Chaos theory also frees us from thinking in terms of linear causality, wherein the magnitude of effects is proportional to that of the "causes," and helps to account for those situations in which even very small changes introduced into a system can have consequences which are very extensive in scope. Although chaos theory is indeed a "systems" theory, it should not be equated with the social system as described in sociological structural-functionalism. There is no reliance upon or reference to system "needs" or "functional requisites." While change in a chaotic system may result from sudden, perhaps violent, conflict, it may just as likely occur in a gradual and orderly manner. In a chaotic system there may be order, there may be conflict; there always is process. It is our position that certain concepts of chaos theory can be applied metaphorically to aspects of the American judicial system in an effort to better understand the relationship between law and social change in society at large. The remainder of this chapter will be devoted to discussion of certain key concepts in chaos theory, namely, attractors, recursive symmetry and symmetry breaking, autopoiesis, and even Maxwell's demon, and an application of these to American judicial processes.

JUDICIAL CHAOTICS

Hayles (1989) has constructed the metaphor "chaotics" to describe and explicate some of the concepts of chaos theory. The concepts of chaotics are used as indicators in order to determine if a system is chaotic. Chaotics indexes six aspects of reality. First, reality contains a level of disorder, of unpredictability, and is a source of information and novelty. Second, reality is composed of irregular, complex forms that are conceptualized as fractional dimensions, as having inexact symmetry, making exact prediction impossible. Third, reality exists as a hierarchy of scales in which statements about one level are not necessarily true at others. Fourth, the scales are coupled to one another. Fifth, causes are non-linearly connected to their effects. Finally, small or minute fluctuations and changes are amplified to a macro level of large-scale change (Hayles, 1989: 7–8). This chapter employs Hayles's idea of chaotics in seeking to describe some of the aspects of judicial process. By viewing the court system through the perspective of judicial chaotics, the relationship between law and social change may be illuminated. Following are some examples of chaotics which can be found in the American court system.

Attractors

Baker (1993) describes an "attractor" as a "core pattern" which "re-creates predictability and unpredictability" in social interactions. An-other way of describing an attractor is a point in "space" that seems to "attract" the system to it. When we say an attractor is a point, we mean to imply that there is an observed pattern in "space" which draws the system to it. In many ways, an attractor is like a magnet. The system, over time, is drawn to the pattern and has its behavior organized by it. This does not, however, imply absolute determinism for the system. There is a special pattern called the strange attractor in which the pattern is predictable, but where the system never repeats the same locus from one time to the next. If a system exhibits a strange attractor, then it lives the paradox of unpredictable order, for the pattern is orderly but evo-lution of the system is not. Court cases which provide a line of legal reasoning can be conceptualized as attractors. They both organize human behavior by providing guidance on what is to be acceptable (normal) behavior, and provide the pattern for the orderly sorting of conflicting claims to reality: criminal, civil, or administrative. Through the coupling of court cases to one another, and through the courts' coupling to other institutions, societal interactions are kept within patterned bounds.

Brion (1991) has utilized a chaos perspective in examining court de-cisions in tort claims. In his attempt to explain the differing outcomes or decisions rendered by the court in two cases with identical fact situa-tions, he discovered that judges make decisions according to certain un-derlying themes. While these themes are many and varied, they are not limitless. The themes are, in essence, attractors which pattern the judges' decisions and the written opinions produced to justify these decisions. Legal decisions are not always predictable because the judge has the discretion to choose from a number of different themes. Brion refers to the judge's choice of theme as the "bifurcation point" or the critical stage which determines which attractor (or theme) the decision-making pro-cess will move toward. By viewing tort cases as chaotic process, Brion demonstrates that although legal decisions cannot be explained by look-ing to the law as a preexistent rational structure set apart from society, they do exhibit a pattern or a sense of order, dependent upon the judge's choice of theme. A chaos perspective thus helps to account for aberrant cases and results while simultaneously refuting the position that there is no order or consistency whatsoever in legal decision-making.

In the American judicial system, judges often decide cases based upon what happened in the past, that is, precedents. Young (1993) has re-marked upon the power inherent in legal precedent in his discussion of non-linear cause and effect within the legal system. He points out how even a small thing, such as a "judge's ire," a "juror's slip of the tongue or a plaintiff's appearance" can have an effect upon the outcome of a particular case. The outcome then becomes a precedent which is "locked in," and will require a whole series of secondary adjustments.

Of course, if courts followed precedent exclusively, there would never be *any* social change. After all, to perform in accordance with the past is to do nothing more than to reify history embodied in textualized court cases. The court's way out of this paradigmatic trap is to realize the essence of case law. The contextual boundaries separating cases are fuzzy. Because legal precedent necessarily is preserved through language, there is opportunity at every new reading for its meaning to be perturbed. When courts and their agents look to precedents, they interpret and reinterpret these to fit a new situation. In effect, meaning is perturbed out of case law and a reality claim is made that the same meaning can also be found in the newly filed case.

Many times, judges and courts are concerned with public policy. By public policy, we refer to a paradigmatic discourse constructed by the political branches of government which expresses the "will of the people." The meaning that becomes paramount, then, is that of the framers or authors of the policies, law, and rules. This is in keeping with the hermeneutic tradition of establishing the meaning embedded in textual artifacts by uncovering the intention of the author. Yet, it should be pointed out that the "intent of the author," be it individual, legislative, or rule-making body, is not always invoked, at the discretion of the court. Sometimes, the intent of the author has been lost or is impossible to ascertain.

Balkin (1987), in his deconstruction of the Rule of Law, has discussed the concepts of "iteration" and "free play of the text." He points out that when a judge's published opinion is invoked as precedent or rationale for decision-making in a subsequent case, it is actually the *interpretation* of the judge's intent which controls the decision-making process, not the judge's intent itself. The words or text of the opinion are iterated in the context of the new case. Because words may be iterated through time while intent or meanings may not, the text of the opinion has been "liberated" from the author and the original intent. While the iteration of precedents through time can be seen as an attractor, or pattern into which subsequent cases are organized, this pattern is subject to abrupt and potentially drastic change. Bifurcation may occur in response to a seemingly small change which then results in a new and different pattern.

Fractals and Recursive Symmetry

Court cases which set precedents can also be viewed as fractals, or irregular shapes which exhibit self-similarity and a recursive symmetry, and the courts' fostering of or accommodation to social change may be seen as symmetry breaking.

When we speak of a hierarchy of precedents or of case law, we speak of cases which are prima facie different, but which have a degree of similarity among claims or causes of action or similar domains of conflict. These precedents, and their additions, are self-organized into a temporal hierarchy (cases precede others in time). Precedent cases are discontinuous yet similar. They each possess a fractal character. In a manner of speaking, the constructed hierarchy is "fractals all the way down." Since there is an iteration through time, and the maintenance of a degree of symmetry, case law and networks of precedents are fractal in nature and possess a level of recursive symmetry.

The vehicle of symmetry and of symmetry breaking is the social and legal context surrounding the newly filed case. The existing body of case law provides the legal context. New cases are interpreted in accordance with similar cases previously decided. If the court interprets and assigns meaning to the newly filed case in accordance with existing case law, then symmetry can be said to exist. Meaning is invariant. If the meaning of the filed case is not interpreted in accord with existing case law, then the symmetry is broken. The court makes the determination as to whether or not meaning is invariant with respect to existing case law. For example, a plaintiff in a civil suit may make a claim that his cause of action is invariant with respect to existing precedent, while the defendant makes a claim that the meaning of the case at bar is somehow different from existing case law. To find in favor of the plaintiff is to validate the symmetry of existing case law, while a finding in favor of the defendant is tantamount to symmetry breaking. Court case symmetry breaking, if the case or result is novel enough, can lead to the erection of a new self-organizing fractal hierarchy. The court's decision to allow symmetry breaking, in effect, bifurcates the legal analytical space of court precedents.

Courts as Strange Attractors

Besides helping us to explain the process of a constantly evolving body of case law, chaos theory can also help us to understand the role of the court system and its relation to other institutions in society. We can view the court itself, apart from the body of case law it generates, as a strange attractor which, within temporal constraints, keeps societal interaction within bounded patterns of behavior. In a criminal case, the court patterns behavior and regulates socio-cultural disorder through the prosecution of norm violators. We must realize, of course, that the court's ability to pattern interactions is only partial, based upon a "scan" of individual behavior which in reality contains a measure of unpredictability. As such, the court cannot control individual behavior completely nor totally specify societal interactions. "Patterned" interaction is not exactly the same day to day, year to year, or moment to moment. It does not preclude nor prevent disorder from erupting. Interaction is bounded in a pattern but the non-linear coupling of individuals and institutions to one another allows for movement through the boundaries and the emergence of disorder; that is, deviance and novelty can be amplified into a new "pattern."

When norms are violated, the deviation, on its face, appears to be disruptive, disorderly. The court steps in to sanction violators and restore a sense of order; sometimes the court is not successful in doing this, sometimes the opposite effect of more disorder results. As time passes, the apparent disorder continues until a new pattern (norm) starts to emerge out of disorder; novelty out of sameness, order out of chaos. In this sense, the court's role in regulating disorder is perhaps illusory over the long term.

The Court as a Maxwell's Demon

Another way in which we can conceptualize the role of the court in society is to consider the court as a type of Maxwell's demon. Lest we stretch this analogy too far, let us consider one of the unresolved paradoxes in Maxwell's thought experiment. James Clerk Maxwell was a thermodynamics scientist who wished to test the validity of the second law of thermodynamics. This law states that under conditions of a closed system, entropy increases. Maxwell asks us to consider the idea of a system as a chamber divided into two compartments, each obtaining a collection of molecules, some fast and others slow (fast molecules have more energy and are considered more orderly). A passageway connects the two compartments and the molecules can move through the passageway, back and forth between the two compartments—the dispersion of fast and slow molecules leads to disorder, or entropy which will continually increase. Maxwell then posits the question of what would happen if some type of being (a demon) existed which could, through an opening in the passageway, control the movement of the molecules by shunting all the fast molecules to one side of the compartment and the slow ones to the other side, keeping them separated. Would this action succeed in keeping the molecules ordered and organized, defeating the law of entropy?

Part of the problem in conceptualizing Maxwell's demon over the years has been the seemingly unresolvable question of whether the demon is actually inside or outside the system. If the demon is outside the system, able to observe the action of the molecules from a godlike vantage point and controlling their movement accordingly, then the system is not in fact "closed," that is, there is input from the environment. In this scenario, the second law of thermodynamics, which describes entropic processes within a closed system, does not seem truly applicable. Conversely, if the demon is found to be within the system, there would seem to be no vantage point from which to observe the action of the molecules, and the demon itself would be subject to the same law of entropy as would other system elements. It is our position that Maxwell's demon is best conceptualized cybernetically. That is, the demon is coupled with the system it is manipulating. It is like a thermostat or servomechanism.

The court as the demon is coupled to the socio-cultural milieu as a whole and to the political branches/legal system specifically. It influences the legal system directly, and the observed level of disorder in the socio-cultural milieu via the legal system. When observed disorder gets out of bounds, the court reacts (in this situation, law is reactive) and influences other institutions (usually the political branches) so as to return society or other disordered institutional relationships to an illusory bounded, yet patterned, order. The court is the demon of self-organization. The order it seeks to preserve is fractal patterning in case law, and its method is recursively symmetrical court cases.

CONCLUSION

The concepts of chaotics, including strange attractors and fractals, can be applied in a metaphorical sense to describe the American judicial system and the body of case law which emanates therefrom.

The court itself may be seen as similar to Maxwell's demon, in that it is an entity which seeks to control or maintain order, decreasing entropy within the social system. As in the case of Maxwell's demon, confusion arises as to whether the court stands in some privileged position, able to view and organize elements of society, or is, in fact, a part of the system it seeks to regulate, itself subject to the same entropic processes as are other elements of the system. Viewing the court as cybernetically coupled with the social system may provide the most helpful way of understanding this relationship.

The court system, however, may also be seen as an agent of change through the instrumentation of case law. Individual cases which evidence even small changes in the traditional line of legal reasoning may have far-reaching effects when perpetuated in a non-linear fashion as precedent.

Court decisions and the developing body of case law can be seen as fractal formations, evidencing patterns of recursive symmetry, and, in the instance of novel questions involving the superseding or reversal of legal precedents, symmetry breaking.

The body of American case law also evidences a self-organizing quality which can be detected when we view courts and the precedents they generate as strange attractors which serve to perpetuate normative patterns.

Employing the concepts of chaos theory metaphorically to aspects of the legal system enables us to entertain a more sophisticated view both of the relation between "order" and "conflict" in society and of the role of the court system in maintaining order and responding to conflict within the social system.

REFERENCES

Baker, P.L. 1993. "Chaos, Order, and Sociological Theory." *Sociological Inquiry* 63(2): 123–38.

Balkin, J.M. 1987. "Deconstructive Practice and Legal Theory." *Yale Law Journal* 96(4): 743–86.

Brion, D.J. 1991. "The 'Chaotic' Law of Tort: Legal Formalism and the Problem of Indeterminacy." Pp. 45–77 in R. Kevelson (ed.), *Peirce and Law*. New York: Peter Lang.

Coser, L.A. 1956. *The Functions of Social Conflict*. London: Free Press of Glencoe.

Francis, R.G. 1993. "Chaos, Order, and Sociological Theory: A Comment." *Sociological Inquiry* 63(2): 239–42.

Hayles, N.K. 1989. *Chaos and Order: Complex Dynamics in Literature and Science*. Chicago: University of Chicago Press.

Kellert, S.H. 1995. "When Is the Economy Not Like the Weather? The Problem of Extending Chaos Theory to the Social Sciences." Pp. 35–47 in A. Albert (ed.), *Chaos and Society*. Amsterdam: IOS Press.

Luhmann, N. 1985. *A Sociological Theory of Law*. Boston: Routledge and Kegan Paul.

Milovanovic, D. 1994. *A Primer in the Sociology of Law*, 2d ed. New York: Harrow and Heston.

Prigogene, I. and I. Stengers. 1984. *Order Out of Chaos*. New York: Bantam Books.

Turner, J. 1991. *The Structure of Sociological Theory*. Belmont, CA.: Wadsworth, Inc.

Vago, S. 1995. *Law and Society*. Englewood Cliffs, NJ: Prentice-Hall, Inc.

Young, T.R. 1991. "Chaos and Social Change: Metaphysics of the Postmodern." *The Social Science Journal* 28(3): 289–305.

———. 1993. "Law and Social Control in Complex Societies," No. 172. Distributed as part of the Red Feather Institute Transforming Sociology Series.

CHAPTER 7

Chaos, Law, and Critical Legal Studies: Mapping the Terrain

Caren Schulman

INTRODUCTION

Chaos, contrary to its common usage, is not, as applied below, anarchy. Rather, chaos theory is a methodology for examination which utilizes newly developed and borrowed scientific principles as they are applied to dynamical systems, revealing a progression from order to disorder and on to new forms of order.

First, we shall discuss the postmodernist versus the modernist perspective for inquiry and discovery, situating chaos theory within the postmodernist paradigm. Second, we shall provide a discussion of the key concepts of chaos theory and how they may be used to quantify American legal thought and the judicial decision-making process that follows. Finally, analogies between chaos theory and Critical Legal Studies are examined as methods to critique the law and judicial process and the implications for further study.

CHAOS THEORY AND POSTMODERN ANALYSIS

From the point in time, some two and one-half millennia ago, at which the discipline of philosophy became less a matter of mankind's relationship with the supernatural and more a study of or attempt to describe an individual's relationships with other individuals, his community, and the natural world (Kitto, 1951) until the last one-third of the twentieth century, mankind employed relatively static models to depict these relationships (Milovanovic, 1995). However, as our tools of analysis became more sensitive to fluctuations within these natural and social systems, and with the rise of analytical social science in the nineteenth century, it became more and more obvious that the fixed models previously employed no longer explained the totality of observed phenomena. Chaos theory is an attempt to quantify and qualify the newly observed, seemingly random movements within our social systems. However, almost by definition, existing chaos theory will disclose new variations unexplainable by that theory as it currently exists (Zukav, 1979).

Previously accepted philosophical doctrines concerned themselves with rational thought and reductionism, or the absolute and linear link between cause and effect (Milovanovic, 1995: 20; Zukav, 1979). These doctrines, employed since the so-called "Age of Enlightenment" in the eighteenth century, have been transformed by the technological advances of the twentieth century. The ability to gather and quantify vast amounts of data over very short periods of time has forced a reexamination of the true nature of systems under study, much as the discovery of the atomic structure of matter forced a reexamination of the perceived solidity of objects (Zukav, 1979).

The modernist paradigm embraces ideation of equilibrium and homeostasis, where balance and stability are sought between organisms or social groups and their environments. The dominant literature of social theorists such as Durkheim, Parsons, and Luhmann rests upon the above underlying models (Milovanovic, 1995). The influence of Newtonian physics on modern social thought is exemplified by celebrating order, quantitative resolutions, and scientific knowledge providing absolute postulates leading to calculated and logical answers with linear predictability (Milovanovic, 1995; Zukav, 1979; Briggs and Peat, 1989). However, these models are rapidly being replaced by a "more intense critique of what is and transformative visions of what could be" (Milovanovic, 1995: 21) known as "Postmodernist Thought."

Analyses through the use of discursive formations by wandering from topic to topic and accepting conditions far from a state of equilibrium as normal or even preferable, and where the diversified and transient elements of pathos are integral considerations of analysis, become the cornerstones of postmodernism (Milovanovic, 1995). When these forms of analysis are coupled with the accessibility of technology for rapid, almost instantaneous calculations, they give rise to chaos theory as a model within which a variety of disciplines, such as psychotherapy and psychology (Bütz, 1993a; Barton, 1994), literature (Hayles, 1990), criminology (Milovanovic, 1994, 1995, 1996; Young, 1992), and business and management (Leifer, 1989) can be profitably and more accurately examined.

Chaos theory, through the use of terms and definitions modified from the "hard sciences," becomes a general, almost generic term (Bütz, 1993: 543; Prigogine and Stengers, 1984; Gleick, 1987; Briggs and Peat, 1989) used to describe the study of apparently random behavior within dynamic systems (Bütz, 1992: 1050–51; Coveney and Highfield, 1990: 362). As such, chaos theory readily adapts itself to "the realities of social breakdown and potential chaos in the late 20th century world which presents the need for [a] new action oriented social theory" (Loye and Eisler, 1987: 53).

As Newton invented calculus in order to express mathematically the relationship of objects in the macro-universe (Briggs and Peat, 1989: 91), so too, new mathematical and mapping methods have been devised and used as tools to describe the relationship and order of a multiplicity of presumably random phenomena (Bütz, 1993: 543; Gleick, 1987). Borrowing both terms and principles from the sciences of physics, biology, and quantum mechanics, chaos theorists develop explanatory models with which to depict simple and complex interactions, and linear and non-linear relationships (Bütz, 1992: 1044; Loye and Eisler, 1987; Chamberlain, 1990). Chaos theory is a landscape which includes non-linearity and phase-space maps, allowing details to be brought into focus which would otherwise be lost as a result of our inability to quantify, conceptualize, and pictorialize these phenomena (Briggs and Peat, 1989: 32; Bütz, 1992).

CONCEPTS OF CHAOS THEORY

Phase Space/Attractors

Disciplines such as psychology and sociology with "no self-consistent mathematics at its disposal" (Abraham, 1992: 111–20; Jung, 1969) find chaos theory to be an appropriate vehicle for expression. Assigning values and mapping variables which represent position and momentum, as in quantum mechanics (Zukav, 1979: 27), to produce visual diagrammatical representations in two or more dimensions, is achieved through the use of phase space. "Phase space is [a region] composed of as many dimensions (or variables) as the scientist needs to describe a system's movement" (Briggs and Peat, 1989: 32). This movement is then tracked by a line which indicates the history of that movement over time or space (Briggs and Peat, 1989: 33). When examining variables of interest over the course of time, the values stay within some limits (Young, 1992: 449), creating a generally identifiable, visualized shape, depending on the number of variables and the period of time over which the variable is tracked. In phase space, an attractor is a representative set of points or lines (Bütz, 1992: 1050) which emerge coherently to describe the behavior being measured.

The four primary two- and three-dimensional portraits of dynamic systems or attractors are identified as: point, limit, torus, and strange (Milovanovic, 1993: 12). The point attractor represents a fixed point to which a tracked, periodic, repetitive behavior will return after the completion of one oscillation or series of movements. The classic example of this activity is a swinging pendulum which returns to its starting point once the momentum of the swing decays and movement stops. A limit attractor is a depiction of a body or activity in motion whose trajectory does not decay to a fixed point, but rather, traces a cyclical path. A torus attractor represents the phase space defined by a collection of individuals or activities which behave in varying paths but follow an overall organized course. Two or more interacting or interdependent systems, such as our solar system, can be pictured by a three-dimensional torus. A strange attractor is a representation of a system which is in turbulence, where the periodic fluctuations create irregular and unpredictable changes in the course of the activity (Briggs and Peat, 1989).

A Poincaré section, a "slice" through the doughnut-shaped torus attractor, provides an opportunity to examine a cross-section of space-time events which allows us to view occurrences at a specific point in time, permitting us to identify "outcome fields or basins: the points at which all systems of a kind behave alike for a given set of conditions" (Young, 1992: 450).

These basics of chaos mapping provide only the means to identify behaviors at fixed points in time. This is analogous to natural systems which will undergo rigid, repetitive movements over extended periods of time and then, at some critical point, mutate into a radical new behavior (Briggs and Peat, 1989: 33).

Mathematical Expressions

Twentieth-century electronic technology and the mathematical language of quantum mechanics provide diverse and almost instantaneous methods of examining phenomena. "Continual reabsorption or enfolding of what has come before" (Briggs and Peat, 1989: 66), such as repeating the product or outcome of one equation as the starting value of a second equation or multiplying a factor by itself, known as *iteration* or feedback looping, has created a new method of pictorializing phenomena (Briggs and Peat, 1989; Barton, 1994; Bütz, 1992). This creates system fragmentation which tends toward chaos, or a period of unpredictability and non-equilibrium evolving eventually into a stabilized new behavior through a series of feedback loops (Briggs and Peat, 1989: 143).

Period doubling or bifurcation in chaos theory denotes moments at which causal basins (points at which doubling exists) expand (Young, 1992: 452; 1991) into behavior variations and chaos (Barton, 1994: 6). When bifurcation is translated into a two-dimensional map, a forking line is depicted, splitting exponentially into what appears to be chaotic darkness. However, along this continuum inexplicably and unpredictably appears a dissipative structure or an organized state beyond the first bifurcation where a system maintains equilibrium (from principles of thermodynamics) (Bütz, 1992: 1050; Coveney and Highfield, 1990: 361). Or, in other words, a spontaneous emergence of order develops when certain parameters built into a system reach critical values (Bütz, 1992: 1050). This period of self-organization may emerge as a result of changes in social or economic conditions, an example of which may be a person who applies for a new credit card to borrow money to pay off other credit card debts. This may result in a temporary stop-gap solution (a period of self-organization), but the ultimate consequences propel the individual into more chaos.

In developing a new language and methods for describing the dynamic energy (Bütz, 1993b: 545) of social as well as natural phenomena, exploration of the heretofore "imaginary" has become common among chaos theorists. For example, *fractals* are infinite numbers between any two numbers on a complex plane (Briggs and Peat, 1989: 97). "A process of iteration in which each step takes on smaller and smaller scale" (Briggs and Peat, 1989: 93) maintains an "unending series of motifs repeated at all lengths of scales" (Bütz, 1992: 1050; Coveney and Highfield, 1990), the most famous of which is the Mandelbrot Set. Here the simple and complex are interwoven and create "evolving shapes which emerge out of an equation's feedback" (Briggs and Peat, 1989: 104). It may mimic actual forms in nature's fine detail.

Entropy and Human Agency

Chaos theory, in measuring the transformations and activity of systems, again borrows from the principles of thermodynamics, co-opting the principle of entropy; or "the measure of the capacity of an isolated macroscopic system to change," when it ceases to exchange energy or matter with its surroundings (Bütz, 1992: 1046, 1050; Coveney and Highfield, 1990: 365; Zukav, 1979).

Like a drop of dark ink disbursing in a bowl of clear liquid until it seems to disappear (Zukav, 1979: 221), we associate this increasing entropy with the forward movement of time (Zukav, 1979: 221). Therefore, the application of chaos theory as a modeling paradigm for human events and environments is appropriate.

Free will and choices in human events motivated by desires are variables which create as well as limit the diversity of activity from which outcome basins develop and from which regions of uncertainty emerge (Young, 1992: 454). Thus, the biological restrictions of humans as well as the actions of human behavior upon their environment are random, seemingly unpredictable variables, which are, however, readily mapped utilizing the tools of chaos theory.

Thus, human beings are not only sentient, aware of their own existence, they are also inquisitive, seeking to understand their relationship to others of their kind and the totality of their environment. As technological and analytical tools for the study of these interrelationships have become more sensitive, we have discovered whole new sets of variables in the social universe which bear implications of randomness and uncertainty heretofore unpredicted and unaccounted for by earlier theories of social organization. However, the same tools which have detected this seeming disorder also serve to describe, pictorialize, and quantify it, leaving us with a deeper appreciation of the complexity of existence, as well as a theoretical approach for the examination of chaos.

APPLICATION OF CHAOS THEORY AND CRITICAL LEGAL STUDIES

Decisions in Space

The ability to predict future conditions on a macro scale based upon past experience and awareness of present circumstances gave our ancestors a visionary power in their universe (Zukav, 1979: 26). However, knowledge of an entity's present state, its current environment, and laws which govern its transformations is not sufficient information to either absolutely predict future behaviors or specific events in the long term (Gregersen and Sailer, 1993: 783; Zukav, 1979).

Social systems, like systems in nature, are characterized in chaos theory as: "iterative recursive systems which can exhibit discontinuous change" (Gregersen and Sailer, 1993: 792), so that graphical representations and modeling can be useful tools to understanding where nonrepresentational methods of prediction fail to provide concrete results. Simple or even elaborately contrived models, applied as didactive devices, become illustrative in the comprehension of discontinuous behavior depicted over time (Abraham, 1992: 111–15).

The character of the transformations of segments within an organization or institution with even virtually identical internal states and embedded in virtually identical environments can exhibit totally different behaviors while still being governed by the same set of rules (Gregersen and Sailer, 1993: 777–78). The process of judicial decision-making, when modeled utilizing the tools of chaos theory, provides an example of a system where choices of outcomes are not always predetermined by antecedent structures (Brion, 1991: 63) and where a variety of factors may greatly influence the ultimate outcome, despite the protestations of the decision makers to the contrary.

Applying a pragmatic view to the decision-making process, determining whether something is "true," or whether an outcome is "just," can be influenced by how consistent that decision is with our personal experiences (Zukav, 1979: 38).

Heresy, Heritage, and Dynamic Models

As Brion describes, value-based judicial decisions tailored to particular or individual cases encompass a "partisan," or "community-based" judgment (Brion, 1991: 65), rather than the syllogistic overlay with which most rulings are glossed.

Brion identifies two factors that influence the decision-making process. The first with an outward look, a flexible accommodation to pluralistic values based in the political process, is termed by Brion as *heresy*. Decisions may be manipulated by such "local" influences as: the political process, peer perception, personal values and morals, education, the family situation and experiences of the judge, and/or the identity, status in the community, or demeanor of the parties involved in the instant litigation (Brion, 1991: 64–65). As judges at the local level are generally elected to their positions on the bench, political considerations may create a tendency toward decision-making based upon these local influences. Variables such as perceived political or social pressure may effect a deviation from the central position of decision-making, based strictly upon precedent and statutory requirements.

The second factor that influences decision-making is called *heritage*. It stands for the application of an inward function reverting to the accumulation of prior decisions for judicial guidance, giving normative weight to outcomes judges have reached in the past (Brion, 1991: 65–66). The American judicial system embraces as an indispensable tenet the principle of "equal justice under law"; therefore, the application of prior judicial rulings to a current set of facts is fundamental to its process. This backward-focusing decision-making necessitates not only academic expertise on the part of the judge, but also a devotion to preparation, research, and an inquiry into scholarly works on the law. Such considerations may not always be possible in the day-to-day business of a court's agenda. Movements between these poles, where conflict exists within the context of cooperation, private conscience, and public accountability (Abraham, 1992: 111–17, quoting Tompkins), create oscillations between the values. It is these oscillations and the attempt at balance between these opposing values which create the dynamics examined here, dynamics which make prediction of court rulings chance at best.

The *heresy* and *heritage* influences on the decision-making process can vary at any point in time (see "t" in Figure 7.1) and each new case ruled upon with comparable issues of law or fact could be considered an iteration. Most decisions will fit neatly within a set, that is, the same gen-

Figure 7.1
Dynamical System Phase Portrait

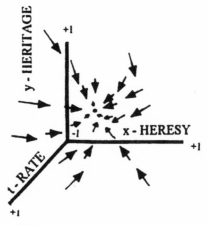

Adapted from Abraham, 1992.

eral facts will result in the same decision. However, as the facts which define the issues of each case tend to vary, so also do the influences which tend to move the decision-making away from the attribute of *heritage*. Each moment of judicial decision amounts to a bifurcation point within the chaos paradigm (Brion, 1991: 70).

Shown as attributes varying from low to high, x-*heresy* represents the occasions where the local influences play a greater part in determining the outcome of a case before the bench. The y-*heritage* variable represents the occasions when a strict adherence to precedent and prior court rulings are dominant. Over time (t-rate) each of these influences create movement or oscillation in a phase-space diagram (Figure 7.1), with the target action being the arrival at a judicial decision. The vector, or trajectory of movement, is shown as arrows (Abraham, 1992: 111–41) describing the movement toward the moment of decision, with most decisions fitting within the set depicting a point attractor.

By applying three variables to a two-dimensional map of a time series shown in Figure 7.2, or bifurcation diagram (Barton, 1994: 6), the process of judicial decision-making, the variables *heresy* and *heritage* represent amplification factors which act as accelerative coefficients (Abraham, 1992: 111-9–10) propelling the system into a dissipative chaotic structure (Abraham, 1992; Young, 1992).

The bifurcation sequence shown represents what might be expected (Abraham, 1992: 111–34) when multiple states change suddenly and a parameter value crosses a critical threshold (Barton, 1994: 8). When the combination of forces behaves as interacting influences, they move the vectors to a new point in space. As an election day approaches, for in-

Figure 7.2
Bifurcation Response Diagram

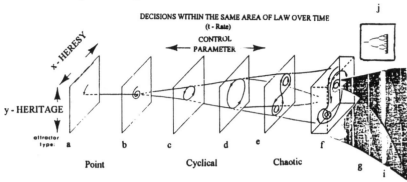

Adapted from Abraham, 1992.

stance, a judge may be more influenced to conclude his/her cases by *heresy* than after he or she has been reelected to a new term.

In the judicial system, localized instabilities (incompatible decisions when either the facts or principles of law at issue are incapable of differentiation) occur based on the *heresy/heritage* dichotomy, leading one part of the system to organize itself differently than another part (Barton, 1994: 8). An increased dependency on *heresy* as opposed to dependence on *heritage* may cause the trajectories to spiral from a point attractor (a) to cyclical attractors (b, c, and d), and then chaotic attractors (e and f) as shown in Figure 7.2. This organization (Abraham, 1992; Kauffman, 1993; Prigogine and Stengers, 1984) denotes a process by which structure or pattern emerges in an open system, giving rise to a variety of complicated temporal, spatial, and behavioral patterns (Barton, 1994: 7; Prigogine and Stengers, 1984). When judicial decisions rendered in relatively identical cases result in inconsistent and contradictory decisions, indeterminacy occurs and chaos emerges to the point where any number of unexpected changes may force a non-linear expansion (Young, 1992: 4) resulting in loss of predictability, the primary virtue of decision by precedent as represented by the *heritage* variable.

Changes unanticipated by the judicial community, such as the acceptance of a new theory of behavior by a significant portion of the scientific community (Young, 1992: 4), can sufficiently ripen an issue of law to the point where the U.S. Supreme Court must make a definitive statement in order to reconcile divergent results in the various circuits or jurisdictions. As a result, a period of order will emerge out of the period of unpredictability represented by the white vertical band embedded within the shadow of chaos (Figure 7.2, i) (Briggs and Peat, 1989: 62). This "window" of order or period of intermittency creates a coherent and unifying approach to the disputes which were previously depicted by inconsistent and conflicting decisions (Brion, 1991: 54). However, as the holding of the Supreme Court's decision based on specific facts becomes attenuated through its application by analogy to wholly different fact patterns, the system may return to the chaotic state as the window of self-organization closes and a new bifurcation series begins (Figure 7.2, Insert "j").

In other words, as the highest Court's decision is utilized by lower courts to resolve the legal issues raised by "fact" patterns more and more divergent from the fact pattern upon which the Supreme Court originally decided, a random or chaotic pattern of results will again emerge, requiring redetermination or reimposition of order by the High Court.

Deconstructionism

As we have already observed, classical methods of analysis were derived from an individual's observation and description of his or her relationships with other individuals, the broader community, and the totality of natural phenomena which could be observed and measured in terms of units agreed upon by those in the same field of observation. Thus, insights into these complex relationships have historically been realized by the individual's powers of observation.

Since the Enlightenment and the development of modern Western scientific research methods, the quest for a universal formula, derived of linear logic, has permeated traditional thought and methods of analysis as applied in both the natural and social sciences. This holistic scientific paradigm provided the climate for Newtonian applications and the "ordered" worldview we embrace today (Baker, 1993: 123–24).

As has been previously discussed: social systems, dynamic relationships, and the fluidity of social, cultural, and political change do not fit easily within these static models derived "snapshot" fashion by observation. "The social world can neither be experimented upon nor taken into the lab: social life is embedded in environments" (Baker, 1993: 125). Despite the fact that rigid application of scientific theories may not suit the investigation of social phenomena, it is nonetheless the renowned of science—Newton, Poincaré, Heisenberg, Einstein, and Bohm—whose works provide the momentum for rethinking our fixed concepts of causality (Baker, 1993: 127; Prigogine and Stengers, 1984), and it is these concepts of causality which define and limit the exploration of traditional social structures.

The glorification of indeterminacy, irregularity, and unpredictability is the hallmark of the postmodernist approach, out of which chaos theory and other critical methods of analysis have emerged. Critical Legal Studies, by adopting these methods to the study of the judicial process, provides a paradigm for analyzing the law and deconstructing legal reasoning, the decision-making process, and the sociology of the legal system (Russell, 1994: 223).

While it is not derived directly from chaos theory, Critical Legal Studies bears a strong resemblance to it, as this application examines an ever-changing dynamic system by comparing internal and external influences, or variables, resulting in a deconstruction process in order to discover new and non-traditional patterns and understandings. However, much of the language and use of computer models so prevalent in chaos theory are notably absent from Critical Legal Studies. The translation of chaos-oriented, computer-generated constructs and language to Critical Legal Studies is a fruitful area for exploration, as the only tool currently employed by this discipline is the analysis of written decisions and the work of other commentators.

Where the more traditional forms of analysis may disregard aberrant outcomes, chaos theory, by the process of deconstruction, utilizes data from phenomena which appear random and without precedent. Organizations such as the common-law, within which the most inherently valuable characteristic is predictability and where reliance upon principles previously determined is axiomatic, can be profitably subjected to scrutiny utilizing the tools of chaos theory. The modern scholarship in Critical Legal Studies applies concepts familiar to chaos theory, displaying a parallel development through the use of some shared terms and similar methods of examination. Chaos theory and Critical Legal Studies each use a broad view to identify both self-similarities and periods of indeterminacy where a bifurcation point may occur.

Some of the principles shared by chaos theory and Critical Legal Studies under often differing nomenclature are:

1. *Indeterminacy*, or the belief that legal doctrine is not systematic and does not offer a definitive answer for all circumstances. Likewise in chaos theory, where behavior variations become unpredictable and outcomes are uncertain as bifurcation points emerge as shown in Figure 7.2;

2. *Anti-formalism*, where it is accepted that no decision is value-free, nor totally determined by legal methodology. In comparison, chaos theory celebrates a sensitivity to initial conditions where otherwise seemingly unrelated scant influences can have an enormous effect on a given outcome;

3. *Contradiction*, that legal doctrine does not provide a single coherent view of human relations, but rather describes competing relations, be they social or economic. In chaos theory this can be compared to the notion of fractals, where there may be an infinite number of fragmentations appearing to lead the system into chaos; and,

4. *Marginality*, or the construct which assumes that law is not a significant variable controlling social behavior. Similarly, chaos theory provides not a predictor of behaviors but an understanding of a system's momentum (Russell, 1994: 224; Trubek, 1984; Unger, 1986).

If one assumes an approach emphasizing culture as a social construct with both competing and interconnected influences upon a system's outcomes, then the system is both autopoietic and dissipative. A process is said to be autopoietic if it is self-maintaining, self-contained, and self-generating. This principle clearly may be applied to the legal system, as its tradition is based upon the principle of *stare decisis*, where case follows case, creating a consistent, though somewhat rigid, and ordered system designed to utilize previously settled questions of law to resolve new factual disputes. At the same time, the legal process is a dissipative structure, dependent upon its environment, and ever changing, based upon the nature of society, the political environment, and social and scientific changes. This paradox raises questions as to whether there is a privileged perspective (Baker, 1993: 131) in our legal culture. As, for example, where courts may apply alternative lines of authority, such as those derived from property law or those derived from civil rights law, to an identical fact pattern and arrive at opposite conclusions, depending on the line of authority chosen.

Science is the study of facts which are regular and reoccur to form patterns. Scientific classification depends on placing facts in an orderly context, be it in an individual, national, international, or universal context (Huber, 1991: 197). Litigation, on the other hand, is often an examination of facts in isolation; each injury, crime, or violation of the law stands as a reinvention, a one-shot decision often made on bases not apparent from the written opinion. It is only when many decisions are examined over time that patterns of order and disorder emerge.

Can a coherent application of these tools be used to amplify our understanding of the "legal culture" which appears to be replete with dichotomy and uncertainty? The structural features of the legal system reflect a distribution of power: there is an ongoing struggle between uniformity and diversity and between centralism and localism, and these are issues for which there may be neither solution (Friedman, 1973: 661–62) nor complete explanation. However, the legal arena is a culture, where its members participate through their distinctive language (Baker, 1993; Lyotard, 1984), practices, and customs, and therefore, the legal system is one which lends itself to examination by means of modeling.

Examining the legal process based upon chaos theory, the iterative nature of repeated decisions becomes evident. An enfolding of concepts whereby new fact patterns are superimposed over previous decisions bearing similar issues of law create self-similar results. However, this is not perfectly deterministic in that it magnifies and brings into focus initial uncertainties (Hayles, 1990: 183). Employing Critical Legal Studies as a methodology, a critique of one or two cases may be made to examine adherence to controlling legal principles (classical formalism), or by looking for decisions based upon norms determined by moral judgment, rather than precedent. It may be common to find decisions which are based on principles borrowed from postulates of economics and a free market (as in the plea bargaining process), or that legal principles are adopted which render the criminal justice process easier to manage and perpetuate influence for those who comprise the system's actors, such as judges, lawyers, and court personnel (Russell, 1994: 226–27). This methodology encompasses those variables which contribute to the initial conditions that may propel the decision-making process into unpredictability and chaos. Therefore, both Critical Legal Studies and chaos theory share non-linear dynamics and deconstruction methods which are not just general attitudes, but specific methods and assumptions (Hayles, 1990: 183).

CONCLUSION

Despite the fact that chaos theory and Critical Legal Studies may have many shared components, it is doubtful whether either can provide reliable methods for prediction. However, the two theories appear isomorphic in that they seem similar in form and substance. Their central ideas seem to emanate from an interconnected network (Hayles, 1990: 184) of analysis. While neither chaos theory nor Critical Legal Studies professes to offer a reliable or steadfast tool for prediction, both seem to be successful in what Hayles (1990) refers to as "retrodiction," or creating a model for examining a dynamic culture based upon a backward look at how that culture has behaved.

REFERENCES

Abraham, F. 1992. *A Visual Introduction to Dynamical Systems Theory for Psychology.* Santa Cruz, CA: Aerial Press.

Baker, P.L. 1993. "Chaos, Order and Sociological Theory." *Sociological Inquiry* 63(4): 123–49.

Barton, S. 1994. "Chaos, Self-Organization, and Psychology." *American Psychologist* 49(1): 5–14.

Benson, R.W. 1991. "Peirce and Critical Legal Studies." Pp. 17–28 in R. Kevelson (ed.), *Peirce and Law.* New York: Peter Lang.

Briggs, J. and F.D. Peat. 1989. *Turbulent Mirror: An Illustrated Guide to Chaos Theory and the Science of Wholeness.* New York: Harper and Row.

Brion, D.J. 1991. "The 'Chaotic' Law of Tort: Legal Formalism and the Problem of Indeterminacy." Pp. 45–77 in R. Kevelson (ed.), *Peirce and Law*. New York: Peter Lang.

Bütz, M. 1992. "Fractal Nature of the Development of Self," Table 1, Modified Working Definitions or Ideas from "Hard Science." *Psychological Reports* 71: 1050–51.

———. 1993a. "Practical Applications from Chaos Theory to the Psychotherapeutic Process, A Basic Consideration of the Dynamics." *Psychological Reports* 73: 543–54.

———. 1993b. "Systemic Family Therapy and Symbolic Chaos." *Humanity and Society* 17(2): 200–222.

Chamberlain, L. 1990. "Chaos and the Butterfly Effect in Family Systems." *Network* 8(3): 11–12.

Coveney, P. and R. Highfield. 1990. *The Arrow of Time: A Voyage Through Science to Solve Time's Greatest Mysteries*. New York: Fawcett Combine.

Friedman, L.M. 1973. *A History of American Law*. New York: Simon and Schuster, Touchstone Books.

———. 1993. *Crime and Punishment in American History*. New York: Basic Books.

Garrity, J. and P. Gay. 1972. *Columbia History of the World*. New York: Columbia University Press.

Gleick, J. 1987. *Chaos, Making a New Science*. New York: Viking Penguin.

Gregersen, H. and L. Sailer. 1993. "Chaos Theory and Its Implications for Social Science Research." *Human Relations* 46(7): 777–801.

Hayles, N.K. 1990. *Chaos Bound*. Ithaca, NY: Cornell University Press.

Henry, S. and D. Milovanovic. 1996. *Constitutive Criminology: Beyond Postmodernism*. London: Sage Publications.

Huber, P.W. 1991. *Galileo's Revenge: Junk Science in the Courtroom*. New York: Basic Books.

Jung, C.G. 1969. "The Structure and Dynamics of the Psyche." *Collected Works of C.G. Jung*, vol. 8. Princeton, NJ: Princeton University Press.

Kauffman, S.A. 1993. *The Origins of Order*. New York: Oxford University Press.

Kitto, H.D.F. 1951. *The Greeks*. New York: Pelican Press.

Leifer, R. 1989. "Understanding Organizational Transformation Using a Dissipative Structure Model." *Human Relations* 41(10): 899–916.

Loye, D. and R. Eisler. 1987. "Chaos and Transformation: Implications of Nonequilibrium Theory for Social Science and Society." *Behavioral Science* 32: 53–65.

Lyotard, J.F. 1984. *The Postmodern Condition: A Report on Knowledge*. Minneapolis: University of Minnesota Press.

MacDonald, S.W., C. Grebogi, E. Ott, and J.A. Yorke. 1985. "Fractal Basin Boundaries." *Physica* 17(D): 125–83.

Maturana, H. and F. Valera. 1980. *Autopoiesis and Cognition: The Realization of the Living*. Boston: D. Reidel.

Milovanovic, D. 1993. "Lacan's Four Discourses, Chaos and Cultural Criticism in Law." *Studies in Psychoanalytic Theory* 2(1): 3–23.

———. 1994. *A Primer in the Sociology of Law*. Albany, NY: Harrow and Heston.

———. 1995. "Dueling Paradigms: Modernist versus Postmodernist Thought." *Humanity and Society* 19(1): 19–44.

New Columbia Encyclopedia. 1975. New York: Columbia University Press.

Pickover, C.A. 1988. "Pattern Formation and Chaos in Networks." *Communications of the ACM* 31(2): 136–51.

Prigogine, I. and I. Stengers. 1984. *Order Out of Chaos: Man's New Dialogue with Nature.* New York: Bantam Books.

Russell, K. 1994. "A Critical View from the Inside: An Application of Critical Legal Studies to Criminal Law." *The Journal of Criminal Law and Criminology* 85(1): 222–40.

Sagan, C. and A. Druyan. 1992. *Shadows of Forgotten Ancestors.* New York: Random House.

Savill, A. 1993. *Alexander the Great and His Time.* New York: Barnes and Noble Press.

Trubek, D.M. 1984. "Where the Action Is: Critical Legal Studies and Empiricism." *Stanford Law Review* 575.

Unger, R.M. 1986. *The Critical Legal Studies Movement.* Cambridge, MA: Harvard University Press.

Van Doren, C. 1991. *A History of Knowledge: The Pivotal Events, People and Achievements of World History.* New York: Ballantine Books.

Young, T.R. 1991. "Chaos and Crime Part II: The ABC of Crime: Attractors, Bifurcations, Basins and Chaos." *Critical Criminologist* 3(4): 13–14.

———. 1992. "Chaos Theory and Human Agency: Humanist." *Humanity and Society* 16(4): 441–60.

Zukav, G. 1979. *The Dancing Wu Li Masters: An Overview of the New Physics.* New York: Bantam New Age Books.

CHAPTER 8

The Chaotic Law of Forensic Psychology: The Postmodern Case of the (In)Sane Defendant

Bruce A. Arrigo

INTRODUCTION

The field of forensic psychology is activated precisely at the point that the criminal justice and mental health systems intersect. We broadly recognize this intersection to affect adult, juvenile, family, and civil adjudication matters (Wrightsman, 1994). One area of deep-seated controversy in forensic psychology is the mentally ill person who appears before a court and/or administrative tribunal and pleads not guilty by reason of insanity (NGRI). Several commentators have assessed the plight of such citizens and the mechanisms by which the state mobilizes the machinery of the law to socially control and discipline the disordered defendant's behaviors (e.g., Scull, 1989; Kittrie, 1972; Rothman, 1971; 1980).

In forensic law, there are several standards which medico-legal decision makers rely upon to accurately assess criminal responsibility. The McNaghten Rule, the Irresistible Impulse Test, the Durham Rule, the Substantial Capacity Test, and present federal law are jurisprudential measures of insanity largely informed by the wisdom of psychiatry (Steadman et al., 1993; Simon and Aaronson, 1988). This is not to say, however, that they are necessarily sound or representative of the interests of the disordered persons so greatly affected by their use and courtroom meaning (Szasz, 1987). Indeed, they are merely standards developed by persons who claim that there is an objective basis to (in)sanity and who further claim expertise to objectively identify and measure it (Arrigo, 1996b).

On closer scrutiny, the various insanity defense doctrines offer only marginal courtroom utility. Research has confirmed this on the basis of empirical (Pasewark, 1981; Steadman and Braff, 1983), case (Levitt, 1984), and statutory (Hagan, 1982; Pearlstein, 1986) analysis. Accordingly, significant challenges have been raised about the capacity of NGRI standards to provide authoritative clinico-legal information (Morris, 1982; National Institute of Justice, 1986; Ellison and Buckhour, 1982) and to facilitate the fact-finding process (Sales and Hafemeister, 1984).

One area of substantial criticism is the extensive and minimally effective use of expert testimony. For example, current research indicates that the witness reporting of mental health and clinical experts predicting the future "dangerousness" of the disordered criminal defendant is only reliable about 33 percent of the time (Monahan, 1981; Brooks, 1984; Arrigo, 1996b). Alternatively, in those jurisdictions where criminal culpability attaches despite psychiatric disability (i.e., guilty but mentally ill verdicts), clinical assessments pertaining to degree and type of mental disorder are also susceptible to gross inaccuracies (Arrigo, 1996a; McGraw et al., 1985; Portes, Wagner and Lore, 1991). Thus, as Morris (1982) concludes, these defendants confront a double stigma; namely, they are labeled "bad and mad" when funneled through the clinico-legal courtroom apparatus. Interestingly enough, despite the limited predictive capabilities of the diagnostic reporting, the legal system regards the evidentiary value of such expert testimony as highly determinative for purposes of the criminal trial (Arrigo, 1996a, 1993c: ch. 6; Klofas and Yandrasits, 1989).

The significance of this psychiatric testimony, especially in its relationship to the insanity plea, is the power that clinico-legal language assumes in assigning meaning to the experiences of the juridic subject (the defendant). Put another way, when examining the legal standards on the insanity defense, it is evident that the coordinates of a highly specialized and dominant communicative market are at work. Thus, the underlying legal praxis question examined in this chapter is the extent to which courtroom discourse, via the tests for insanity, represents the interiorized (linguistic) reality of the psychiatric citizen.

In order to understand more fully the NGRI defense doctrine, the methodological contributions of postmodern science will be utilized. Of particular concern here is the potential contribution, if any, for Lacanian psychoanalytic semiotics (Lacan, 1975, 1977, 1978, 1985, 1991) and chaos theory (see e.g., Briggs and Peat, 1989; Gleick, 1987; Stewart, 1989) to further our knowledge of this complex, socio-legal issue. In the United States, the vitality and integration of both analytical paradigms have only recently been examined in the broad domain of the social sciences. Particularly in the area of law and criminology, what work has been conducted, while indeed fascinating, is, nonetheless, mostly theoretical and speculative. Selected topics explored include such matters as: the chaotic law of torts (Brion, 1991); chaos and crime (Young, 1991); psychoanalytic semiotics and juridic exegeses (Milovanovic, 1992a, 1993); chaos theory and humanistic sociology (Young, 1992); and critical social theory and psychiatric justice (e.g., Arrigo, 1994a, 1996b, 1996c).

At issue in this chapter will be something more pragmatic. Thus, many of the perplexing terms incorporated into the largely technical and idiosyncratic vocabulary of Lacanian psychoanalysis and chaos theory will not be closely examined here. Instead, this chapter will explore how the insurgent code of the decentered subject in law (the insane criminal defendant's discourse) is depathologized, is semiotically cleansed, by the juridico-linguistic communicative market (Milovanovic, 1986). Thus, this chapter will first examine Lacan's four discourses (Lacan, 1991; see also Bracher, 1988; Lee, 1990; Melville, 1987) and appropriately apply them to the storytelling that occurs in law as distinguished from the thought and language patterns of the psychiatrically disordered criminal defendant. In the context of this theoretical application, the affinity Lacan's work shares with that of chaos theory will also be explored. Some discussion, too, on forging replacement discourses (Henry and Milovanovic, 1991, 1996) in forensic psychology will be incorporated into the analysis.

LACAN'S FOUR DISCOURSES AND CHAOLOGY

As a matter of broad inquiry, comprehending Lacan's schematization on the four discourses (including the Discourse of: the Master, the University, the Hysteric, and the Analyst), the four critical positions (i.e., agent, truth, other, production) and the four terms/factors (i.e., S1: the master signifier, S2: knowledge, S: the divided subject, and a: le plus-de-jouir) is no simple task. Moreover, as a matter of particular focus, Lacan's insights are cumbersome when considering how such concerns as storytelling in law and the often unintelligible utterances of the disordered defendant relate to his thesis at all. Notwithstanding, the aim here is mostly integrative and practical; that is, I will explore the linkages between Lacan's semiotic formalizations and chaos theory's "disorderly order" concept through an assessment of the not-guilty-by-reason-of-insanity defense. Thus, my treatment of this socio-legal phenomenon will inevitably be reduced to the germane and essential aspects of both theories. In the last section of this chapter, the targeted expository analysis will be most significant. There I will comment not only on the assimilability of both models but also on their paradigmatic utility in advancing critical inquiry on the subject, including the potential contribution psychoanalytic semiotics and chaos theory offer for the development of a replacement discourse.

Law Speak as Discourse of the Master

Milovanovic (1992a, 1993) maintains that law and law-finding assume the discourse of the Master. In this context, he argues that case and statutory law, notions of fairness, equity, autonomy, proprietorship, due process, and so on, function as master signifiers (S1). Master signifiers are primordially situated in the flow of signifiers embedded in one's unconscious. Thus, legal phenomena (like those described above) symbolize "key linguistic forms which are [laden] with the illusory potential [for intersubjective and intrapsychic] fulfillment" (Milovanovic, 1993: 317; see also Milovanovic, 1992b). This understanding of fulfillment resonates with Lacan's use of the construct *jouissance*. In short, master signifiers in law, imbued with ideological content, announce a truth, a meaning, abstractly designed to encompass the interests (both linguistically and socially) of all juridic subjects.

Following Lacan's schematization on the Discourse of the Master, however, its discursive structure produces a circumscribed knowledge (S2). Knowledge is understood to be mediated by language and, thus, to be structured by a host of signifiers. Elsewhere I have argued that in Lacan's phallocentric Symbolic Order (i.e., the "agent of paternity" through which childhood identity is recognized as a masculine endeavor), phallic *jouissance* perpetuates a limited knowledge or *pas tout* (Arrigo, 1993b; see also Caudill, 1993: 131–34). This certain left-out understanding or fulfillment has tremendous implications for the establishment of an *écriture féminine* in general (Sellers, 1991; Grosz, 1990) and for an uncultivated discourse for and about women in the domain of feminist jurisprudence in particular (Arrigo, 1992a, 1995).

Law, as the legitimized master signifier assuming the position of agent (i.e., the dominant factor activated and at work in the person transmitting a message), produces in the receiver of the message (i.e., the other) a perspectival awareness (Merleau-Ponty, 1962, 1963). The receiver, as constituted by and responsive "to the overdetermining effects of the omnipotent master signifier" (Milovanovic, 1993: 319), must become receptive to the transmitted message (Bracher, 1988). The result is a particular juridico-linguistic product, a specialized juridico-linguistic meaning. In Lacanian grammar, the "lack" in this product is recognized as the *a, le plus de jouir*. This is the locus of *jouissance*, the saturated linguistic realm of "more than enjoyment," denied affirmative codification in legal discourse. Put another way, *jouissance* is that beyond or excess that is repressed in the juridic citizen through law speak.

In addition, as Lacan (1985: 150–56, 176–68) himself tells us, this *a*, as the "beyond of enjoyment" or as *objets petit a* (i.e., coded words or even entire sign systems), resists the self-referential form that knowledge assumes (note that if knowledge is mediated by language then knowledge must, by necessity, be anchored by the preconfigured limits of its linguistic coordinates). This *a*, then, as *jouissance*, represents resistance to the symbolization embedded in the signifier. It is the not-all. It is the presence of the divided subject (S) denied, repressed, decentered, during the juridic citizen's exchange between his/her S1 and its circumscribed S2. Thus, it is the presence of an absence (Derrida, 1976); it is that residual discourse which is *pas tout* and "left out in [one's] articulations of S1 with S2" (Milovanovic, 1993: 319).

When considering the function of law and the process of law-finding—particularly the determination of a criminal defendant's degree of mental illness, dangerousness, and criminal responsibility—the basic, discursive structure of Lacanian psychoanalytic semiotics (understood as the Discourse of the Master) is represented as follows:

$$S1 \dashrightarrow S2$$
$$S \dashleftarrow a$$

The storytelling that occurs at the criminal trial where the central controversy addresses the defendant's sanity includes a constellation of master signifiers. The promulgators of such signifiers are lawyers (here, I am specifically referring to the defense attorney, including the rebel advocate). Such notions as "formal equality," "reasonableness," "equal protection," "due process," and the like, symbolically function as pivotal semiotic forms infused with the imaginary possibility for collective *jouissance*. However, these master signifiers are activated in the presence of psychiatric consumers who defy, who resist, the citizen homogeneity implied in and linguistically privileged by these illusory terms. Said in another way, the deductive and syllogistic logic of the criminal law assumes that fulfillment is a relatively stable concept that can be homeostatically attainable through the court system. However, since knowledge (here, juridico-linguistic knowledge informed by psychiatric medicine) is always governed by preconstituted linguistic parameters consistent with the internal dynamics of advanced, state-regulated capitalism (Althusser, 1971), assigning meaning to signifiers like "mental illness," "dangerousness," "incompetency," "diminished capacity" will yield a perspectival knowledge. This perspectival knowledge will tend to reduce multiaccentuated experience (discursive semiotic meanings) to uniaccentuality (prestructured and narrowly defined meaning), advancing the linguistic and social reality of the clinico-legal apparatus (Arrigo, 1996a, 1996b, 1996c, 1994a, 1993c).

Moreover, this reductionism in the court includes the denial of alternative constructions of *jouissance* (the non-normalizing articulations of the insane criminal defendant). This supplemental discourse, this *a* which falls below the bar, is recognized as linguistically non-justiciable and is, therefore, repressed through the courtroom storytelling. The testimony of psychiatrists and clinical consultants includes the *re-presentation* of the defendant's "flight of ideas," "perseverations," "delusions," "loose associations," and so on, into justiciable dialogue. Put another way, defense advocates, in order to do "good" law, must construct a narrative sequence consistent with the preconstituted master signifiers from which juridical knowledge is conceived. Thus, the decentered subject is *pas tout*, is semiotically cleansed.

While the psychiatrically disordered criminal defendant is seemingly represented by critically anchored master signifiers (recall those mentioned above contained in the juridical sphere), such signifiers fail to include the linguistic coordinates that promote the disabled citizen's reality. The divided subject, ostensibly representing the client, then engages in reification. This is a process wherein the producer of legal discourse (the rebel advocate included) promulgates system-maintaining master signifiers by turning to the criminal court and the legal apparatus to locate the criminal defendant's *jouissance*. The result is a system-sustaining cycle wherein linguistic oppression perpetuates itself.

Law Speak and Chaology

The fractal geometry of chaos theory amplifies and elucidates Lacanian psychoanalytic semiotics. The dynamics of chaos theory delegitimize the linearity, reductionism, and determinism implied in the structuralist approach to investigating social systems and human phenomena (Gleick, 1987). Put another way, chaos theory resists the enduring positivism and linear causality of Newtonian physics, Aristotelean logic, and Euclidean geometry. The theory holds that there are no preordained or inevitable conditions. Instead, the social life-world is situated in unpredictability and natural systems stably perpetuate themselves "precisely because they are 'unprincipled,' i.e., they behave nonlinearily" (Young, 1992: 445).

This view of the world (and by implication human agency in the form of storytelling in law) challenges conventional wisdom on the role of disorder in mapping out events in spatio-temporal or "phase" space. In subsequent sections of this chapter I will comment more in depth on this matter. For the present, however, I simply wish to indicate how chaology further clarifies the Discourse of the Master.

As previously described, master signifiers provide primordial sense data by which personal identity and entrance into the Symbolic Order take place. Thus, these seminal linguistic forms offer the citizen the potential for *jouissance*. The Discourse of the Master, however, is governed by what chaologists term *point* attractors. These are the fixed and static "points of subjectification" (Deleuze and Guattari, 1987: 129), perpetuating the positivistic and formalistic (logocentric) aims of legal thought. Thus, law in pursuit of justice promotes equilibrium conditions or stasis. Following Young (1990: 112), this notion in law is compatible with the "politics of sameness." Elsewhere I have commented on how legal stasis governs decisions in mental health law, promoting the logic of identity (Arrigo, 1992b).

As a practical matter, the defense advocate, while zealously representing his/her client and while cognizant of the client's quest for *jouissance*, is situated within and interpellated by the juridico-linguistic communicative market. Put another way, the rebel advocate discovers that the *only* discourse codifying as justiciable the NGRI defense is that discourse which revalorizes the preconstituted master signifiers from which clinico-legal knowledge is constructed. Thus, the "what happened" in the case, as conveyed by the disordered citizen to the defense lawyer, is semiotically purified. Moreover, this filtration process renders the enactor of master signifiers (even the activist attorney) as constituted by the point attractors, that is, the lawyer becomes the embodiment of key juridico-linguistic forms governing the courtroom storytelling. As legal signs, the McNaghten Rule, the Irresistible Impulse test, the Durham Rule, the Substantial Capacity test, and present federal law all are composed of signifiers (e.g., "mental illness," "wrongfulness," "knowing," "responsibility," "diminished control") that assume precise spatiotemporal meaning in law. To engage in the practice of legal defense work, then, the manifest level of meaning contained in each NGRI test (i.e., the linguistic coordinates that define the juridical parameters of the particular doctrine) must be appropriately registered and articulated if the advocate is to have any hope of successfully advancing the defendant's case.

Psychotic Communication and the Discourse of the Hysteric

The Discourse of the Hysteric is produced by two quarter turns in the basic discursive structure. In short, Lacan's schematization depicts the divided subject as endeavoring to transmit his/her interiorized reality (desire) to the other in the furtherance of alternative master signifiers, resulting in decentered or newly constructed knowledge.

$$S \dashrightarrow S1$$
$$a \longleftarrow S2$$

In this model, key linguistic forms symbolizing the illusory potential for citizen *jouissance* (i.e., master signifiers) are semiotically inadequate in incorporating the divided subject's personal expression of desire. The agent, as above the bar, attempts to locate in the other some master signifier (or cadre of master signifiers) that will embody the divided subject's existential search for meaning, for centeredness, for *plenitude*. The other, as producer of circumscribed knowledge, perpetuates a discourse consistent with preconstituted master signifiers. It is within this linguistic realm that the hysteric, as agent, experiences only partial fulfillment. Alternatively expressed, there remains in the *manque d'être* (the hole in being) a gap; that is, the divided subject's desire remains essentially repressed or *pas tout*. Thus, this *a* and its *plus-de-jouir* character (i.e., the divided subject's existential reality as both source and product of desire) perpetuates the ossified and alienated position of the divided subject.

The psychiatrically disordered criminal defendant turns to the court apparatus, through her/his legal counsel, for representation. The coordinates of the juridic sphere are constituted by a battery of master signifiers that are highly specialized and known only to the legally trained or the well initiated. The juridic subject (the defendant) is in search of meaning, consistent with her/his desire, in the plethora of master signifiers promulgated by the juridico-linguistic market. The other, relying upon the machinery of the clinico-legal system, attempts to incorporate, to embody, the disordered citizen's *jouissance* in the courtroom process. In this regard, the defendant's quest for personal fulfillment is realized; after all, the advocate is moving forward on the client's request for representation.

Notwithstanding, this representation only minimally satisfies the disordered citizen's longing for "meaning, stability, and embodiment of his/her desire" (Milovanovic, 1993: 326). Even when the rebel attorney makes good on the promise that the case will go to court, the circumscribed knowledge of the other, of law as articulated by the defendant's counselor, fails to embody the discourse of the mentally disabled criminal defendant. The clinico-legal apparatus *re-presents* the ostensibly unintegrated storytelling of the disordered citizen so that it is compatible with law speak. All of the inconsistencies, contradictions, ambiguities, incompletenesses, and the like, are removed, are semiotically purged, by the rebel advocate, from the "what happened" in the case. The result is that the fact-finding is consistent with master signifiers and rigid point attractors, thereby perpetuating what is understood to be "good" law.

In this regard, however, an essential element of the disordered citizen's reality is conspicuously left out from courtroom consideration. The integrated linguistic coordinates of the clinico-legal apparatus superimpose themselves upon (oppress) the discourse of the mental health defendant.

The result is that trial outcomes addressing the mental competency and legal accountability of a criminal defendant are nothing more than the affirmation of "law speak." As Pfohl (1984: 201) argues, assigning meaning to signifiers like "mental illness," "dangerousness," "criminal insanity," and the like, is simply the privileging and reaffirmation of a well-defined linguistic perspective, a social construction of psychiatric and legal reality. Therefore, the insanity defense, while designed to mitigate or even neutralize the element of criminal intent, necessarily fosters the invalidation of the disordered citizen's languaged experiences as *jouissance* and concomitant social reality.

Psychosis and Chaology

The relationship between chaology and Lacanian psychoanalytic semiotics is also evident in the Discourse of the Hysteric. The bizarre and often unintegrated communication of a criminal defendant signals something profound about the irreducibility and irrepressibility of meaning for the decentered subject. At the macro-sociological level, order and predictability prevail because signifiers (like master signifiers in law) are regarded as system-sustaining generators of culture. Chaologists invoke the image of a tube-like structure called a *torus* attractor to convey this experience and, as such, its geometry implies completeness, determinacy, constancy.

However, the torus also includes Poincaré sections. These are divisions, or "ruptures" in the established pathways to meaning. Within the structure and stream of signifiers these ruptures represent the possibility for new meaning. They signify the potential for alternative or multiple iterations (Balkin, 1987), extending the linguistic parameters of the sign system (like the law), to take on semiotic form. At the micro-sociological level, at the level of particularity, Poincaré sections are most pronounced. Here, regularity, predictability, stasis, hallmarks of the point (and limit) attractor, give way to irregularity, uncertainty, and far-from-equilibrium conditions (Prigogine and Stengers, 1984). Thus, "orderly disorder" governs the life-world and events in it.

The formalism of the law presumes that established premises or precedents can be, through deductive logic, rigidly and prescriptively applied to all cases, regardless of factual differences, inconsistencies, or anomalies among the litigants in the respective suits (Milovanovic, 1993; 1992a). This is the prevailing paradigm in law; it is linear, reductionistic, and totalizing. In Lacanian grammar this is the presence of S2 or circumscribed (juridico-linguistic) knowledge. However, the cross-section of the torus attractor represents the birth of an epistemological break in the core of meaning. The disordered defendant, in search of his/her *jouissance*, experiences the inadequacy, the emptiness, of the master signifiers in law. As divided subject, the discourse of the hysteric resists the circumscribed knowledge implied in the juridico-linguistic communicative market. Seeking to situate desire, attempting to valorize and codify the ruptures in meaning that breathe life into the divided subject's being, the insane criminal defendant eventually learns that any hope of such *plenitude*, as expressed in the embodiment of the law's master signifiers, is illusory. The discursive and unintegrated communication of the decentered subject (the hysteric's knowledge) becomes re-presented according to the iterative modality of the legal apparatus. The linguistic coordinates that define the psychiatric citizen's *a* as *le plus de jouir*, as fulfillment, as more than excess, are invalidated, even by the defense lawyer. The despairing subject, experiencing psychic meaninglessness, absence, alienation, finds solace and consolation in the dominance of the divided subject assuming the privileged position of agent. Again, the psychiatrically disordered criminal defendant pinpoints truth/knowledge in its *plus de jouir*. Thus, the Discourse of the Hysteric perpetuates itself. The far-from-equilibrium truth claims embedded in the defendant's linguistic ruptures (i.e., torus attractor) remain uncodified and long for something more.

LACAN, CHAOS, AND FORGING A REPLACEMENT DISCOURSE

Lacan's Discourse of the Analyst and the protean dimension of its discursive structure provide the necessary ingredients for making a preliminary excursion into the realm of the imaginary possible. The emphasis given to the imagination is critical for purposes of rendering a more humanistic, participatory, and empowering linguistic reality for marginalized citizens. Included within this cadre of subjects is the psychiatrically disordered, criminal defendant. Thus, the appeal to the imagination, understood as the Discourse of the Analyst, is, at some fundamental level, inexorably linked to the linguistic coordinates that define the experiences of disenfranchised citizens.

In addition, as we shall see, chaos theory (especially in its notion of a *strange* attractor) contributes to the future development of a new linguistic order in which far-from-equilibrium conditions advance the divided subject's quest for meaning and *plenitude*. It is within this realm of uncertainty, change, and flux that the disordered defendant's *jouissance*, as an insurgent sign system constituted by new forms of master signifiers, could conceivably usher in a *mythic knowledge* or linguistic structure sufficient to render as sustainable a replacement discourse.

The Discourse of the Analyst

The Discourse of the Analyst is produced by three quarter turns in the basic discursive structure.

$$a \dashrightarrow S$$
$$S2 \longleftarrow\!\!-\!\!-\!\!-\!\!- S1$$

Following Lacan's schematization, the analyst is situated in the *a*, the not-all, and is cognizant of that saturated linguistic realm that assumes the position of agent and is the *manque d'être* (the lack-in-being). This *pas tout* stems from the analyst's circumscribed knowledge/truth (S2) which finds affirmation in the production of distancing, alienating and, therefore, limiting master signifiers (S1) that the divided subject (the hysteric or, in our case, the insane criminal defendant) embodies, albeit temporarily and falsely, with desire.

It is the presence of the absence, the *a*, and its *le plus de jouir* character, that permits a foray into the realm of the imaginary. Here, embedded in this untapped, uncultivated discourse is the potential for relanguaging and reconstituting the juridico-linguistic communicative market such that hegemonic practices and ossified reification no longer receive legitimation. Specifically, the analyst validates and revalorizes the certain left-out knowledge of the hysteric. Put in another way, the exchange of signifiers entertained by the analyst and analysand encompass, at both an intrapsychic and intersubjective level, a certain element of prestige. Recall that in the model pertaining to the Discourse of the Analyst, the *pas tout* is above the bar. It is the dominant factor that is activated in the divided subject, the other.

In my own previous work as a social activist, employed mostly as a community organizer for the disenfranchised (especially the homeless mentally ill), the underemployed, and the non-served, cultivating the rediscovery of primitive and primary experiences (embodied master signifiers) that gave meaning to the lives of such citizens entailed a validation of their own language, culture, and dissipative structures (Briggs and Peat, 1989; see also Arrigo, 1994b, 1993c, 1993d: 46–50). These structures were typically rooted in both stasis and flux (recall that "orderly disorder" is a cornerstone of chaos theory). Thus, many of the normative rituals (and the point attractors by which human agency represses desire) associated with such practices as celebration, work, play, initiation, companionship, and so on, were discarded. All of the apparent inconsistencies, ambiguities, indeterminacies, contradictions, incompletenesses, and uncertainties by which the desiring subjects (the disenfranchised citizens) communicated their needs, their circumscribed knowledge, and their non-legitimized master signifiers were "sutured" in our discourse (see Lacan, 1978: 214–19).

This notion of suture, developed by Lacan and further refined by Silverman (1983) and Smith (1988), *re-presents* to the decentered subject the *a*, the not-all, enabling this person to experience *plenitude*. As Silverman (1983: 231) explains: "[Suture] is the process whereby the inadequacy of the subject's position is exposed in order to facilitate (i.e., create the desire for) new insertions into cultural discourse, which promises to make good the lack." In the context of community-building for the disempowered, McKnight (1987) describes a number of cultural cues that offer important conceptual insight relevant to storytelling in law and adjudicating the psychiatrically disordered, criminal defendant. In sum, McKnight argues that developing a progressive social system (community) sensitive to the desiring subjects' longing for inclusivity, participation, and empowerment necessarily entails that the structural milieu remain malleable and informal. Unger (1987), too, has assessed this phenomenon of promoting a self-actualized society in his discussion of an empowered democracy. Unger's point is that far-from-equilibrium conditions, in the form of diversity, multiplicity, and heterogeneity, must govern the operation of institutions (e.g., schools, the media, the press, the law) if cultural sedimentation and stasis are to be neutralized.

Both McKnight and Unger anticipate the chaologist's agenda. Indeed, such openness to and tolerance of difference is compatible with that of a torus or, more particularly, a strange attractor. As various citizens observe and experience situations differently, predictions about their perception, attitude, behavior, and response are impossible. However, in time and with continuous iterations, a pattern does develop. The ostensibly unintegrated ramblings of a serial killer include the repetition of dissociative themes. The horrifically inspired activities of a pedophile include a series of iterative rituals. The seemingly crazed thoughts of a cannibal include recurring images consistent with his/her desire to digest human flesh.

The point that chaologists strive to make through their notion of a strange attractor is that disorder, uncertainty, chaos, and confusion abound at the micro-sociological level but not so at the macro-sociological level. At the trial, the mentally disabled defendant is interpellated as *in opposition to* the principles embodied in the master signifiers, constituting the law. The defendant signifies all that the clinico-legal apparatus resists (i.e., difference, the body, contradiction, in short, chaos). But again, the master signifiers to which the law claims allegiance produce a circumscribed knowledge that already, even before the trial unfolds, fails to include the divided subject's linguistic reality expressed as *jouissance*. Indeed, such articulations are rendered as nonjusticiable. The analysis here is not intended to legitimize killing, sexual deviance, or cannibalism. Rather, following the insights of Lacanian psychoanalytic semiotics and chaos theory, these comments are designed to identify the inadequacy with juridical discourse and the criminal court apparatus as *the* mechanisms by which to adjudicate the disordered defendant. Alternatively expressed, legal standards on the insanity defense are nothing more than the privileging of clinico-legal discourse, which linguistically invalidates the non-normalizing articulations and experiences of the mentally ill understood as that lack which seeks fulfillment in the law.

CONCLUSIONS

Chaologists remind us that the only real mechanism by which to address the problem of order is through the instrumentation of chaos. This chapter shows that the not-guilty-by-reason-of-insanity defense is a linear, predictable, and counterproductive criminal justice response to what is a social justice phenomenon. Following Lacanian psychoanalytic semiotics we see that the dangerous behaviors of the psychiatrically ill, including their desire and search for meaning and being, are vastly different from the discourse of the clinico-legal apparatus. The result is that law speak, through its master signifiers and circumscribed knowledge, oppresses the juridic subject, invalidating the lack that is the defendant's *jouissance*. Situated within this *pas tout* is the possibility for cultivating a replacement discourse, especially in the context of valorizing stories, and ways of knowing for and about the mentally disabled. Thus, the law and forensic psychology must be more open to instability if they are to embody those master signifiers that announce the contours of this juridic citizen's mythic knowledge.

NOTE

This is a revised version of a previously published manuscript.

REFERENCES

Althusser, L. 1971. *Lenin and Philosophy*. New York: Monthly Review Press.

Arrigo, B. 1992a. "Deconstructing Jurisprudence: An Experiential Feminist Critique." *The Journal of Human Justice* 4(1): 13–30.

———. 1992b. "The Logic of Identity and the Politics of Justice: Establishing a Right to Community-based Treatment for the Institutionalized Mental Disabled." *New England Journal on Criminal and Civil Confinement* 18(1): 1–31.

———. 1993a. "Civil Commitment, Semiotics, and Discourse on Difference: An Historical Critique of the Sign of Paternalism." Pp. 5–32 in R. Kevelson (ed.), *Flux, Illusion and Complexity in Law*. New York: Peter Lang.

———. 1993b. "An Experientially Informed Feminist Jurisprudence: Rape and the Move Toward Praxis." *Humanity and Society* 17(1): 28–47.

———. 1993c. *Madness, Language, and Law*. Albany, NY: Harrow and Heston.

———. 1993d. "Paternalism, Civil Commitment and Illness Politics: Assessing the Current Debate Outlining a Future Direction." *The Journal of Law and Health* 7(2): 131–168.

———. 1994a. "Legal Discourse and the Disordered Criminal Defendant: Contributions from Pscyhoanalytic Semiotics and Chaos Theory." *Legal Studies Forum* 28(4): 93–112.

———. 1994b. "Rooms for the Misbegotten: On Social Design and Social Deviance." *Journal of Sociology and Social Welfare* 21(4): 95–114.

———. 1995. "Feminist Jurisprudence and Imaginative Discourse: Toward Praxis and Critique." Pp. 23–46 in R. Janikowski and D. Milovanovic (eds.), *Legality and Illegality: Semiotics, Postmodernism, and Law*. New York: Lang.

———. 1996a. "The Behavior of Law and Psychiatry: Rethinking Knowledge Construction and the Guilty but Mentally Ill Verdict." *Criminal Justice and Behavior* 23(4): 572–592.

———. 1996b. *The Contours of Psychiatric Justice: A Postmodern Critique of Mental Illness, Criminal Insanity, and the Law*. New York, London: Garland.

———. 1996c. "Toward a Theory of Punishment in the Psychiatric Courtroom: On Language, Law, and Lacan." *Journal of Crime and Justice* 19(1): 15–32.

Balkin, J. 1987. "Deconstructive Practices and Legal Theory." *Yale Law Journal* 96(4): 743–86.

Bracher, M. 1988. "Lacan's Theory in the Four Discourses." *Prose Studies* 11: 32–49.

Briggs, J. and F.D. Peat. 1989. *Turbulent Mirror: An Illustrated Guide to Chaos Theory and the Science of Wholeness*. New York: Harper and Row.

Brion, D. 1991. "The Chaotic Law of Tort: Legal Formalism and the Problem of Indeterminacy." Pp. 45–77 in R. Kevelson (ed.), *Peirce and Law*. New York: Peter Lang.

Brooks, A.D. 1984. "Defining the Dangerousness of the Mentally Ill: Involuntary Civil Commitment." Pp. 280–307 in M. Craft and A. Craft (eds.), *Mentally Abnormal Offenders*. New York: Vintage.

Caudill, D. 1993. " 'Name of the Father' and the Logic of Psychosis: Lacan's Law and Ours." Pp. 124–43 in R. Kevelson (ed.), *Flux, Illusion and Complexity in Law*. New York: Peter Lang.

Deleuze, G. and F. Guattari. 1987. *A Thousand Plateaus*. Minneapolis: University of Minnesota Press.

Derrida, J. 1976. *Of Grammatology*. Baltimore: Johns Hopkins University Press.

Ellison, K. and R. Buckhour. 1982. *Psychology and Criminal Justice: Common Ground*. New York: Harper and Row.

Gleick, J. 1987. *Chaos: Making a New Science*. New York: Penguin Books.

Grosz, E. 1990. *Jacques Lacan: A Feminist Introduction*. New York: Routledge.

Hagan, C.A. 1982. "The Insanity Defense: A Review of Recent Statutory Changes." *Journal of Law and Medicine* 3: 617–41.

Henry, S. and D. Milovanovic. 1996. *Constitutive Criminology: Beyond Postmodernism*. London: Sage.

———. 1991. "Constitutive Criminology: The Maturation of Critical Theory." *Criminology* 29: 293–315.

Kittrie, N.N. 1972. *The Right to Be Different: Enforced Therapy*. Baltimore: John Hopkins University Press.

Klofas, J. and P. Yandrasits. 1989. "Guilty but Mentally Ill and the Jury Trial." *Criminal Law Bulletin* 24: 420–36.

Lacan, J. 1975. *Encore*. Paris: Edition du Seuil.

———. 1977. *Ecrits: A Selection*, trans. A. Sheridan. New York: W.W. Norton.

————. 1978. *The Four Fundamental Principles of Psychoanalysis*, trans. A. Sheridan. New York: W.W. Norton.

————. 1985. *Feminine Sexuality*. New York: W.W. Norton and Pantheon Books.

————. 1991. *L'Envers de la psychanalyse*. Paris: Editions du Seuil.

Lee, J.S. 1990. *Jacques Lacan*. Amherst: University of Massachusetts Press.

Levitt, A. 1984. *Insanity and Incompetence: Case Studies in Forensic Psychology*. Cincinnati: Pilgrimage.

McGraw, B.D. et al. 1985. "The Guilty but Mentally Ill Plea and Verdict: Current State of the Knowledge." *Villanova Law Review* 21: 18–42.

McKnight, J.L. 1987. "Regenerating Community." *Social Policy* 17: 54–58.

Melville, S. 1987. "Psychoanalysis and the Place of Jouissance." *Critical Inquiry* 13: 349–70.

Merleau-Ponty, M. 1962. *Phenomenology of Perception*. New York: Humanities Press.

————. 1963. *The Structure of Behavior*, trans. A.L. Fischer. Pittsburgh: Duquesne University Press.

Milovanovic, D. 1986. "Juridico-linguistic Communicative Markets: Toward a Semiotic Analysis." *Contemporary Crises* 10: 281–304.

————. 1992a. *Postmodern Law and Disorder: Psychoanalytic Semiotics, Chaos and Juridic Exegeses*. Liverpool: Deborah Charles.

————. 1992b. "Rethinking Subjectivity in Law and Ideology: A Critically Informed Psychoanalytic Semiotic View." *The Journal of Human Justice* 4(1): 31–52.

————. 1993. "Lacan, Chaos, and Practical Discourse." Pp. 311–37 in R. Kevelson (ed.), *Flux, Illusion and Complexity in Law*. New York: Peter Lang.

Monahan, J. 1981. *Predicting Violent Behavior*. Beverly Hills, CA: Sage.

Morris, N. 1982. *Madness and the Criminal Law*. Chicago: University of Chicago Press.

National Institute of Justice. 1986. *Crime Study Guide: Insanity Defense*, by N. Morris. Washington, DC: U.S. Department of Justice.

Pasewark, R.A. 1981. "Insanity Plea: A Review of the Research Literature." *Journal of Law and Psychiatry* 9: 357–401.

Pearlstein, S. 1986. *Forensic Psychiatry and Legal Protections of the Insane*. New York: Oceana.

Pfohl, S.J. 1984. "Predicting Dangerousness: A Social Deconstruction." Pp. 201–26 in L. Teplin (ed.), *Mental Health and Criminal Justice*. Beverly Hills, CA: Sage.

Portes, P., D. Wagner and E. Lore. 1991. "How Just Is the Guilty but Mentally Ill Verdict? An Exploration into Personality and Intellectual Factors." *Journal of Criminal Justice* 19: 471–79.

Prigogine, I. and I. Stengers. 1984. *Order Out of Chaos*. New York: Bantam Books.

Rothman, D.J. 1971. *The Discovery of the Asylum*. Boston: Little, Brown.

————. 1980. *Conscience and Convenience: The Asylum and Its Alternatives in Progressive America*. Boston: Little, Brown.

Sales, B. and T. Hafemeister. 1984. "Empiricism and Legal Policy on the Insanity Defense." Pp. 253–78 in L. Teplin (ed.), *Mental Health and Criminal Justice*. Beverly Hills, CA: Sage

Scull, A.T. 1989. *Social Order/Mental Disorder: Anglo-American Psychiatry in Histor-ical Perspective*. Berkeley: University of California Press.

Sellers, S. 1991. *Language and Sexual Difference*. New York: St. Martin's Press.

Silverman, K. 1983. *The Subject of Semiotics*. New York: Oxford University Press.

Simon, R.J. and D.E. Aaronson. 1988. *The Insanity Defense: A Critical Assessment of Law and Policy in the Post-Hinckley Era*. New York: Praeger.

Smith, P. 1988. *Discerning the Subject*. Minneapolis: University of Minnesota Press.

Steadman, H.J. 1985. "Empirical Research on the Insanity Defense." *Annals of American Academy of Political and Social Sciences* 14: 67–90.

Steadman, H.J. and J. Braff. 1983. "Defendants Not Guilty by Reason of Insanity." Pp. 84–102 in J. Monaham and H.J. Steadman (eds.), *Mentally Disordered Offenders: Perspectives from Law and Social Science*. New York: Plenum.

Steadman, H.J. et al. 1993. *Before and After Hinckley: Evaluation Insanity Defense Reform*. New York, London: Guilford.

Stewart, I. 1989. *Does God Play Dice?* New York: Basil Blackwell.

Szasz, T.S. 1963. *Law, Liberty, and Psychiatry: An Inquiry into the Social Uses of Mental Health Practices*. New York: Collier Books.

———. 1987. *Insanity: The Idea and Its Consequences*. New York: John Wiley & Sons.

Unger, R.M. 1987. *False Necessity*. New York: Cambridge University Press.

Volosinov, V. 1986. *Marxism and the Philosophy of Language*. Cambridge, MA: Har-vard University Press.

Wrightsman, L. 1994. *Psychology and the Legal System*. Pacific Grove, CA: Brooks/ Cole.

Young, I. M. 1990. *Justice and the Politics of Difference*. Princeton, NJ: Princeton University Press.

Young, T.R. 1991. "Chaos and Crime: Nonlinear and Fractal Forms of Crime." *The Critical Criminologist* 3(2): 3–4, 10–11.

———. 1992. "Chaos Theory and Human Agency: Humanist Sociology in a Post-modern Age." *Humanity and Society* 16(4): 441–60.

PART III

Chaos Theory, Social Justice, and Social Change

CHAPTER 9

Surfing the Chaotic: A Non-Linear Articulation of Social Movement Theory

Robert C. Schehr

I say unto you: one must still have chaos in oneself to be able to give birth to a dancing star.

Friedrich Nietzsche

Standing on the shoulders of giants leaves me cold....

R.E.M., "King of Birds"

INTRODUCTION

What I will contend in this chapter is that our zest to categorize, label, and in so doing ontologize collective behavior as befitting one or the other paradigms comprising classical and some contemporary social movement theory serves to launch perhaps the most prodigious segment of movement potential, that activity occurring within the life-world, into theoretical obscurity. What is called for, I believe, is a reconceptualization of social movement theory. Most radical and potentially contentious in my proposition is to explode the boundaries constituting previous conceptualizations to eliminate morphological accounts of social movements which privilege what are incidences of collective behavior which are both historically rare and relatively recent (Cohen and Arato, 1992; Scott, 1990; Welch, 1985). What is needed is a theory of social movements capable of capturing the potential of actors hovering in the life-world, a theory which can capture what I perceive is the *persistence of resistance*. What is needed, I contend, is a sociological adaptation of the theory of chaos as a logical extension of the existing insights offered by new social movement theory (NSM) theory.

SOCIAL MOVEMENT THEORY AND INTENTIONAL COMMUNITIES

Social movement theory can generally be said to comprise one of three contemporary paradigms: collective behavior, resource mobilization, and from Europe what is referred to as new social movement theory (NSM) or the identity paradigm (Jamison and Eyerman, 1991). I would like to initiate in this chapter a discussion of a possible fourth approach to social movement theory, one which builds primarily upon the insights of the NSM literature, but which endeavors to move beyond what is conceptualized here as a still limited articulation of movement potential. For while it is true that NSM theory has advanced conceptualization of movement actors, issues, environments, demands, and the like, it continues to cling to conventional articulations of social movement, resulting in a still restrictive ontologization. That is, while Touraine (1985, 1988), Offe (1985), Cohen (1985), Melucci (1980, 1988, 1990, 1995), and the others associated with NSM theory have expanded the field of conceptualization regarding NSM status and significance, they reproduce the emphasis on state-directed conflict or other modes of political organization as comprising a defining moment in its morphological composition, a proposition it shares with the resource mobilization and classical traditions.[1] This is, in my view, too narrow a conceptualization of social movement. Remaining within the confines of traditional theorizing on social movements limits our capacity to identify forms of resistance occurring within civil society at the level of the life-world. We do so at the risk not only of poor scholarship but also of the potential danger involved in not identifying those issues, actors, circumstances, and cultural capital (e.g., indigenous constructions of folklore, myth, language, song, and the like) constituting the cultural milieu of oppressed peoples. For as Laclau and Mouffe (1985) have argued, inefficacious attention to alternate modes of resistance and movement potential from Left academics leaves the discourse of opposition, identity formation, alienation, and anomie to those traditionally on the political Right who may appropriate the language of pain and suffering by offering a regressive return to tradition.

The considerable urgency with which sociologists must confront global expressions of oppression concern the struggle over naming, the ability of academics, politicians, political think tanks, and the media complex to frame issues and people in such a way that humanistic or progressive solutions are marginalized in the public discourse. It is my belief that sociologists play a role (how significant a role is debatable) in the struggle to liberate the voices of the dispossessed. Inadequately recognizing the multiple layers of resistance existing within civil society leaves us with the grand narrative of dominant culture. That is, and Paulo Freire has written extensively on this, without a conscientization of identity which seeks to reconcile agentic struggles over signification with material conditions and ideology (Milovanovic, 1995: 39), all we are left with is the message of the status quo. Marginalization of localized voices occurs within sociological theorizing on social movements when efforts are made at composing grand theories of social movements, what historians have referred to as "covering law" theory. Operating at macro-structural levels of abstraction requires by methodological fiat the prioritization of a linear cognitive framework for viewing social change. That is, social change must be determined as having moved from one point on the chess board of history to another, the assumption being that if we have information on a specific starting point, we can predict with relative accuracy future manifestations. The assumption is not only at odds with the predictive capacity of social scientific methods, but it also tends to gloss over the richness of subaltern resistance which is seldom ever articulated in grandiose ways. While a sociological interest in the everyday life-world behaviors of people is not new, I contend that even where this emphasis does exist within the literature comprising analyses of social movements (e.g., Evans and Boyte, 1986; Fantasia and Hirsch, 1995; Flacks, 1988; Hirsch, 1990; Jenson, 1995), overt, typically state-directed political activity is privileged. Application of chaos theory will encourage us to pay closer attention to those subaltern modes of resistance.

While anthropologists have long lamented the neglect of peasant rebellion, not merely the fact of, but equally the ways in which they rebel, as a serious omission in sociological scholarship on social movements, sociologists, for their part, have traditionally shaped their analyses of social movement phenomena by drawing upon the influential but flawed work of the collective behavior school initiated by Herbert Blumer (1951), Talcott Parsons (1971), and Turner and Killian (1972), but catapulted to disciplinary prominence in the early 1960s by Neil Smelser (1962). Resource mobilization (e.g., della Porta, 1988; Jenkins, 1989; Klandermans and Tarrow, 1988; McAdam, 1988; McCarthy and Zald, 1977; Tilly et al., 1975; Tilly, 1985), while an advance over the collective behavior paradigm in its reassurance that collective behavior is not irrational but a normative component of human interaction, nevertheless, perpetuates the collective behaviorists' exposition of social movements as vying primarily for political recognition at the level of the state, and has tended to neglect the construction of collective identity, that is, the multiple ways in which actors interpret images within and beyond the life-world, leading them to participate in social movements.

In an effort to address perceived weaknesses in prevailing social movement theories, NSM theory emerged in the 1980s to advance a conceptualization of movement actors, issues, and environments which illuminated the manifold ways in which movement actors engage representations of power to (re)create identities. Research on NSMs continuing into the present decade suggests a general multidisciplinar theoretical thrust challenging traditional structuralist interpretations of social movements, emphasizing instead the unique cultural innovation inspired by NSM actors (Taylor and Whittier, 1995: 163). Theorists as sessing NSM actors and activities have advanced social movement the orizing by adding a layer of complexity to traditional explanation: focusing their analytical interests on cultural efforts to reappropriat temporal, spatial, and interpersonal perceptions of meaning. It is th struggle to rearticulate the meaning of norms, values, and beliefs, struggle initiated within the life-world, which distinguishes NSMs from previous social movements, and in particular intentional communitie (ICs) as a NSM. NSMs have strategically refrained from totalizing rev olutionary strategy to focus on the foundations, to penetrate the root of domination in postindustrial society, to strive, as Sassoon (1984) con cludes, to "take possession of representation opportunities . . . to impos the codes of relation with the world (with social life, with nature, with one's own body)" (864). NSM actors like those living in ICs must engag adversaries at the level of symbolism, and to the extent that they offe alternative life-world experiences (imagination, play, love, nature, femi nism, art, spirituality), they embody a significant challenge to contem porary postindustrial society. A point which must be set aside for the moment.

What has been neglected in each of these literatures is the bountifu spectrum of resistance as practiced by oppressed peoples, directed no at the state but at the level of the life-world. As Scott (1990) clearly dem onstrates in his work on peasant rebellion, the oppressed, by virtue of their status as oppressed people, have constructed modes of resistance which intentionally deflect attention away from state-directed activitie to focus on issues emerging within civil society. Crucial in this work and still others (Benjamin, 1969; Bernal, 1994; Bloch, 1995 [1955]; Bone and Gilliam, 1994; de Certeau, 1984; Foucault, 1976; Gilmore, 1987; Gross 1992–93; Gyani, 1993; Heehs, 1994; Laclau, 1990; Nandy, 1987; Rao, 1994 Scott, 1990; Welch, 1985), is the historically relentless preservation of lo cal myth and folklore, including what Hobsbawm and Ranger (1983 refer to as the act of "inventing tradition," procured by the oppressed and reinscripted in daily activities to buffer the intrusion of dominant cultural capital (Bourdieu 1984). The active interpretation and reinter pretation of the habitus of oppressed people, by and for oppressed peo ple, are what is overlooked in classical application of social movemen theory. Indeed, to the extent that it is recognized as, for example, whei Tilly (1985) argues that there is "nothing new in new social movements," that the demands and activities of NSM actors can locate their origins in movements past, it is clear that he, and others within the resource mo bilization paradigm, neglect attention to the preservation and rearticu lation of the life-world. It seems clear that our contemporary moment differs, in some ways dramatically, from our pre-1960s predecessors (Boggs, 1985; Brand, 1990; Johnston and Klandermas, 1995; Melucci, 1988; Offe, 1985; Touraine, 1971, 1988). Whether perceived as postmodern, postindustrial, or hypermodernity (Luke, 1991), sociological analyses of social movements, including NSM theory, must be reconceptualized to absorb a broader array of resistance potential. To further my point, in the section to follow I will apply insights culled from chaos theory to an interpretation of the role played by members of ICs in exhibiting an alternate mode of resistance, one clearly directed at the transformation of the life-world. For its part, contemporary social movement theory, operating as it does within linear constructions of movement activity, lacks both the theoretical and conceptual tools necessary to privilege members of ICs as movement actors. Let us turn now to a discussion of ICs.

There are probably as many ways to elaborate on the *intentional* in intentional community as there are community members to respond to the question. According to Dan Questenberry (1995), himself a member of Shannon Farm community in Virginia, responses range from the utilitarian:

Intentional community . . . has its own clear borders and membership. Some people call it a "utopian" community. The essential element in any intentional community, ours included, is that people who want to live in it will have to join, be accepted by those who already live there, and go by its rules and norms, which may in some ways differ from those in society at large. (Kat Kincade, Twin Oaks)

the sociological:

Community, like love, is so craved, adored, and overused, it seems to have lost its meaning, except as a kind of political/new-age slogan. We're becoming interested in more specific words, such as cooperative business, support group, neighborhood, and even commune. (Niche Community)

and the holistic:

[Community represents] An interdependent, cooperative grouping of aligned humans, animals, plants, earth energies, and benevolent multidimensional beings who together comprise a sensitive, sustainable ecosystem. (Mariah Wentworth, Rainbow Hearth Sanctuary)

While it remains quite difficult to know precisely how many ICs are currently in operation in the United States, we do know, as Geoph Kozeny writes in the 1995 edition of the *Communities Directory*, that unlike the more rapid turnover of the 1960s communal efforts, the current *Director* identifies over 160 communities which have lasted over a decade or more, and 80 which have lasted more than two decades (24). In all, the *Directory* identifies over 500 ICs in both the United States and Canada alone.[2] Furthermore, conversations with numerous members of ICs at the annual Conference on International Communities held in Oneida, New York, confirmed what numerous secondary literatures, and my own work with communitarians were saying: there appears to be an emerging interest among community members in the proliferation and cultivation of social movement status.

There are a number of factors distinguishing contemporary ICs from their predecessors, and while there are equally numerous lines of intersection with previous generations of communitarians relative to values, goals, and methods, it is the differences noted below which designate contemporary members as comprising a NSM. Briefly, there are perhaps eight significant characteristics which distinguish contemporary ICs: (1) they exhibit an aggressive pursuit of innovative modes of enhanced human cohabitation through the application of numerous spiritual, philosophical, psychological, and sociological insights; that is, neither urban co-housing nor rural land trusts signify "regression"; (2) they are typically non-hierarchical, often selecting feminist-inspired consensus decision-making models; (3) they are both innovators and practitioners of psychologically sophisticated methods for non-violent conflict resolution and personal growth (e.g., Creative Conflict, Clear-Mind Training based on Zen philosophy, Gestalt); (4) they utilize appropriate technology where it is not ecologically intrusive (e.g., tractors, solar-powered computers); (5) there is a strong philosophical dedication to community outreach often pursued through slide shows, book publications, newsletters, and conferences; (6) there is an effort to maintain balance in the pursuit of cultural, economic, and personal liberation and awareness leading to inspired and ostensibly more humane experiences of love, sex, play, work, childcaring, self-identity, relationships to time, space, and the like; (7) there is a firm belief in economic self-sufficiency, which is experienced in many ways, including innovative efforts at alternative farming cooperatives (concentrating on organic whole foods), food circles (organization of multiple community land trusts within a specific region to produce diversified food stuffs for circulation among the communities), production and circulation of alternative money, and experimentation, production, and marketing of alternative energy devices; and finally, (8) there is a firm commitment to non-violence, race and gender harmony, and peace. It is when viewing contemporary ICs in totem that their levels of sophistication in all aspects of human experience reveal their differences relative to their predecessors.

With specific regard to social movement theory, members of ICs, while

not profoundly interested in pursuing partisan politics or finding redress
for grievances at the level of state legislatures, do have what McLaughlin
and Davidson (1990) recognize as a "planetary consciousness." That is,
they are active participants in community activities with some, like the
Farm in Tennessee, establishing networks of humanitarian aid for people
in less-developed countries. Moreover, and in keeping with Gusfield's
(1994) proposition that a social movement exists when actors believe it
does, it is the members of ICs themselves who view what they are doing
as potentially transformative, as when, for example, a member of the
Twin Oaks community in Virginia acknowledges:

My life has political meaning, just by living here and doing what I'm doing. It's
a message, an example to people, something they can look at, come to visit, and
talk to us and get inspired to change their own life. (in McLaughlin and Davidson: 37)

My own research on ICs in central New York produced similar responses. Members of ICs are, sometimes excruciatingly, aware of their
status as innovators, something which is confirmed with each new request from a "seeker" to visit their community. Members of Birdsfoot
Farm in Canton, those at Common Place in Truxton, and members of
the emerging community Common Ground in Camden were each thoroughly aware of their activities as having both symbolic and literal political and cultural significance. However, despite multiple and
innovative modes of life-world activity characterizing contemporary ICs
as forerunners in human and environmental relations, they are not recognized as a social movement. The reason, as will become clear, is the
seemingly rigid entrenchment of social movement theory.
    Actors in ICs, operating at the level of civil society and without state-
directed conflict as their *modus operandi*, can only be recognized as participants in a social movement if the boundaries of the classical social
movement tradition are transformed. Even within the prevailing NSM
paradigm, significant theoretical confusion continues to pervade efforts
to precisely operationalize social movements as a collective phenomena.
Specifically, NSM theory reiterated the one dimension indicative of all
previous conceptual efforts, that in order to qualify as a social movement
actors and organizations must express overt, typically state-directed conflict. Italian theorist Alberto Melucci, who, along with French sociologist
Alain Touraine, was largely responsible for propelling NSM theory to
disciplinary prominence, has persistently emphasized the necessity of
conflict as a requisite condition of social movement status. Melucci identifies the three most significant dimensions of social movements as: (1)
solidarity, (2) conflict, and (3) breaking the limits of compatibility of a
system (1990: 29). Conflict is defined as struggling against an opponent

to secure the same goods or values (29). Similarly, in his earliest attempt to distinguish social movements from other collective behavior, Melucci argues that collective action must "go beyond the rules of the political system and/or . . . attack the structure of a society's class relations" (1980: 202). Melucci's closest empirical reference to ICs is his disapproving reference to "regressive utopia." In his identification of the qualifying characteristics of NSM phenomena, Melucci celebrates the "end of the separation between public and private spheres," but simultaneously cautions against movement actors slipping into a "regressive utopia," articulated as a group identification with traditional values, often having a religious component. His critique of regressive utopia clearly signifies his allegiance to overt forms of conflict as a significant dimension of effective social movements, that is, social movements which do not break the limits of compatibility of the system.

Alain Touraine (1988) has further disaggregated societal conflict to include collective behavior, struggles, and social movements. The former are typically defensive in nature and primarily seen as efforts to preserve or adapt "sick" elements of social structure. Struggles seek direct access to decision-making power within the confines of political parties. But social movements are viewed as a special category of collective behavior where actors are engaged in conflictual actions seeking "to transform the relations of social domination that are applied to the principal cultural resources (production, knowledge, ethical rules)" (64). In a way, analogous to Melucci's conceptualization of "regressive utopia," Touraine also identifies the political and cultural ramifications of slipping into "anti-movements." For Touraine, anti-movements consist of collective actions appealing to community in defense of some external enemy. Doing so impedes the expansion of group interests, prohibiting its blossoming into a social movement, leaving the door open for further domination and exploitation.

Each of these typological articulations of social movement, if taken alone, preclude the inclusion of ICs. While it is true that one of the defining characteristics of contemporary ICs is their commitment to the cultivation of a "planetary consciousness" (e.g., localized community activism), with few exceptions (e.g., The Farm, The Movement for a New Society), overt conflict as expressed in the establishment of, say, an "Intentional Community Party," or direct pleas to state agencies, is not characteristic of the movement in totem. What then should we make of ICs? While NSM theory initiated efforts to conceptualize contemporary movement actors within the broader context of a postindustrial West, and articulate modes of resistance to domination linking movement expressions to life-world concerns, they nonetheless continue to cling to the conflict-centered litmus test inherited from classical social movement research. In my estimation, NSM theory cannot carry us far enough in being able to successfully identify actors, like members of ICs, who have channeled their energies toward the reconstitution of localized space. For this, we must move to a rearticulation of social movement theory consistent with recent sociological interpretations of chaos theory. If I am successful, what we will be left with is a theory of social movement which is at once heterogeneous, non-linear, and perhaps most importantly, "radically morphological." What I mean by "radically morphological" is an abandonment of the classical social movement emphasis on birth, growth, and decay, an Enlightenment-inspired evolutionary model (Bernal, 1994; Bond and Gilliam, 1994; de Certeau, 1984; Nandy, 1987), to be replaced by a rhizomatic articulation of structure and form which recognizes in global actors a resounding mosaic of resistance. Perhaps it is true that it is not "deviance" which needs explanation, but rather, order.

ENTER CHAOS: BUTTERFLIES, FRACTALS, AND AFTERIMAGES

Perhaps most compelling for sociologists is the degree to which the recognition by chaos theorists of the non-linearity of systems, the correlation between numerous unpredictable occurrences at the micro-level and their consequent patterned emergence at the macro or system level, can be reconceptualized to include variables relating to, for example, social movements. Is it conceivable that Wilson's (1983) metaphor of the transition from boiling water to steam has applications to such seemingly unrelated a topic as the relationship between localized forms of resistance and the preservation of civil society via state-based preservation of rights of assembly, speech, and so on? Has the sociology of social movements ignored micro-level diversity due to its commitment to positivism? Following Shaw (1981), who comes dangerously close to Nietzsche, isn't it conceivable that it is sociologists, who have traditionally busied themselves with the construction of conceptual boxes in which to locate and analyze cultural phenomena, who can be partially to blame for impeding the proliferation of cultural forms at the level of the life-world? For as Shaw would suggest, it is chaos which produces all new forms of information, and, I would add following Nietzsche, a myriad of diverse life-world options where creativity, opportunity, and alternatives abide, each emerging from the unpredictability of the micro. Mandelbrot, Shaw, Serres, and others affiliated with the strange attractor analysis of chaos theory view the chaos inherent in nature as what constitutes its beauty, its majesty. Serres (1977) has identified, in the work of Epicurean physicist Lucretius, the application of chaos to illuminate the origin of the universe. According to White (1991),

Lucretius images this state of disorder as the eternal fall of atoms through space. ... At uncertain times and indefinite places, the universal fall of the atoms is interrupted by what Lucretius calls the *clinamen*, "the smallest conceivable condition for the first formation of turbulence." (265)

As the atoms begin to collide and spiral, we have the beginning of the universe and, subsequently, the world. Lucretius proposes a theory of chaos to resolve the most prodigious philosophical question in Occidental philosophy, "why is there something rather than nothing?" It all happened by chance. A state of negentropy emerges from the volatile sea to render the manifest, "pockets of local order in rising entropy" (Serres in White: 265).

Finally, and as if he were directly addressing our concerns for IC and heterogeneity, White (1991), following Serres, asserts:

We ourselves must become improvisational artists, *bricoleurs* who live close to the clinamen, where Nature is born, close to the fertile chaos from which form is continually emergent. (in White, 1991: 265; original emphasis).

This is what Serres refers to as the "wisdom of the Garden," the significance of the local, the improvisational. Here Serres's work, particularly his publication of *The Parasite*, begins to round out the correlation between chaos theory and my critique of classical social movement theory, resource mobilization, and some components of the NSM conceptualization of social movements.

In *La Naissance*, Michael Serres contributes further to the distinction between indigenous knowledges and master narratives by conceptualizing the mythological figure of Venus as the manifestation of the wisdom of the Garden. Venus, the goddess of love, emerged as the product of the torrid flux of the sea. If we are to expand the parameters of sociological theorizing on social movements, that is, if we are to embrace the wisdom of the Garden and promote an alternative vision of social movement consistent with recognition of local (i.e., life-world) autonomy and forms of resistance, we must battle that other formidable mythological figure Mars, the war god, who, according to Serres, "proposes a science and an ethics of totalization, force, mastery, and empire" (1977: 236). Venus and Mars are antithetical. Venus promotes the value of stochastic processes, where Mars promotes the " 'science of death' according to which reality can be reduced to deterministic trajectories" (White: 266). To assure system predictability Mars must resort to violence and control; control over identity construction, sexuality, leisure, work, nature. For Serres, Mars initiates a "thanatocratic" world order in which "there is nothing new to be learned, to be discovered, to be invented," since hegemonic ontologization has reduced in theory that which exists as diversity to the status of anomaly. What follows is the "reduction of difference to sameness" where there exists a prevailing belief that there is "nothing new under the sun." Serres offers us a convenient transition enabling us to document the evolution of intentional communities. It is my contention that prevailing sociological analyses of communes and the commune "movement" as originally conceived in the work of Zablocki (1980), Kanter (1973), Berger (1981), and others, shared a similar conclusion. What this initial section on chaos theory and the following section on post-Marxism and poststructuralism have and will contend is that these sociological interpretations, and particularly the extensive research of Zablocki, are limited in their exposition of the social movement potential of ICs, due to their conceptualization of social movement within the classical tradition. Classical social movement theory and resource mobilization each are constituted by the Enlightenment-based positivistic search for Truth. They hover, much like Mars, in the linear milieu of deterministic predictability and cause and effect. What they miss, and what chaos theory alerts us to, is the myriad diversity of organic interaction sempiternally constructing and reconstructing lifestyle options, flirtations with identity, alternate expressions of sexuality, innovative forms of consensus decision-making, renewed respect for the earth, for life, for peace.

What emerges in the theory of chaos is recognition of the life-giving force of heterogeneity, multiplicity. Just as with physical systems, in cultural systems too, chaos enhances opportunities for creativity. In Serres's novel *The Parasite*, closed cultural systems are destabilized by the parasite lurking within. Ensuing turmoil created by the introduction of the parasite produces innovative options, or as White (1991) suggests, "alternative logics," to address the perceived instability. What this means for us and for our efforts to reconstruct an alternate theory of social movement, particularly as it applies to ICs, is a reliance upon "parasitic dissonance" (White) at the level of the life-world.

While it is perhaps an unfortunate choice of metaphor, since parasites are usually perceived as organisms drawing life from another without offering comparable return, members of ICs do perceive themselves as purveyors of the possible. And since they exist for most of us at the fringe of society, they are well positioned to exemplify effective alternatives to the numerous components of cultural capital comprising our national popular.

Perhaps a more efficacious metaphor can be located in Pirsig's (1991) *Lila: An Inquiry Into Morals*. In attempting to ascertain the distinction between *static* and *dynamic* good, Pirsig refers to a passage in Ruth Benedict's (1934) *Patterns of Culture*. To establish the pervasiveness of culturally specific deviance designations, Benedict relates the story of a charismatic Pueblo Indian living in Zuni, New Mexico, in the nineteenth century. Benedict describes this man in the following way:

In a society that thoroughly distrusts authority of any sort, he had native personal magnetism that singled him out in any group. In a society that exalts moderation and the easiest way, he was turbulent and could act violently on occasion ... Zuni's only reaction to such personalities was to brand them as witches. (in Pirsig, 1991: 110)

For Pirsig, this tale foretold considerably more than cultural relativism. Pirsig concludes that the man accused of being a witch was actually a *shaman*, or more precisely, a *brujo*, "a Spanish term used extensively in that region that denotes a quite different kind of person." A *brujo* is a person who "claims religious powers; who acts outside of, and sometimes against local church authorities" (112).

The story of the *brujo* related here is significant for us on two levels. First, the *brujo* comprises a more accurate metaphorical figure than the parasite related in the work of Serres to exemplify the complicated role played by members of ICs in contemporary American culture. To genuinely encompass the significance of ICs, a metaphor must communicate the imagery of an organism which is of, but not of. That is, ICs must be conceptualized as having emerged from dominant culture, but now, standing in many ways opposed to it, be simultaneously viewed as exogenous actors sempiternally engaged in a process of agitation and integration. The *brujo*, by challenging the authority of priests, stood on the cultural fringe offering alternative interpretations of traditional cultural capital. The image of the *brujo*, the cultural critic, presents us with a metaphorical character possessing attributes which contribute to the vitality and heterogeneity of civil society. In his capacity as critic and contributor to the vivacity and enrichment of his culture, the *brujo* approximates members of ICs.

The metaphor of the *brujo* equally offers us a critique of essentialism. One of the more interesting components of Pirsig's work is his effort to promote subjectivity while mindful of deterministic systems. In his effort to define Quality, Pirsig, drawing upon the tale of the *brujo*, determines that there are two distinct forms of "the good," one static and the other dynamic. Static good refers to sedimented cultural practices: language, folkways, mores, myth, norms, and values. Static good is what makes the persistence of culture possible, predictable. In this context, the *brujo*, one who challenged tradition, was viewed as deviant, dangerous, one deserving of punishment. The priests, in contrast, are the embodiment of tradition. They are good. This classic Derridean bifurcation of good and evil holds a lesson for students of social movement theory. Let me explain.

It is my contention that neither classical social movement theory nor resource mobilization considers the significance of actors acting at the level of the life-world, due to their allegiance to positivistic interpretations of social scientific phenomena. In the metaphor of the *brujo*, Pirsig cites the work of anthropologist E.A. Hoebel to confirm the restrictive power of sedimented interests:

I]n the more highly developed cultures in which cults have become strongly organized churches, the priesthood fights an unrelenting war against shamans. . . . Priests work in a rigorously structured hierarchy fixed in a firm set of traditions. Their power comes from and is vested in the organization itself. They constitute a religious bureaucracy. Shamans, on the other hand, are arrant individualists. Each is on his own, undisciplined by bureaucratic control; hence a shaman is always a threat to the order of the organized church. (in Pirsig: 113)

In this sense, ICs present classical social movement theory with a curious problem. They do not fit the mold of classical conceptualizations of movement actors. Indeed, they signify chaos at the level of the life-world. As such, they are morphologically perceived by social scientists as perhaps amusing historical phenomena possessing an uncanny capacity to rekindle during various historical epochs. This interpretation would certainly satisfy the structural concerns of social movement theorists like Tarrow (1989, 1994), and sociologists like Kanter (1973) and Zablocki (1980). But in my estimation, metaphorical interpretation of the *brujo* corresponds nicely with my efforts to reconceptualize social movement theory by focusing greater attention on potential movement actors contemporaneously perceived as existing on the fringe (and, therefore, not in need of serious attention), and relatedly in the way that it enables us to see that an academic commitment to specific Enlightenment-inspired, methodological assumptions leads us to overlook cultural phenomena occurring at the level of the life-world.

Milovanovic's (1993a, 1993b, 1994) and Brion's (1991) adaptations of chaos theory to criminology and law suggest possible avenues for our conceptualization of social movement theory and my articulation of the role played by members of ICs as social movement actors. Let us consider for a moment Lorenz's butterfly attractor. Strange attractors are conceptualized diagrammatically as two wings of a whole, a butterfly attractor, constituted by "infinite variation within a finite space" (Milovanovic, 1993a: 13). In practice this has been interpreted as suggesting the presence of "two (or more) outcome basins . . . within which any accurate prediction is impossible" (13); that while order reigns at the global level, there is disorder at the local. Brion's application of the butterfly attractor to law is instructive. He argues that one wing of the butterfly be conceptualized as legal heritage, while the other contains heresy, alternative or subversive legal views. Contemporary communitarians constitute a heterogeneous rearticulation of dominant cultural capital. Innovations in sexual relations, gender and race/ethnic relations, conflict resolution, modes and means of production, child rearing, play, relationship to the environment, commitment to organic and holistic (diversified agriculture, aquaculture) food production, planetary consciousness, education, spirituality, and the like, distinguish contemporary communitarians not only from dominant culture, but when taken holistically, from their communitarian predecessors. When located within the lexicon of chaos theory, members of ICs are hovering at the archimedean nucleus of the two wings of the butterfly. One wing re-presents dominant cultural capital, the familiar. The other wing signifies the unfamiliar, the entropic, a torrent of possibility, Nietzsche's dancing star. It is here, in this instability, where creativity flourishes, where the cultural revolutionary emerges to rearticulate critical memory, or quite possibly to activate nostalgic utopia.

Now it becomes apparent that this is the possible link between essentialism and civil society, between daily ritualized forms of resistance to oppression expressed at the level of the life-world, and those social movements indicated by sociologists as having a morphological composition. Operating in the entropic wing of the butterfly attractor, cultural revolutionaries articulate a new master signifier (counterhegemonic), founded on local knowledge, myth, folklore, and the like. This new knowledge is qualitatively different from the master discourse of dominant culture, since only critical memory

can avoid excluding [intense enjoyment], because it offers not absolute, clearly established, self-referential identities, but rather a system of oppositions embodied in images and fantasies that offer no unequivocal identities, meanings, or values (Bracher in Milovanovic, 1994: 18).

That is, what conceptualizing social movements within the context of chaos theory enables us to do is recognize the relevance and continuity of those social movements most clearly identified in the work of collective behaviorists and resource mobilization theory, one wing of the butterfly attractor, while we remain aware of the entropic other wing. For if my interpretation of the postindustrial or postmodern malaise as represented in the NSM literature is accurate, then those "disenfranchised, marginalized, colonized, and repressed subjects" hovering at the archimedean nucleus of the butterfly attractor have the capacity to (re)create meaning consistent with critical memory or nostalgic utopia. More specifically, what this means is that the entropic wing of the butterfly attractor offers no specific direction for the disenfranchised. It is out of entropy that negentropy has arisen in the form of intentional community.

A new master signifier materializes to act as a counterhegemonic alternative to dominant cultural capital. The fragmented and unsituated self returns to an ordered state.

AFTERIMAGES AND PLATEAUS

Let us return for a moment to an earlier effort to establish the significance of entropy as it relates to social movement actors through the use of metaphor. You will recall that I offered to replace the metaphor of the parasite suggested in Michael Serres's novel of the same name with that of the *brujo* found in the philosophical work of Pirsig. It was the *brujo* who stood on the periphery of dominant culture, simultaneously a product of that culture and potentially its most threatening iconoclast. Now it is possible to further loosen conceptually the metaphorical constitution of social movement actors. Doing so explodes the dissipative structures established by chaos theory to articulate a perpetual state of *(dis)order*.

Conceptualization of plateaus, as discussed by Deleuze and Guattari (1987) in their publication of *A Thousand Plateaus: Capitalism and Schizophrenia*, is seminal to our efforts to understand the role played by social movement actors who resist, not by directing their energy at the level of the state, but rather, through a multifarious juxtaposition of resistances at the level of the life-world culminating in a multiplicitious weave. These are forms of resistance that generally go unnoticed in contemporary social movement research. In the "Translator's Foreword," for example, Brian Massumi illuminates the derivation of Deleuze and Guattari's use of the concept plateau as emanating from an essay on Balinese culture by Gregory Bateson. In his research, Bateson "found a libidinal economy quite different from the West's orgasmic orientation." Massumi contends that:

In Deleuze and Guattari, a plateau is reached when circumstances combine to bring an activity to a pitch of intensity that is not automatically dissipated in a climax. The heightening of energies is sustained long enough to leave a kind of afterimage of its dynamism that can be reactivated or injected into other activities, creating a fabric of intensive states between which any number of connecting routes could exist. (xiv)

More specifically, perceiving global social movement actors as comprising myriad plateaus sempiternally acting and interacting at the level of the life-world, and occasionally the state, liberates social movement theory from confounding and, in my estimation, deleterious constraints. It is more likely, and probably more efficacious (as they seem well aware), for movement actors to resist oppression in ways producing the *afterimage of a plateau*, rather than initiate efforts to confront images of power directly through the use of force. In this way what movement actors, like those in ICs do, is constitute one of the numerous strands comprising the complex weave of resistance which indelibly designates for current and future generations an alternate path, a counterhegemony. It is in the afterimage of the plateau that oppressed people rely upon myth, folklore, tradition, and the like, to (re)construct critical memory (Welch), or as Benjamin contended, a nostalgic utopia.

While spatial concerns limit thorough explication of the concepts critical memory and nostalgic utopia, I would like to briefly state their relevance given our present interest in afterimages. Seminal to my establishing the significance of ICs as a NSM is their capacity to draw upon and enhance remnants of history, what Heehs (1994) refers to as the cultivation of *mythistory*. Myth, for Heehs, amounts to

a set of propositions, often stated in narrative form, that is accepted uncritically by a culture or speech-community and that serves to found or affirm its self-conception. "Myth" in this sense includes most traditional narratives as well as some modern literature, but also "texts" such as performance wrestling, certain advertisements, and so on. (3)

To the extent that these perceptions are accepted uncritically, that is, they exhibit a certain taken-for-grantedness, they closely resemble Bourdieu's (1984) insightful articulation of habitus. Myths can be viewed as scripts for articulating cultural history. Here, it is the process of storytelling through mythic transposition of cultural artifacts and symbols which permits, indeed encourages, the free and creative play with history. Moreover, myth facilitates clarification of often opaque life-world experiences. It is this process of presentation and interpretation which constitutes in myth a transformative capacity. The power of myth to inspire action in defense of custom and illuminate alternate modes of thinking on contemporary issues is juxtaposed to Enlightenment-based rationalism, which directs behavior through the cognitive vehicle of logical thought. Specifically, mythic representation can be viewed as the narrative juxtaposition of antinomies. Potent combinations of myth and tradition as expressed in contemporary struggles for liberation or, as in the case with ICs, in structural details outlining alternate modes of living, have been referred to by Hobsbawm and Ranger (1983) as invented traditions. Invented traditions are unique in that they are fabricated mythological constructs grafted from components of historical memory to suit contemporary situations. In many ways then, the manipulation and digestion of historical memory operate in a way similar to the appeals made by Barthes for the sempiternal interpretation of the text. That is, there are countless ways to interpret the stock of accumulated knowledge for contemporary activation. David Gross (1992–93) makes this point quite clear when he states:

By juxtaposing rather than integrating the past and the present, the nonsynchronous and the synchronous, it may become possible not only to see the present from an entirely new perspective but to raise questions about some of the otherwise hardly noticed cliches of contemporary life. (6)

Each of the cross-cultural references to folklore, music, festivals, dinners, work processes, agriculture, *gemeinschaft*, spirituality (and many more) comprises the stock of cultural memory from which members of ICs derive their mechanisms for producing the structures of community. Members of ICs seeking to generate their own legitimate codes in keeping with the values of non-violence, spiritual awakening, simplicity, diversified agriculture, and the like, freely appropriate relevant references to historical memory, and often its symbolic composition, regardless of its ethnic, geographic, or spiritual origin. In essence they themselves appear to symbolize the embodiment of the postmodern. References to nostalgic utopia and critical memory force a radical juxtaposition with contemporary political, economic, and cultural conditions necessary to inspire fractured consciousness. It is in this way that the afterimages created by generations past are appropriated by contemporary cultural actors and infused with new life. Much like NSM theorists, Deleuze and Guattari contend that to effectively conceptualize the multiple we must confront "the dint of sobriety" through our recognition of life-world activities. It is here that we discover the rhizome, the language of the people, the language of the oppressed, critical memory.

One of the most intriguing correlations between Deleuze and Guattari's deliberations of rhizomes and my interests in intentional community can be found in their contention that the proliferation of multiplicity referred to above stems from the capacity of rhizomes to emerge from events which splinter or shatter a particular strand by grafting on to vestiges of weaves spun in historical memory, or by constructing entirely new strands. That is, "every rhizome contains lines of segmentarity according to which it is stratified, territorialized, organized, signified, attributed, and so on, as well as lines of deterritorialization down which it constantly flees" (9). There are obvious correlations here between contemporary intentional communities and their predecessors. While contemporary ICs are being presented here as unique relative to their pre-1960s predecessors, primarily based on a more total, holistic agglomeration of communal living skills, there remain, without doubt, vestiges of communal efforts past.

CONCLUSION

In this chapter I have sought to illuminate possible insights offered by chaos theory as a theoretical alternative to prevailing social movement theories. It is my contention that through the privileging of one or another mode of overt conflict and the construction of social movement organizations and political lobbies, prevailing social movement theory is incapable of capturing the full panoply of diverse modes of resistance sempiternally operating within the life-world. This, I argue, is due in part to a continued effort by social scientists to ontologize movement actors and to view movement successes through a narrowly defined and delimiting morphological lens.

Conceptualizing ICs within the context of chaos theory serves to punctuate my interest in elevating indigenous modes of resistance to a position of prominence among movement theorists. That intentional communities are not viewed as comprising a social movement, I argue, is due primarily to the continued reliance of social scientists on tidy theoretical boxes in which to locate movement actors. In the end, chaos theory alerts us to the endless array of potential furiously moving about at the quantum level of analysis, for me at the level of the life-world. For it is from this frenzied activity within the life-world that new patterns emerge at the level of the system. Here it is conceivable that the persistence of indigenous modes of resistance mobilizing, for example, over greater community autonomy on issues ranging from recycling probgrams to education and health care, will spiral upward and outward, effecting broader structural-level changes. While this could mean, on the one hand, the preservation of those political spaces necessary for free expression of local issues and activities, that is, the preservation of civil society, it may equally mean structural-level policy innovations in education, environmental healing, dispute resolution (as with victim/offender reconciliation projects which typically emerge as community efforts), work generation projects, and so forth. Like chaos theorists, Deleuze and Guattari encourage us to value the rhizome, the creative, the unpredictable as the true source of social change. I am convinced that doing so requires social scientists studying social movements to move beyond prevailing theoretical paradigms. This is indeed an uncomfortable proposition, since it means, while not relinquishing entirely the numerous insights offered by prevailing theory, moving beyond contemporary theory to privilege those actors, issues, and activities which may not fit so nicely into our more familiar theoretical boxes. ICs stand as but one of many examples of social movements which defy contemporary social movement theory. Having little interest in structural-level confrontations, they work to bring about social change within the life-world. They operate with very little organizational infrastructure, indeed, they often proudly perceive themselves as a working antithesis of organizations. And yet they persist. Recognizing intentional communities as a social movement requires exploding the boundaries of social movement theory.

NOTES

1. In fairness, Melucci has recently begun to "expand" his conceptualization of movement composition to include a broader array of movement potential. Interested readers should refer to his "A Strange Kind of Newness: What's New in New Social Movements?", pp. 101–130 in E. Larana, H. Johnston, and J. Gusfield (1994) (eds.), *New Social Movements: From Ideology to Identity*. Philadelphia: Temple University Press.

2. Relatedly, Dan Questenberry of Shannon Farm makes the point that an additional 500 requests for information were mailed to known ICs without producing any responses. Many of the ICs listed in the 1990 edition of the *Communities Directory* found they were overwhelmed with numerous requests for visits and information from "seekers," what often amounted to a substantial burden for those ICs making maximum use of resources, both human and material, for daily survival.

REFERENCES

Benedict, R. 1934. *Patterns of Culture*. Boston: Houghton Mifflin.

Benjamin, W. 1969. *Illuminations*. H. Arendt (ed.), trans. H. Zohn. New York: Schocken Books.

Berger, B. 1981. *The Survival of Counterculture*. Berkeley: University of California Press.

Bernal, M. 1994. "The Image of Ancient Greece as a Tool of Colonialism and European Hegemony." Pp. 119–28 in G.C. Bond and A. Gilliam (eds.), *Social Construction of the Past*. New York: Routledge.

Bloch, E. [1955] 1995. *The Principle of Hope*, vols. I and II. Cambridge, MA: MIT Press.

Blumer, H. 1951. "Social Movements." In A.M. Lee (ed.), *New Outline of the Principles of Sociology*. New York: Barnes and Noble.

Boggs, C. 1985. *Social Movements and Political Power*. Philadelphia: Temple University Press.

Bond, G.C. and A. Gilliam. 1994. "Introduction." Pp. 1–22 in G.C. Bond and A. Gilliam (eds.), *Social Construction of the Past*. New York: Routledge.

Bourdieu, P. 1984. *Distinction: A Social Critique of the Judgement of Taste*, trans. R. Nice. Cambridge, MA Harvard University Press.

Brand, K-W. 1990. "Cyclical Aspects of New Social Movements." In R. Dalton and M. Kuechler (eds.), *Challenging the Political Order: New Social and Political Movements in Western Democracies*. Cambridge, MA: Polity Press.

Brion, D. 1991. "The Chaotic Law of Tort: Legal Formalism and the Problem of Indeterminacy." Pp. 45–77 in R. Kevelson (ed.), *Peirce and Law*. New York: Peter Lang.

Cohen, J. 1985. "Strategy or Identity: New Theoretical Paradigms and Contemporary Social Movements." *Social Research* 52(4) (Winter): 664–716.

Cohen, J. and A. Arato. 1992. *Civil Society and Political Theory*. Cambridge, MA: MIT Press.

de Certeau, M. 1984. *The Practice of Everyday Life*. Berkeley: University of California Press.

Deleuze, G. and F. Guattari. 1987. *A Thousand Plateaus: Capitalism and Schizophrenia*. Minnesota: University of Minnesota Press.

della Porta, D. 1988. "Recruitment Processes in Clandestine Political Organizations." *International Social Movement Research* 1: 155–69.

Evans, S. and H. Boyte. 1986. *Free Spaces*. New York: Harper and Row.

Eyerman, R. and A. Jamison. 1991. *Social Movements: A Cognitive Approach*. University Park, PA: The Pennsylvania State University Press.

Fantasia, R. and E. Hirsch. 1995. "Culture in Rebellion: The Appropriation and Transformation of the Veil in the Algerian Revolution." Pp. 144–62 in H. Johnston and B. Klandermans (eds.), *Social Movements and Culture*. Minneapolis: University of Minnesota Press.

Flacks, R. 1988. *Making History*. New York: Columbia University Press.

Foucault, M. 1976. *The Archeology of Knowledge*. New York: Harper and Row.

Gilmore, D. 1987. *Aggression and Community: Paradoxes of Andalusian Culture*. New Haven, CT: Yale University Press.

Gross, D. 1992–93. "Rethinking Traditions." *Telos* 94 (Winter): 5–10.

Gusfield, J. 1994. "The Reflexivity of Social Movements: Collective Behavior and Mass Society Theory Revisited." Pp. 58–78 in E. Larana, H. Johnston, and J. Gusfield (eds.), *New Social Movements*. Philadelphia: Temple University Press.

Gyani, G. 1993. "Political Uses of Tradition in Postcommunist East Central Europe." *Social Research* 60(4) (Winter): 893–913.

Heehs, P. 1994. "Myth, History and Theory." *History and Theory* 33(1): 1–19.

Hirsch, E. 1990. *Urban Revolt: Ethnic Politics in the Nineteenth Century Chicago Labor Movement*. Berkeley: University of California Press.

Hobsbawm, E. and T. Ranger 1983. *The Invention of Tradition*. London: Cambridge University Press.

Jamison, A. and R. Eyerman. 1991. *Social Movements*. University Park, PA: The Pennsylvania State University Press.

Jenkins, J. 1989. "States and Social Movements: Recent Theory and Research." *Social Science Research Council Newsletter*.

Jenson, J. 1995. "What's in a Name? Nationalist Movements and Public Discourse." Pp. 107–26 in H. Johnston and B. Klandermans (eds.), *Social Movements and Culture*. Minneapolis: University of Minnesota Press.

Johnston, H. and B. Klandermans. 1995. "The Cultural Analysis of Social Movements." Pp. 3–24 in H. Johnston and B. Klandermans (eds.), *Social Movements and Culture*. Minneapolis: University of Minnesota Press.

Kanter, R.M. 1973. *Commitment and Community*. Cambridge, MA: Harvard University Press.

Klandermans, B. and S. Tarrow. 1988. "Mobilization in Social Movements: Synthesizing European and the American Approaches." *International Social Movement Research* 1: 1–38.

Kozeny, G. 1995. "Intentional Communities: Lifestyles Based on Ideals." *Communities Directory*. Langley, WA: Fellowship For Intentional Community: 18–24.

Laclau, E. 1990. *New Reflections on the Revolution of Our Time*. London: Verso.

Laclau, E. and C. Mouffe. 1985. *Hegemony and Socialist Strategy*. London: Verso.

Luke, T. 1991. "Touring Hyperreality: Critical Theory Confronts Information Society." Pp. 1–26 in P. Wexler (ed.), *Critical Theory Now*. New York: The Falmer Press.

McAdam, D. 1988. "Micromobilization Contexts and Recruitment to Activism." *International Social Movement Research* 1: 124–54.

McCarthy, J. and M. Zald. 1977. "Resource Mobilization and Social Movements: A Partial Theory." *American Journal of Sociology* 82(6): 1212–41.

McLaughlin, C. and G. Davidson. 1990. *Builders of the Dawn: Community Lifestyles in a Changing World*. Shutesburg, MA: Sirius Publishing.

Melucci, A. 1980. "The New Social Movements: A Theoretical Approach." *Social Science Information* 2(19): 199–226.

———. 1988. "Getting Involved: Identity and Mobilization in Social Movements." *International Social Movement Research* 1: 329–48.

———. 1990. *Nomads of the Present: Social Movements and Individual Needs in Contemporary Society*. Philadelphia: Temple University Press.

———. 1995. "The Process of Collective Identity." Pp. 41–63 in H. Johnston and B. Klandermans (eds.), *Social Movements and Culture*. Minneapolis: University of Minnesota Press.

Milovanovic, D. 1993a. "Borromean Knots and the Constitution of Sense in Juridico-Discursive Production." *Legal Studies Forum* XVII (2): 171–92.

———. 1993b. "Lacan's Four Discourses, Chaos and Cultural Criticism in Law." *Studies in Psychoanalytic Theory* 2(1): 3–23.

———. 1994. "The Decentralized Subject in Law: Contributions of Topology, Psychoanalytic Semiotics, and Chaos Theory." *Studies in Psychoanalytic Theory* 3(1): 93–127.

———. 1995. "Dualing Paradigms: Modernist versus Postmodernist Thought." *Humanity and Society* 19(1): 19–44.

Nandy, A. 1987. "Cultural Frames for Social Transformation: A Credo." *Alternatives* XII: 113–23.

Offe, C. 1985. "New Social Movements: Challenging the Boundaries of Institutional Politics." *Social Research* 52(4) (Winter): 817–68.

Parsons, T. 1971. *The System of Modern Societies*. Englewood Cliffs, NJ: Prentice-Hall.

Pirsig, R. 1991. *Lila: An Inquiry Into Morals*. New York: Bantam Books.

Questenberry, D. 1995. "Who Are We: An Exploration of What 'Intentional Community' Means." *Communities Directory*. Langley, WA: Fellowship For International Community, 33–38.

Rao, N. 1994. "Interpreting Silences: Symbol and History in the Case of Ram Janmabhoomi/Babri Masjid." Pp. 154–64 in G.C. Bond and A. Gilliam (eds.), *Social Construction of the Past*. New York: Routledge.

Sassoon, J. 1984. "Ideology, Symbolic Action and Rituality in Social Movements: The Effects on Organizational Forms." *Social Science Information* 23(4/5): 861–73.

Scott, J. 1990. *Domination and the Arts of Resistance.* New Haven, CT: Yale University Press.

Serres, M. 1977. *La Naissance de la physique dans le text de lucrece.* Paris: Minuit.

———. 1982. *The Parasite.* Trans. L.R. Schehr. Baltimore: Johns Hopkins University Press.

Shaw, R. 1981. "Strange Attractors, Chaotic Behavior, and Information Flow." *Zeitschrift für Naturforschung* 36a: 79–112.

Smelser, N. 1962. *Theory of Collective Behavior.* New York: Free Press.

Tarrow, S. 1989. *Democracy and Disorder: Protest and Politics in Italy, 1965–1975.* Oxford: Clarendon Press.

———. 1994. *Power in Movement: Social Movements, Collective Action, and Mass Politics in the Modern State.* New York: Cambridge University Press.

Taylor, V. and N. Whittier. 1995. "Analytical Approaches to Social Movement Culture: The Culture of the Women's Movement." Pp. 163–87 in H. Johnston and B. Klandermans (eds.), *Social Movements and Culture.* Minneapolis: University of Minnesota Press.

Tilly, C. 1985. "Models and Realities of Popular Collective Action." *Social Research* 52(4) (Winter): 717–47.

Tilly, C. et al. 1975. *The Rebellious Century.* Cambridge, MA: Harvard University Press.

Touraine, A. 1971. *The May Movement.* Trans. L. Mayhew. New York: Random House.

———. 1985. "An Introduction to the Study of Social Movements." *Social Research* 52(4) (Winter): 750–87.

———. 1988. *The Return of the Actor.* Minneapolis: University of Minnesota Press.

Turner, R. and L. Killian. 1972. *Collective Behavior.* Englewood Cliffs, NJ: Prentice-Hall.

Welch, S. 1985. *Communities of Resistance and Solidarity: A Feminist Theology of Liberation.* New York: Orbis Books.

White, E. 1991. "Negentropy, Noise, and Emancipatory Thought." Pp. 263–77 in N.K. Hayles (ed.), *Chaos and Order.* Chicago: University of Chicago Press.

Wilson, K. 1983. "The Renormalization Group and Critical Phenomena." *Reviews of Modern Physics* 55: 583–600.

Zablocki, B. 1980. *Alienation and Charisma.* New York: Free Press.

CHAPTER 10

Dimensions of Social Justice in an SRO (Single Room Occupancy): Contributions from Chaos Theory, Policy, and Practice

Bruce A. Arrigo

INTRODUCTION

Research exploring single room occupancy (SRO) facilities as a viable source of affordable and supportive housing for the poor is a somewhat recent phenomenon (e.g., Arrigo, 1994b; Hoch and Slayton, 1989; Smithers, 1985). One dimension of SRO living not developed in the literature is the conceptual paradigms explaining how these communities are conceived and implemented (Siegal, 1978). More particularly, there is a dearth of studies examining social engineering models which produce minimal crime and deviance outcomes while utilizing the peer-focused philosophy of empowerment and inclusivity (HUD, 1989; McKnight, 1987).

This chapter represents an attempt to apply selected aspects of the chaos paradigm to the cultural identity and structuring of one large, urban SRO in Pittsburgh, Pennsylvania. We contend that the residents of this neighborhood maintained peer-directed social relationships and engaged in supportive communal events which effectively limited the extent of their personal harm and property damage. We intend to show how several orderly disorder practices were instrumental in this process.

The chapter begins by presenting aggregate crime data on the building's two phases of development. This information is useful for demonstrating how the second stage (based on principles of chaos theory) produced crime and deviance figures substantially lower than the first stage (based on linear cause-effect logic). We then more closely examine the SRO neighborhood's second phase of development. This requires a more careful, though provisional, consideration of where and how chaos principles helped structure the facility's internal ecology. We conclude by evaluating the justice policy relevance of orderly disorder practices. This policy assessment addresses the applicability of SRO social designing concepts to community systems theory and to creating and sustaining thriving neighborhoods in the postmodern age. Before these matters are addressed, however, some background details on SROs in general and the Pittsburgh community in question are warranted.

ON SROs, HOUSING THE POOR, AND WOOD STREET COMMONS

The development of single room occupancy housing in the twentieth century can be traced to the rise of business and commerce associated with most major metropolitan cities (Barak, 1992; Rossi, 1989). The growth of industry produced sweeping changes in the way people lived. Migrant workers, day laborers, travel enthusiasts, commuting students, and others found that the activity of the downtown marketplace provided a veritable kaleidoscope of essential services and satisfied an assortment of daily needs (Coons, 1987). Single room lodging was an affordable means of housing that ensured easy access to virtually all of the city's many wonders.

The enthusiasm for inner city life waned in the decades of the 1970s through the 1980s. Large hotels and other housing facilities (especially YMCAs and YWCAs) were ill- and underequipped to meet the residential demands wrought by a changing and devastating political economy (Arrigo, 1994b: 96). The successful SROs of the past became safe, though temporary, havens for welfare recipients, the mentally ill, the chemically addicted, the displaced poor, day laborers, AIDS victims, Vietnam-era veterans, and the homeless (e.g., Hopper and Hamberg, 1984; National Coalition for the Homeless, 1989; Barak, 1992). Single room occupancies once regarded as convenient, low-cost dwellings situated amid thriving city environs were transformed into shelters, welfare hotels, flop houses, and asylums (Arrigo, 1994b: 96–98). These facilities were the only available sanctuaries for a deeply troubled population (Caton, 1990: 12); a constituency encompassing the country's growing poor and disenfranchised citizenry.

A typical example of the twentieth-century SRO phenomenon is Wood Street Commons (WSC) (Arrigo, 1996b: 3–7). Wood Street Commons is an urban facility located in the heart of downtown Pittsburgh, Pennsylvania. This housing resource, formerly a YMCA, accommodates 259 adult men and women. There are approximately 26 apartment-style rooms on each of the 11 tenant floors. Each tenant occupies his/her own private room. Each room consists of a wash basin and mirror, a chest of drawers and chair, a single bed with night stand, and a walk-in closet. Several private hallway bathrooms are located on each of the building floors. There is a Congregate Space in the lower level of the facility. This space consists of several rooms, all of which serve various tenant functions. There are a kitchen and dining area, a library and meeting room, a health and fitness station, a recreation and activities area, and several counseling offices.

Originally, Wood Street Commons was a YMCA and, comparable to many urban SROs, was not able to meet the social service needs of its troubled occupants, despite offering very affordable housing. In the mid-1980s, a locally based redevelopment and property management company, in conjunction with one of Pittsburgh's major nonprofit entities, purchased the YMCA. Together, these corporations saw the building's potential as an attractive housing resource providing respite and shelter to the city's homeless and working poor within a safe, supportive, and affordable environment. Following a year of renovations, the former YMCA was renamed Wood Street Commons and its housing agenda was implemented.

CRIME IN THE COMMUNITY: AN ASSESSMENT OF TWO DEVELOPMENT PHASES

The data described below are based on WSC's two phases of development. By "phases of development" we mean: (1) how staff and residents perceived the social space they inhabited; (2) how staff viewed resident skills; and (3) and how staff interacted with tenants. Thus, these phases reflect different strategies for creating and sustaining a sense of community in vertical high-rise facilities like SROs. Elsewhere, we have described these two strategies in the context of social work and community organization practice (Arrigo, 1994b: 98–100). The Phase 1 model, in operation from 1985 to 1987, was termed the *need-focused* approach. The Phase 2 model, implemented from 1988 to the present, was termed the *strength-focused* approach.

The nomenclature for the two phases essentially telegraphs how the building's ecology was organized, particularly in relation to the three principles referenced above. The *need-focused* model responded to the social conditions in which tenants lived through sustained, trust-inducing staff counseling. Believing that the pathology level of the overall tenant population contributed to the facility's "asylum-like" atmo-

Table 10.1
Prevalence of Criminality Scales*

	PHASE 1 (1985-1987)	PHASE 2 (1988-1991)
A. *Evictions*	Average Number Per Week**	
1. Drug Abuse	2	0
2. Alcohol Abuse	4	2
3. Violence (Toward Others)	2	0
4. Violence (Toward Property)	3	0
5. Other Minor Infractions	2	1
6. Failure to Pay Rent	3	2
Totals	16	5
B. *Incident Reports*	Average Number Per Week	
1. Drug Abuse	3	1
2. Alcohol Abuse	6	2
3. Violence (Toward Others)	2	1
4. Violence (Toward Property)	2	0
5. Other Minor Infractions	2	2
Totals	15	6

*Adapted from Arrigo, 1994b: 105.
**Evictions and Incident Reports* are based on an average weekly occupancy rate of 245
  residents.

sphere, the ongoing, one-on-one interaction generated between residents and staff was a calculated effort to address deep-seated tenant deficiencies (e.g., deviance, illiteracy, unemployment, addiction).

The *strength-focused* model utilized the social space as a vehicle for cultivating tenant skills through peer-oriented activities (e.g., newsletter, Sports League, cooking). Recognizing that residents needed to improve their lives and social skills, the SRO functioned as an incubator readying tenants for work, sobriety, family reunification, education, and so on. Deliberately emphasizing the creation and implementation of recreational initiatives requiring group participation, staff encouraged residents to assume greater responsibility for the cultural identity of the SRO.

Based on the implementation of these two organizational strategies, data were collected over a seven-year period related to the prevalence of crime and deviance in the SRO community. Table 10.1 summarily presents the results. The findings list aggregate data based on two measures of criminality. These indices include *Evictions* and *Incident Reports*. Evictions in the SRO referred to termination of residency due to serious or excessive building infractions. These violations were generated through staff and tenant write-ups. Incident Reports represented more formal instances of house rule infractions accumulated by residents. These were drafted by both residents and staff.

Based on the total Eviction figures, the data indicate that the Phase 1 model experienced more than three times as many weekly terminations as its Phase 2 counterpart (16 to 5). Further, based on the total Incident Report figures, the data indicate that the Phase 1 model experienced two and a half times as many weekly write-ups as its Phase 2 counterpart (15 to 6). More particularly, we note that the Phase 2 period was not characterized by *any* resident terminations for drug abuse, violence toward others, or violence toward property.

The dramatic reduction in aggregate crime data throughout the second stage of WSC's development raises important questions relevant to the conceptual dimensions of the *strength-focused* strategy. In the following section we more closely assess how the internal ecology of the SRO was, knowingly or not, organized around non-linear dynamics during the building's Phase 2 cycle. The work of T.R. Young (1997) in this volume succinctly and accessibly describes the essential tenets of orderly disorder practices (see also Arrigo and Young, 1997; Arrigo, 1994a: 98–104; 1996a: 192–200 for linkages to postmodern law and criminology). Our aim here is to provisionally apply some of the more salient insights of chaos or transformation theory (Gregersen and Sailer, 1993) to the creation of the SRO, particularly those notions which we contend contributed to WSC's crime-reduced and community-oriented milieu.

CHAOS THEORY AND WOOD STREET COMMONS: ANALYSIS OF PHASE 2

There are six core principles which we identify as integral to chaos theory (Milovanovic, 1995: 268–70; see also Milovanovic, 1994: 108–9; 1992 for applications to law) that can be amplified through a consideration of the SRO's Phase 2 stage of development. These include: (1) non-linearity; (2) fractal space; (3) attractors; (4) self-similarity; (5) bifurcations; and (6) dissipative structures.

1. Non-linearity. Several ecological components socially and psychologically structured the Wood Street Commons community. Some of these building features consisted of rent collection, the Sports League, housekeeping services, breakfast and dinner meals, the Resident Newsletter, and so on. Figure 10.1 lists several of the current SRO characteristics where sustained tenant involvement was crucial to the overall environment. As the diagram indicates, many of the building's ecological features were generated from the Congregate Space. In Figure 10.1, this is signified by the large circle. This region of the SRO, then, represented a hub for much resident-centered activity. The smaller, though different-sized, circles situated within the Congregate Space area identify the variability of tenant involvement within a given ecological attribute. By "variable tenant involvement" we mean differences in resident partici-

Figure 10.1
Present WSC Model*

Congregate Space

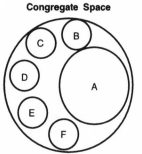

A   Kitchen Project:
    2 meals run by residents
B   Fall Bazaar
C   Resident Council   **Community as Therapeutic**
    Advocacy group for   • Empowerment
    residents   • Self-governance
D   Stretch and Relaxation   • Negotiated Identity
E   Self-Help Group
F   Resident Newsletter

*Each circle signifies an ecological expression of the community culture residents participated in or conducted.

pation levels. This variability includes fluctuations related to frequency, duration, and intensity. The presumed therapeutic effect increased tenant empowerment, self-governance, and negotiated identities. This last observation suggests that residents were not regarded as the sum total of their deficiencies; but, rather, were acknowledged for their competencies, despite their fallibilities.

Chaos theory's notion of non-linearity presupposes that some minor increase in an input value may produce vast disproportional effects in some outcome value (Milovanovic, 1995: 268). As tenant involvement in the SRO changed, so, too, did the configuration of the ecological components which functionally structured Wood Street Commons. More particularly, as resident engagement in building the community increased or decreased, dramatic effects were realized regarding the frequency and intensity outcomes for the existing ecological facets of the facility.

One example of non-linearity in Wood Street Commons was the creation of the Sports League and its impact on the city's perception of and attitude toward homelessness and poverty following the League's introduction to the SRO. Similar to other major metropolitan localities, the community of Pittsburgh largely regarded these matters as social and public health problems (Wilson and Kouzi, 1991). Often, such perceptions unwittingly stigmatize disenfranchised citizens as passive, incompetent, and pathological (Arrigo, 1992: 21–26). In the spring of 1988, Wood Street Commons initiated an effort to dispel deep-seated myths surrounding the residents of the SRO. Cultivating a Sports League in which tenants demonstrated their competencies through organized athletics became a vehicle for producing meaningful personal and societal change.

Commencing with the softball division of the League, teams were formed from various shelters and soup kitchens throughout the city of Pittsburgh. In total, six teams were formed constituting 100 players. The League received immediate print media attention. This attention garnered political support from the mayor's office and members of the city council. Local radio and television personalities began discussing the city's "homelessness and poverty" problem by inviting members of the League to participate in several talk shows. The League received corporate sponsorship. The volleyball, basketball, and flag football divisions of the League were formed. The number of teams per division doubled within one year. The number of players increased threefold. Residents of Wood Street Commons assumed full responsibility for organizing and running the League. Pittsburgh residents mailed in contributions on behalf of the League and its commitment to "giving homelessness and poverty a fresh, new face."

What the League initially symbolized, particularly as a very minor input value regarding perceptions of homelessness and poverty, was the profound uncertainty and instability characteristic of dynamic systems like Wood Street Commons. In other words, by adding the phenomenon of athletics into the cultural mapping of the SRO community, the city's attitude toward the building's tenants was substantially transformed. Moreover, Pittsburgh's response to and appreciation for the skills of disenfranchised citizens in general was dramatically altered.

2. Fractal Space. Decision-making in WSC was based on a loose confederation of rules and procedures. The operating assumption during Phase 2 was that tenants needed adequate adjustment time. For many individuals, inhabiting an urban SRO was a very foreign experience. Coming to terms with basic life issues such as sociability, self-esteem, trust, caring, and so on, was painful. Years of depression, homelessness, chemical dependency, unemployment, and so on, left deep emotional scars. House rules were therefore flexibly designed to accommodate tenants within reason.

Chaos theory points out that truth values assume a fractal nature. In other words, rather than identifying a behavior as right or wrong, good or bad, just or unjust, chaos theory takes the position that such determinations are matters of degree. Elsewhere, we have used the example of the televised beating of Rodney King by Los Angeles County police officers to explain the fractal dimension of what "really" happened (Arrigo, 1995: 117). Milovanovic (1995: 268), too, describes how our existences are more appropriately fragmented in his illustration of the Anita Hill–Clarence Thomas confrontation. In both instances, people were caught up in a binary logic of phase space, thereby creating absolute categories of reason, truth, and justice. However, we can see where a more honest and complete reading of the circumstances suggests that interpreting reality is about shades of meaning, degrees of accountability. We have previously explored the fractal nature of space as it relates to Wood Street Commons in the context of researcher deviance (Arrigo, 1997b). Here we examined how reality construction and truth making were fragmented and partial rather than whole and complete. The investigator's engagement with residents, staff, and corporate sponsors produced homeless programming and policy acutely sensitive to the residents' voices and ways of knowing.

Another illustration of fractional life in the SRO was the tenant drug culture. In a related study, we provisionally determined that a "drug peace" philosophy significantly characterized the community (Arrigo, 1996b). This philosophy acknowledged that illicit chemical use was not per se grounds for an eviction notice nor necessarily even reason for a tenant write-up. The community's position on such matters typically considered the condition of the tenant in question and evaluated: (1) whether the behavior was mostly private or public; and (2) whether the resident or other tenants were visibly suffering from or harmed by the illicit drug use. Thus, "chemical dependency was the inability to inconspicuously conceal behavior presumed to be unacceptable" (Arrigo, 1996b: 5). This description of drug use takes into account both the conduct of the individual resident and the perception of other SRO tenants in the context of their daily, routine interactions. It therefore creates a more fluid reality on the meaning of drug use in the community and its (il)legitimacy.

3. *Attractors.* The trajectory of dynamic systems like communities tends toward chaos (Schehr, 1996a, 1996b). In Wood Street Commons, the daily activity of the building produced cumulative patterns over time that could eventually be plotted. For our purposes, however, we wish only to indicate how the cultural mapping of the SRO was non-linear and complex, thereby producing, more appropriately, the butterfly or "strange" attractor. Figure 10.2 returns us to the ecological attributes of the community generated from within the Congregate Space. In this diagram, we note that there are two drawings. The first depicts the daily movement of residents within the space. There is a high degree of disorder and indeterminability that pervades the convening area. Tenants appear to wander from place to place, from activity to activity. Confusion and uncertainty abound. However, when considering the movement of residents and their involvement in the community's ecology over time, a pattern emerges. The second drawing illustrates the degree of order, predictability, and constancy that developed during the Phase 2 period of the building's development. Each circle signifies some corresponding permanence regarding particular cultural forms over time. Tenants created an ecological identity which included, through their direction, important building features. These features experienced variability on a

Figure 10.2
Congregate Space Ecology

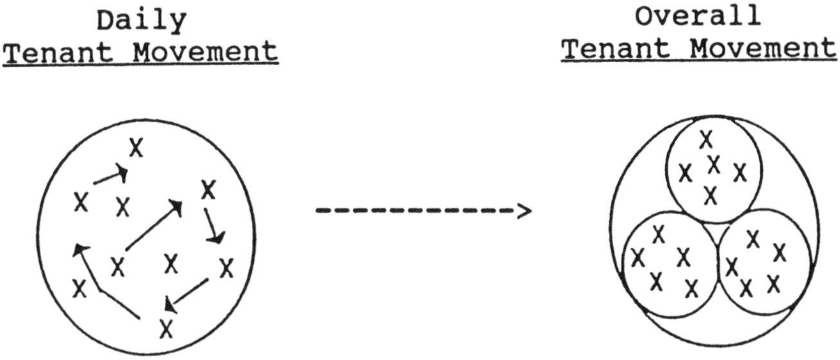

day-to-day basis. The newsletter, the kitchen project, the self-help groups, and so on, became avenues through which residents explored and experimented. Fluctuations in their duration, frequency, and intensity were very prominent. At the same time, though, as social engineering ingredients, their overall meaning to the community took on a certain predictability, contributing to a discernible SRO identity.

4. *Self-similarity.* The internal structure of WSC's daily ecology shared much in common with the facility's overall social, psychic, and organizational reality. This is not to say that the two were identical. There was no precise fit. In the logic of chaos theory, such precision is not possible. For the SRO, routine and local activity produced modest approximations of the community's more global contours. Thus, for example, the manner in which tenants participated in the building's advocacy outlets, meal programs, and health initiatives were estimates of how such structural conditions took on meaning in and value to the community over time.

The explanation for this degree of similarity is partially rooted in iteration. The effect of iteration shows us that there is some imprecision with initial conditions (Hayles, 1990: 143–74; Gregersen and Sailer, 1993). The sensitive dependence on such original circumstances can produce disproportionate outcomes after several attempts at repeating or replicating a given situation. Baudrillard's (1983) work on simulations suggests how this phenomenon exists within the conspicuous consumerism of late capitalism (for criminological applications see Arrigo, 1997a). In a related sense, Derrida (1973) examines how words have slightly different meanings when uttered in new contexts (for legal applications, see Balkin, 1987).

Applying the principle of iteration to Wood Street Commons, we note that the cultural charting of the community required daily tenant engagement in a variety of activities and events. While these ecological features remained relatively constant, their ongoing expression varied sometimes slightly and sometimes dramatically. One example was the tenant Advocacy Group. Each floor either elected or appointed one to two representatives to voice the needs of that floor. In addition, interested residents could become members of the Advocacy Group through sustained participation in its weekly meetings. As tenants moved in and out of the community, there were different interpretations of what "resident advocacy" entailed and the extent to which the group was empowered to make decisions affecting the community. Indeed, as new members joined the Advocacy Group and as old members left it, there was a constant reinterpretation of what the group was doing, why it was doing it, and who was responsible for what it was doing. Thus, as the membership changed, the collective's position on its scope and purpose increasingly deviated from what the original members had envisioned.

5. *Bifurcations.* In the ecology of Wood Street Commons, its internal structure produced elements of order at the macro level. As we explained, however, there was some variability with the initial conditions in which these building characteristics were conceived and implemented. Further, as was shown, the replication of an event (e.g., the Advocacy Group) produced elevated degrees of unpredictability and uncertainty because of iteration. Bifurcations refer to some eventual splitting due to increasing levels of chaos. This excess of disorder eventually and spontaneously produces order. It is a something-out-of-nothing thesis (Milovanovic, 1995: 270) or an order-out-of-chaos phenomenon (Prigogine and Stengers, 1984).

Wood Street Commons repeatedly encountered this experience during its Phase 2 stage of development. As change became a stable ingredient in mapping out the cultural identity of the community, the expression of various cultural forms was subjected to heightened levels of unpredictability. The example of the Advocacy Group is again illustrative here.

Originally, the Advocacy Group was run much like a dictatorship with "officers" elected from the pool of floor representatives. The president of the Advocacy Group endeavored to create a tightly managed collective, allowing for little dissension in decision-making. As floor representatives changed, increasing degrees of animosity developed among the residents, largely directed at the Advocacy Group leadership. This tension produced a splitting. The dictatorial Advocacy Group disbanded, succumbing to a great deal of anger, rage, and frustration generated by floor representatives and other tenants. Out of this disorder emerged a spontaneous new order. This new order was a system of resident advocacy based on floor elections and/or tenants volunteering. This was a decision arrived at by the building's occupants. Thus, the election of officers from the pool of floor representatives was discarded altogether.

These same dynamic, bifurcation effects were realized when chaos in the meal program, the building security system, the Resident Newsletter, and so on, developed. New paradigms were naturally forged out of the chaos that prevailed in each of these ecological components.

6. *Dissipative Structures.* A crucial ingredient in the bifurcation of the building's internal ecology was the presence of far-from-equilibrium conditions. In other words, many ecological facets of the SRO were continuously breaking down but were, as well, spontaneously reconstructed anew. The impetus for this dynamic state was the mixture of order and disorder, or far-from-equilibrium conditions. The community of Wood Street Commons, as a social system, was repeatedly undergoing change; a transformation that spiraled to greater residential autonomy, decision-making, self-governance, and empowerment. The cultural identity of the community therefore hinged, in part, on the active engagement of residents who shaped the communal reality. As we indicated, changes in the resident constituency contributed to modifications with the texturing of the SRO's social fabric and how this social fabric was embodied by tenants. Thus, a blend of structure and disorganization was essential to the cultural mapping of the community.

CREATING AND SUSTAINING COMMUNITIES: A JUSTICE POLICY ASSESSMENT

Community systems theory or, more broadly, social movement philosophy, has recently spawned a different model of community-building termed "the identity paradigm." This new social movement (NSM) prototype is perhaps best reflected in the work of sociologists such as Melucci (1990, 1995) and Touraine (1985, 1988). Regrettably, their model remains somewhat wedded to the baggage of the resource mobilization approach and the classical tradition of movement potential (Scott, 1993; Laclau and Mouffe, 1985).

A fourth paradigm, building on the insights of the NSM literature, links principles of chaos theory and postmodernity with intentional communities (ICs) (Gusfield, 1994; McLaughlin and Davidson, 1990) thereby forging a radical reconceptualization (Schehr, 1996b). In such a model, what is at issue is not the centrality of deviance and disorder in plotting the cultural identity of a given locale but, rather, the blending of it with conformity and order.

Embedded in this observation is the lingering belief that thriving communities are generated by a "resounding mosaic of resistance" (Schehr, 1996c: 6; Laclau, 1991). This resistance is a reaction to structures of stability, permanence, and completeness. It is a call for reconstructing and recovering the self in which new cultural forms emerge. Thus, this opposition is a method for cultivating replacement expressions of identity, sexuality, truth, leadership, and neighborhood. As the constituents of a "just community" (Scharf, 1977: 104), this resistance symbolizes the birth of innovative, non-linear models for decision-making, consensus, participation, inclusivity, and empowerment.

Unger's (1987) work on self-governing democracies and superliberalism, Freire's (1972, 1985) insights into pedagogical policy and practice, and Cornell's (1991, 1993) observations on feminist jurisprudence and utopian possibilities each, in their own way, represent purposeful efforts establishing new vistas of meaning in politics, education, and law, respectively. Collectively, the aim is to foster deeper, richer expressions of community in various institutional contexts.

The just-community concept, and its relationship to intentional communities, new social movement theory, and chaology, returns us to Wood Street Commons, and policy setting for SROs in particular and social engineering models in general. The sense of place and home woven by tenants was a tapestry of difference. Through this difference, cultural identity became an uncertain product of residential input and decision-making. This approach was beyond rehabilitation (for applications to criminology and penology, see Henry and Milovanovic, 1996: 223–24; Whittmore, 1992: 5). There was a rejection of cause-effect explanations for crime and deviance (Phase 1 strategy). Instead, residents were treated as *if* they were athletes, business entrepreneurs, cooks, counselors, and so on, despite feeling, perhaps, that they were somehow incompetent, inadequate, inconsequential.

We note, therefore, that the *strength-focused* strategy of WSC's Phase 2 period was anchored by a policy of deconstruction and reconstruction. Pivotal to this reclamation effort were the non-linear features of the social space and how these ecological determinants were continuously reconfigured again and anew by residents. It is here, then, that we can keenly locate the vitality of orderly disorder principles in mapping out the building's internal ecology. The justice policy pertaining to single room occupancy dwellings would do well to consider the extent to which healthy social engineering models genuinely and actively incorporate the participation of communal members. We contend that, in the case of Wood Street Commons, the heightened degree of tenant engagement in the SRO during Phase 2 substantially contributed to the facility's lower levels of crime and deviance.

Further, we maintain that this same thesis resonates with creating and sustaining thriving neighborhoods in the postmodern age. In other words, the multiple voices and ways of knowing for residents of *any* community seek expression and embodiment in the institutional facets of that locality. Here, too, non-linearity, fractal space, attractors, self-similarity, bifurcations, and dissipative structures play a prominent role in charting the cultural forms of the neighborhood's ecology. In the postmodern age, a mix of predictability and unpredictability is essential to creating and sustaining places. Without such a blend, order, stability, and permanence saturate social living and create conditions that are ripe for destruction and failure. This is the lesson of Wood Street Commons. It is a lesson that may, unwittingly, wring familiar for society if we neglect or reject the possibilities implied in disorder. The example of Wood Street Commons is a vivid reminder of how just communities, by design, thrive through chaos.

CONCLUSIONS

This chapter examined the usefulness of several core chaos theory principles for explaining the prevalence of crime in an urban SRO. Under consideration was Wood Street Commons, situated in Pittsburgh, Pennsylvania. We found that this facility's Phase 2 cycle of development emphasized a *strength-focused* strategy producing markedly lower aggregate crime data than its Phase 1 counterpart. On closer scrutiny, we explained this phenomenon by assessing how the internal ecology of the SRO was structured. Our provisional treatment of this matter emphasized several building features generated through the facility's Congregate Space. We argued, with pertinent examples, that integral to the ecology of WSC was the presence of non-linear dynamics, fractal space, strange attractors, self-similarity, bifurcations, and dissipative structures. Because these chaos principles clearly operated within the community milieu of Phase 2, we concluded that sound social justice policy relevant to creating SROs in particular and thriving neighborhoods in general would do well to introduce social engineering models based upon and sensitive to orderly disorder practices.

In the postmodern age, change, flux, uncertainty, unpredictability, serendipity, absurdity, and chaos loom large. This does not imply, however, a destruction or death of all that is familiar, all that is sacred. Rather, with the illustration of Wood Street Commons, we note that new vistas for expressing identity and community became the cornerstone of the facility's second stage of development. By mixing at the local level the ingredients of chaos, a discernible pattern of social life and human social interaction within the SRO emerged over time. We contend that the same salubrious effects could be witnessed by society in general if city planners, urban sociologists, criminologists, civic leaders, politicians, and corporate sponsors were educated to the possibilities borne out of chaos. Our assessment should not, in any way, be read as implying that no other variables had an impact on fashioning the Phase 2 ecology. Rather, our objective has been to describe the significance of orderly disorder dynamics in conceptually underpinning the *strength-focused* strategy during the building's second evolutionary cycle.

REFERENCES

Arrigo, B. 1992. "The Logic of Identity and the Politics of Justice: Establishing a Right to Community-Based Treatment for the Institutionalized Mentally Disabled." *New England Journal On Criminal and Civil Confinement* 18(1): 1–31.

———. 1994a. "Legal Discourse and the Disordered Criminal Defendant: Contributions from Psychoanalytic Semiotics and Chaos Theory." *Legal Studies Forum* 18(1): 93–112.

———. 1994b. "Rooms for the Misbegotten: Social Design and Social Deviance." *Journal of Sociology and Social Welfare* 21(4): 95–114.

———. 1995. "New Directions in Crime, Law, and Social Change: On Psychoanalytic Semiotics, Chaos Theory, and Postmodern Ethics." *Studies in the Social Sciences* 33: 101–29.

———. 1996a. *The Contours of Psychiatric Justice: A Postmodern Critique of Mental Illness, Criminal Insanity, and the Law.* New York: Garland.

———. 1996b. "Recommunalizing Drug Offenders: The 'Drug Peace' Agenda." *Journal of Offender Rehabilitation* 25(1): 33–55.

———. 1997a. "Media Madness as Crime in the Making: On OJ Simpson, Consumerism, and Hyperreality." In G. Barak (ed.), *Representing OJ: Murder, Criminal Justice, and Mass Culture.* New York: Harrow and Heston.

———. 1997b. "Shattered Lives and Shelter Lies: Anatomy of Researcher Deviance in Homeless Programming and Policy." In J. Ferrell and M. Hamm (eds.), *True Confessions: Law, Crime, and Field Research.* Boston: Northeastern University Press.

Arrigo, B. and T. R. Young. 1997. "Chaos, Complexity, and Crime: Working Tools for a Postmodern Criminology." In B. MacLean and D. Milovanovic (eds.), *New Directions in Critical Criminology,* 2d ed. Vancouver, Canada: The Collective Press.

Balkin, J.M. 1987. "Deconstructive Practice and Legal Theory." *Yale Law Journal* 96(4): 743–86.

Barak, G. 1992. *Gimme Shelter: A Social History of Homelessness in Contemporary America.* Westport, CT: Praeger.

Baudrillard, J. 1983. *Simulations.* New York: Semiotext(e).

Caton, C. (ed.). 1990. *Homeless in America.* New York: Oxford University Press.

Coons, C. 1987. "The Causes and History of Homelessness." In *The National Teach-In on Homelessness.* New Haven, CT: Student Homeless Action Campaign.

Cornell, D. 1991. *Beyond Accommodation: Ethical Feminism, Deconstruction, and the Law.* New York: Routledge.

———. 1993. *Transformation: Recollective Imagination and Sexual Difference.* New York: Routledge.

Derrida, J. 1973. *Of Grammatology.* Baltimore: Johns Hopkins University Press.

Freire, P. 1972. *Pedagogy of the Oppressed.* New York: Herder and Herder.

———. 1985. *The Politics of Education.* South Hadley, MA: Bergin and Garvey.

Gregersen, H. and L. Sailer. 1993. "Chaos Theory and Its Implications for Social Science Research." *Human Relations* 46(7): 777–802.

Gusfield, J. 1994. "The Reflexivity of Social Movements: Collective Behavior and Mass Society Theory Revisited." In E. Larana, H. Johnson, and J. Gusfield (eds.), *New Social Movements*. Philadelphia: Temple University Press.

Hayles, K. 1990. *Chaos Bound*. Ithaca, NY: Cornell University Press.

Henry, S. and D. Milovanovic. 1996. *Constitutive Criminology: Beyond Postmodernism*. London: Sage.

Hoch, C. and R. Slayton. 1989. *New Homeless and Old: Community and the Skid Row Hotel*. Philadelphia: Temple University Press.

Hopper, K. and J. Hamberg. 1985. *The Making of America's Homeless: From Skid Row to the New Poor, 1945–1984*. New York: Community Service Society.

HUD. 1989. *The 1988 National Survey of Shelters for the Homeless*. Office of Policy Development and Research. Washington, DC: Government Printing Office.

Laclau, E. 1991. *New Directions on the Revolution of our Time*. London: Verso.

Laclau, E. and C. Mouffe. 1985. *Hegemony and Socialist Strategy*. New York: Verso.

McKnight, J. 1987. "Regenerating Community." *Social Policy* 17: 54–58.

McLaughlin, C. and G. Davidson. 1990. *Builders of the Dawn: Community Lifestyles in a Changing World*. Amherst: University of Massachusetts Press.

Melucci, A. 1990. *Nomads of the Present: Social Movements and Individual Needs in Contemporary Society*. Philadelphia: Temple University Press.

———. 1995. "The Process of Collective Identity." In H. Johnston and B. Klandermans (eds.), *Social Movements and Culture*. Minneapolis: University of Minnesota Press.

Milovanovic, D. 1992. *Postmodern Law and Disorder: Psychoanalytic Semiotics, Chaos Theory and Juridic Exegeses*. Liverpool, England: Deborah Charles.

———. 1994. "The Decentered Subject in Law: Contributions of Topology, Psychoanalytic Semiotics, and Chaos Theory." *Studies in Psychoanalytic Theory* 3(1): 93–127.

———. 1995. "Moral Philosophy, Social Justice, and the Question of Punishment in a Just Society." In W.R. Janikowski and D. Milovanovic (eds.), *Legality and Illegality: Semiotics, Postmodernism and Law*. New York: Peter Lang.

National Coalition for the Homeless. 1989. *American Nightmare: A Decade of Homelessness in the United States*. New York: NCH.

Prigogine, I. and I. Stengers. 1984. *Order Out of Chaos*. New York: Bantam Books.

Rossi, P. 1989. *Down and Out in America: The Origins of the Homeless*. Chicago: University of Chicago Press.

Scharf, P. 1977. "The 'Just Community.' " *New Society*, 21 (April): 104–5.

Schehr, R. 1996a. *Communities of Resistance*. New York: Peter Lang.

———. 1996b. *Dynamic Utopia: Establishing Intentional Communities as a New Social Movement*. Westport, CT: Praeger.

———. 1996c. "Surfing the Chaotic: A Non-linear Articulation of Social Movement Theory" (unpublished manuscript).

Scott, J. 1993. *Domination and the Art of Resistance*. New Haven, CT: Yale University Press.

Smithers, J. 1985. *Determined Survivors: Community Life among the Elderly*. New Brunswick, NJ: Transaction Books.

Siegal, H. 1978. *Outposts of the Forgotten*. New Brunswick, NJ: Transaction Books.

Touraine, A. 1985. "An Introduction to the Study of Social Movements." *Social Research* 52(2): 75–787.

———. 1988. *The Return of the Actor*. Minneapolis: University of Minnesota Press.

Unger, R. 1987. *False Necessity*. New York: Cambridge University Press.

Whittmore, H. 1992. "Hitting Bottom Can Be the Beginning." *Parade Magazine*, March 15: 4–6.

Wilson, C. and A. Kouzi. 1991. A Social-Psychiatric Perspective on Homelessness: Results from a Pittsburgh Study. In J. Momeni (ed.), *Homelessness in the United States*. Westport, CT: Praeger.

Young, T.R. 1997. "Challenges: For a Postmodern Criminology." Pp. 29–51 in D. Milovanovic (ed.), *Chaos, Criminology, and Social Justice: The New Orderly (Dis)Order*. Westport, CT: Praeger.

CHAPTER 11

Visions of the Emerging Orderly (Dis)Order

Dragan Milovanovic

INTRODUCTION

Chaos theory, one of the constitutive threads of postmodernist thought, is becoming more prevalent in applications to criminology and law. It also has relevance to social change, social movements, and conceptions of social justice. In this chapter we would like to provide some alternative visions as to social structure, political economy, community, agency, criminology, law, and replacement discourses. There is no pretense of providing a blueprint. We merely want to suggest lines of inquiry using chaos theory that provide alternative vistas.

SOCIAL STRUCTURE

There are various modernist notions of social structure that exist in the literature (Henry and Milovanovic, 1996: 45–73). Many of them, however, follow the principles of structural functionalism. Here an analogy is often drawn with organisms that are made up of functioning parts related to the overall well-being of the organism. Underlying the model is often a drive toward homeostasis or equilibrium. When the organism varies from some norm, reactions are set in motion that bring it back to its normal orbit. Through evolution, structures emerge that are said to be the most adaptive. An overall logic emerges that keeps the system on a linear progression, even while being faced with various challenges. This logic, such as formal rationality, or the forces of rationalization that are the basis of law and bureaucracies (Weber, 1978), or the equivalence principle which is derived from the commodity of fetishism dynamics spelled out by Karl Marx (Pashukanis, 1978), becomes the dominant force in the construction of conceptions of social justice. In the terminology of chaologists, what is being privileged by modernists is: equilibrium conditions (homeostasis); point and limit/periodic attractors (movement toward some valued position); rigid structures (as opposed to emergents); linearity (historical progression that follows some prescribed logic); and rigid couplings of each part to each of the other parts in an overall plan.

Theorizing new forms of social structure from a chaos theory would suggest alternative images. First, the notion of the desirability of equilibrium conditions is replaced by the desirability of "far-from-equilibrium" conditions. In this view, all is constantly in flux. Change permeates all interactions and movements. There is no ideal end point toward which the system tends in a linear way. Rather, in this dynamic flux various structures referred to as "dissipative structures" emerge. These forms are unusual in that they are constantly in the process of emerging *and* dissipating. There is no permanent structure such as in bureaucracies, which often become detached from the milieu and remain self-serving. What is critical in these far-from-equilibrium conditions is the entropy principle. Here various dissipative structures live in a milieu that offers the maximal interchange among the various forms, encouraging the emergence of temporary forms sensitive to the surrounding environment, and yet having the propensity to change into yet new forms with perturbation. These forms answer the call for a need for a degree of planning, predictability, and calculability, whether by a person, business firm, or other forms in the society. But they are not rigid.

Elsewhere (Henry and Milovanovic, 1996; Milovanovic, 1996), we have developed the notion of COREL sets, built on conceptions from chaos theory, to indicate how a social system is structured. COREL sets stand for constitutive, interrelational sets. Instead of assuming an objective reality, a reality that privileges "particles," we view all being relational. Accordingly, our term suggests that society is composed of interlocking, intersecting, and interpenetrating relational sets which are in dynamic change. These have been modeled elsewhere (Milovanovic, 1996) as constellations of iterative loops and reflected by the Mandelbrot set. An elementary iterative loop stands for how feedback affects some ongoing functioning of some form. It is non-linear insomuch as variations in initial conditions produce disproportional effects after many iterations, and even with similar starting conditions, feedback produces disproportional change, or the "butterfly effect." Thus, our vision is one where a multiplicity of COREL sets exist that are interconnected and interpenetrate, producing dynamic, non-linear change. Here, rather than a point or a periodic/limit attractor being privileged, we see tori and strange attractors. In other words, we have various degrees of indeterminacy. We do have global stability, hence a degree of order within which planning, calculation, and predictability exist (the shape of the various tori and strange attractors), but at the local level we have indeterminacy. Here there is no possibility of precisely predicting outcomes. Variability pervades the milieu. Accordingly, conceptions of the desirable, good, ethical, beautiful, moral, and so on, must take on new definitions as chance, spontaneity, irony, contradiction, and the serendipitous are ubiquitous.

POLITICAL ECONOMY AND COMMUNITY

Chaos theory has yet to be integrated into conceptions of desirable political economies. Suggestive, however, are the works of Unger (1987) and Reiman (1990). Future studies will look more deeply into this integration in developing models of a more just society. Relatedly, emerging approaches in social movement theory are integrating chaos insights.

Unger's work on the desirability of "superliberalism," although not presented in the language of chaos, has much in compatibility with it (see also Milovanovic, 1992; Henry and Milovanovic, 1996: 235–41). He lays out various ideas for organizational change whereby a milieu is created that denies otherwise ossifying structures, such as bureaucracies and political machinery, their support. His call is for a maximal benefit from the entropy principle and for the prevalence of far-from-equilibrium conditions, where change is ubiquitous (see also Leiffer, 1989). He outlines protections against (1) any limitations placed on "effective challenge and revision," and (2) "instruments of subjugation" (Unger, 1987: 516).

For Unger, a radical vision of an alternative political economy and community is predicated on constructive principles that prioritize the notion that "the security of the individuals should be established in such a way that minimize both the immunity of institutional arrangements to challenge and conflict and the ease with which some individuals can reduce others to dependence" (1987: 513). To this end he advocates enlarging the scope of "context-revising conflict" and "context-preserving routine." These would remain in a disequilibrium state which assures far-from-equilibrium conditions. He also advocates expanding the protections for persons from any possible retaliatory efforts. He outlines various rights: (1) market rights, which would provide capital to teams of workers with the small interest accumulated in an overall fund; (2) destabilization rights, which assure persons their rights to challenge and criticism of existing arrangements; (3) immunity rights, which include many of the protections from various oppressive practices as well as rights to welfare entitlements and other resources to well-being such as health care, housing, work, education, food, and so on; and (4) solidarity rights, which assure mutual, cooperative development reflective of trust and good faith dealings (1987: 514, 516).

Unger's suggestions support a new vision of community building. Even though "a zone of heightened mutual vulnerability" (1987: 562) would develop, "people gain a chance to resolve more fully the conflict between the enabling conditions of self-assertion: between their need for attachment and for participation in group life and their fear of the attachment and their fear of the subjugation and depersonalization with which such engagement may threaten them" (1987: 562). A person in this milieu "is able to accept an expanded range of conflict and revision without feeling that it threatens intolerably his [her] most vital material and spiritual interests" (1987: 579). The peacemaking perspective would be in accord (see Pepinsky, Chapter 5, this volume).

Reiman's (1990) suggestions are usefully incorporated in this transformation. He offers a distributive principle that he calls the "labor theory of moral values." He insightfully develops a distributive principle that, in the short run, benefits both the disenfranchised as well as the well-to-do. Although many of his thoughts lie squarely in the modernist enterprise, especially as to the worth of existing wage-labor relations, certainly it could be seen as a provisional position that may, in the short run, provide some impetus for social change benefiting society as a whole (see also Milovanovic, 1995b).

Emerging social movement literature incorporating chaos theory (Schehr, 1996a, 1996b, Chapter 9, this volume) has provided new vistas for "innovative, non-linear models for decision-making, consensus, participation, inclusivity, and empowerment" (Arrigo, Chapter 10, this volume). This is not just theory building, but as Arrigo (Chapter 10) has shown in his study of single room occupancy in a large urban area, an exciting and productive new development. Schehr's suggestion for a fourth approach in the social movement literature which incorporates chaos theory certainly provides much promise.

AGENCY

Given the conditions briefly outlined in the above section, we must then ask how agency can be envisioned. Our guide is the notion of a "subject-in-process" developed from feminist analyses (Kristeva, 1980), Lacan's four discourses (1991), Henry and Milovanovic's notion of the recovering subject (1996), Unger's role-jumbling (1987), and the "border crosser" developed out of critical pedagogy (Freire, 1972, 1985; Giroux, 1992; JanMohammed, 1994; McLaren, 1994). There is no "death of the subject," often attributed to affirmative postmodernist analysis, and better identified with some of the earlier skeptical/nihilistic forms. The subject would be better conceptualized by the tori and strange attractors. And signs (i.e., words) do not simply float in a sea of indeterminacy, but take on degrees of stability in active social struggle.

When speaking of the subject, much modernist thought, on the one hand, imprisons it in various roles it plays, but on the other, attributes unlimited free self-consciousness and determination. For chaologists, neither will do. Postmodern analysis sees a more desirable picture portrayed by the butterfly attractor: a person can find her/himself in various states. Unlike traditional modernist thought, postmodernists see the subject in a constant movement from identification to dis-identification and re-identification with various discursive subject-positions. In this way the person becomes a transient border crosser (Giroux, 1992), constantly becoming sensitized to the plight of her/his fellow person.

Yet another portrayal of this process by the use of chaos theory can be found in Lacan's topological explanation of the subject. In his view, the subject's desire is what constantly seeks expression, or embodiment. Inherent states of incompleteness, the price paid for the inauguration into the Symbolic Order where potency, control, and mastery are promised—by, for example, the use of various discourses which allow one to overcome one's sense of incompleteness—is a force that mobilizes the subject (see also Arrigo, Chapter 8, this volume). Desire can be conceptualized as either the more passive form, as a response to an inherent lack, as in Freud's more equilibrium model of the psychic apparatus, or as more active, a search for the ever-illusive possible (Lecercle, 1985). Lacan has expressed this best, topologically, by the torus. A torus looks very much like an inflated inner tube. Picture the middle region of the tube as desire, a line that circumvents the outside of the tube without meeting as demand, and the void in the middle as the various objects of desire, and we have a portrayal of a quasi-periodic torus attractor (Milovanovic, 1997). Said in another way, Lacan indicates that at the center of being there is a great void, a castration from the Real established with the inauguration into the Symbolic Order. Desire is what activates the subject. And demand is the particular expression of desire. Demand always attempts to overcome the central void by making use of the numerous objects of desire offered by a political economy and advertisement industry, but always fails, always misses its mark. Hence, the outside line traced on the torus never hooks up. The quasi-periodic torus indicates indeterminacy while at the same time a degree of global stability (the shape of the torus). Determinacy and indeterminacy exist side by side with the subject-in-process.

Postmodernists are well-advised to incorporate many of the ideas developed by chaos theory in conceptualizing the subject. The "death of the subject" has no place in the affirmative forms of postmodernist analysis. Rather, the subject is seen as potentially variable and operating within certain fuzzy limits (global) but with local indeterminacy. In many ways, George Herbert Mead's discussion of the dialectics between the "I" and the "me" as constitutive of self anticipated some of this inquiry. Modernists' honeymoon with the centered subject is over. We need to get on with an understanding that the subject is inherently a relational entity connected in a myriad of ways with its surrounding milieu. Given a milieu that is in far-from-equilibrium conditions, given the dissipative structures that develop, the subject, too, will be an on-going border crosser expanding its limits of possibility while at the same time recognizing the other as constitutive of her/his very being.

CRIMINOLOGY

Applications of chaos theory to critical criminology are beginning to appear in the literature (Young, 1991a, 1991b; Pepinsky, 1991; Chapters 3, 4, and 5, this volume). There have also been emerging applications that have focused on the "foreground" factors (Katz, 1988; O'Malley and Mugford, 1994; Ferrell, 1995) and the "invitational edge" (Matza, 1969; Lyng, 1990). Studies incorporating both (Henry and Milovanovic, 1996; Milovanovic, 1996, 1997) indicate that integrating chaos theory into an overall critically informed postmodernist agenda promises to provide new vistas for understanding crime.

Foreground factors (as opposed to the traditional background factors that look more at materialistic differences and motivations that arise) focus more on the sensual, adrenalin rushes, visceral pleasures, and excitement in crime production. Chaos theory suggests (and so, too, does catastrophe theory) that non-linear effects are especially noteworthy phenomena. That is, many forms of crime are not of the linear variety often found in traditional modernist literature.

Modernist literature is often focused on the search for rational constructs that may be attributed to deviants. These are investigated by empirical research that follows principles of linear progression, as in regression analysis. Results are laid out in two-dimensional path analysis models indicating various contributions of independent variables. A linear flow from left to right in the various diagrams indicates the causal arrow. Prediction (variance explained) is often the valued ideal behind the model. Positivism, the search for underlying deterministic structures, is a guide throughout the research. Many times, "minor" contributing factors are rounded off as unimportant. And, finally, the models are often static, insomuch as a snapshot in time is frozen and brought to life by the various inferences made by the researcher.

Chaos theory questions these assumptions. Chaos theory suggests that feedback mechanisms exist that are non-linear. Knowing some starting values cannot be an adequate basis of knowing precisely where the dynamic system will be at some future point in time. In fact, the "minor" factors can, after iteration, produce disproportional effects. Elsewhere (Milovanovic, 1996), we have shown how the construction of the Mandelbrot set is suggestive of this phenomenon. There, following the suggestive analysis by Gregerson and Sailer (1993), we demonstrated that two persons found in similar starting positions may, after some iterative polynomial (accounting for the laws of transformation) is run, remain in the "prisoner set" of the Mandelbrot set, meaning, they engage in law-breaking behavior; whereas a third person, whose starting values are in between these two, will, after the same amount of iterations, *not* engage in law-breaking behavior.

The Mandelbrot set is also suggestive as to phenomena taking place at the boundaries, the so-called "invitational edge" (Matza, 1969) where "edgework" (Lyng, 1990) takes place. Here, maximal variability exists. Put in another way, as we approach the boundaries the number of possible outcome basins increases to the point of unpredictability. The boundaries are fractal. Matza, Lyng, and O'Malley and Mugford's (1994) integration suggest that the boundaries, in a society tending toward disempowerment, rigidity, and alienation, tend to become attractors in their own right. The boundaries offer momentary escapes and alternative challenges that may provide fulfillment. Here adrenalin rushes, excitement, and the visceral—the foreground factors—tend to be more pronounced. Chaos theory suggests, at best, we can engage in explanation, not prediction.

Along with the Mandelbrot set, we (Henry and Milovanovic, 1996; Milovanovic, 1992, 1995a, 1996) have suggested that "trouser diagrams" are better suited for postmodern research than path analysis models. This model is borrowed from emerging views in quantum mechanics. Picture a series of tube-like forms with varying radii, some of which merge into each other, others discontinue, yet others seem to spontaneously develop. This depicts various phenomena in movement. The radius of each "tube" suggests that indeterminacy prevails; not a line but a "line of continuous variation" (Deleuze and Guattari, 1987) is traced indicating variability. There is some degree of stability (the outline of the tube); but yet within the tube (the radius), we see indeterminacy. Various tubes may merge, producing effects. Yet others may diverge or just discontinue, not producing profoundly noticeable effects. This depiction moves us away from the rigidity implied in lines traced in path analysis models.

Chaos theory suggests that we look at various interconnected iterative loops and their effects (Gregerson and Sailer, 1993). These constellations of iterative loops can be, in a more fanciful way, related to iterative polynomials said to be the "laws" of transformation of a dynamic system. Our notion of the COREL set, or constitutive interrelational sets (Henry and Milovanovic, 1996; Milovanvoic, 1996b), is in accord with this idea. We argued that the search for objectivity or for essences is misguided and that, rather, all is relational. Moreover, not only relational, but we view various factors as being interrelated, interpenetrating, and sometimes running parallel and interlocking. The trouser diagrams model this complexity quite well. Movement of various forces is likened to the "rhizome" spelled out by Deleuze and Guattari (1987). Here movement is non-linear, often more a result of various interpenetrating iterative loops found in historically formed constellations of iterative loops. These are, however, in continuous movement. They are more likened to dissipative structures with the qualifier that the rate of change is greater for some than for others. Foucault's "genealogical method" developed from Nietzsche is well in tune with this model (see Love, 1986: 67–111). Schehr's study on new social movements suggests (Chapter 9, this volume) that the concept of the "rhizome" accounts for the creative and unpredictable in social change.

Because of the non-linearity in the model, the development of disproportional effects must be accepted. Accordingly, any science attempting to idealize strict prediction must be doomed. At best, as T.R. Young tells us (see Chapters 2, 4, this volume), a more humanistic society would set parameters that tend toward more favorable outcomes, but always with an understanding that the unpredictable will emerge. Thus, rather than attempting to use more linear sciences, such as in the syllogistic reasoning of law, what would be more applicable are conflict-regulation models that are sensitive to non-linear flow and foreground factors.

Criminologists incorporating a chaos-informed, postmodernist analysis will certainly need to reconceptualize their investigative methods. The challenge will certainly be demanding. But given the continuous use of old theoretical models of modernist sciences (including various forms of dogmatic Marxism) with seemingly few contributions to an understanding of much of the apparently increasing crime, new models must be developed. We do not discount the importance of some of the findings of modernist scholars, but suggest that new integration and synthesis are necessary.

LAW

Applications of chaos theory to law have begun to emerge in the scholarly literature (Brion, 1991; Milovanovic, 1992, 1993, 1995a, 1995b; see Chapters 6, 7, and 8, this volume). More recent applications are beginning to integrate chaos theory with other perspectives within postmodern analysis. Psychoanalytic semiotics (Lacan, 1977) has been one such integrated perspective (Milovanovic, 1996; Arrigo, Chapter 8, this volume). Another integration has been with constitutive theory (Henry and Milovanovic, 1996). More integration is surely needed. Critical Legal Studies, for example, has not been quick to take this emerging view into account. Schulman's and Simon and Stroup's chapters 7 and 6, respectively, in this volume have certainly suggested further integration. Brion's (1991) work has also been well argued.

Much of chaos theory can be brought to bear against the classical view of law. Here, formal rational thinking rests on syllogistic reasoning, a linear model. We start with some assumed major premise (some constitutional principle), apply it to a minor premise (the "facts" of a particular case), and in a linear way arrive deductively at a conclusion in law. The totality of this reasoning sets precedents. There is a tendency toward greater fine-tuning in developing a "gapless" system of law as envisioned by Weber (Milovanovic, 1994). Increasingly, the courts intrude on every aspect of human existence. There would seem to be little counter to this logic that has been created and increasingly applied. Chaos theory offers a challenge.

Godel's theorem seems to counter the possibility of a "gapless" system in law. For Godel, there will always be a case which cannot be subsumed into a system of axioms that cover all cases. If, indeed, we have even some exceptions, or minor variations, chaos theory suggests that through iteration unexpected results will appear. This is not hyperbole. Chaos theory has convincingly argued that dynamic systems maintain a sensitive dependence on initial conditions. Initial social conditions are always dissimilar. Who would argue that exactness exists, even given the Fourteenth Amendment's equal protection clause, where it stipulates that equally situated should be equally treated? Given the variability in the human conditions, no "equally situated" exist, but at best we may say closely equally situated exist. This imprecision, when iterated, is what produces disproportional effects. The use of formal rationality and syllogistic reasoning can be successful only to the extent that differences, however minor, in initial conditions can be rounded off, or factored out, or discounted as "noise." Early critical theorists in legal realism and sociological jurisprudence, as well as more recent critical legal studies theorists and "fem-crits" have convincingly argued that extralegal factors are often at work in decision-making, and, only after the fact, legal constructions can give the appearance of syllogistic reasoning (for a summary, see Milovanovic, 1994: Chapter 4).

A useful discussion of non-linear effects has been provided by Brion (1991; see also Schulman's critique, this volume) as well as Balkin (1987). Brion has indicated that decision-making can be better understood as the interplay of formal and informal factors, better represented by the two wings of a butterfly attractor. Balkin, explicating Derrida's notion of "iteration," has shown that legal words (signifiers) always undergo change as their meaning is constructed differently in different settings (consider, for example, how the words "person," "liberty," and "property" have been defined over the years). In other words, for both, indeterminacy pervades the otherwise presented linear model of formal reasoning. Modernist legal scholars, lawyers, and judges continuously delude themselves that theirs is an exact science.

Where do we go from here? A chaos-informed critical postmodernist view on law could provide vistas for alternative theorizing. The notion of iteration and non-linear effects would question any notions such as "original intent" of some "Founding Fathers" of the Constitution. Major premises, therefore, would at best be dissipative structures resisting formal closure. Rather than debating the merits of deductive (formalist's) versus inductive (legal realist's) logic, the principle of "abduction" developed by Peirce becomes especially noteworthy. Here *both* induction and deduction are brought into legal reasoning, with ever new principles emerging. Consider Brion: "the movement is not from chaos to order, but rather is from each level of a definitive and orderly arrangement of meaning thus far to a new level of disorder and meaning not yet ascertained but still vague" (1991: 109; see also Uusitalo, 1991; see also the summary of Peirce by Milovanovic, 1994: 110–14). Directions that have recently emerged that lend themselves to further integration of chaos theory include those based on notions of a "reflexive law" (Uusitalo, 1991), "autopoietic law" (Teubner, 1988), "social-principles orientation in civil law" (Uusitalo, 1991; Wilhemsson, 1989), and constitutive law (Henry and Milovanovic, 1996). In each case, the notions of far-from-equilibrium conditions, dissipative structure, iteration, non-linearity, and tori and strange attractors become substitutable for modernists' metaphysics of equilibrium conditions, structural functionalism, formal structure, syllogistic reasoning, linearity, and point or limit/cyclic attractors. In doing postmodernist law informed by chaos theory, at best we can construct "contingent universalities" (Butler, 1992), provisional and contingent truths that become the basis of social action, but "truths" that are always subject to subsequent reflection, modification, deletion, and substitution. This overcomes the debate between those who advocate essentialism and those who advocate relativism.

A chaos-informed postmodernist analysis in law would take seriously the notion that multiple, parallel, intersecting, and interpenetrating factors are constitutive of different forms of harms of repression and harms of reduction (Crenshaw, 1993: 111–32; Henry and Milovanovic, 1996: 99–121). Here, our constitutive interrelational sets (COREL sets) would be implicated. The challenge in developing contingent universalities, forms of dissipative structures, is to understand and verbalize (name) the dynamic systems that have high probabilities of producing harms of reduction or repression. Following Young (1992), various parameters could be redesigned so as to minimize harms and maximize benefits without, at the same time, making any pretense that the "truths" established are definitive, static, objective, and universal.

REPLACEMENT DISCOURSES

Postmodernists advocating social change face a critical problem with language: if, in the use of language, one is indeed imprisoned in constructing narratives and "realities," then how is one to generate visions of the new order? Modernists, generally, see this as non-problematic; for, language is but a neutral instrument for conveying thoughts. Alternative positions are rooted in the linguistic determinism of Whorf (1956), in the importance of a political economy circumscribing the basis of pinning signifiers to signifieds (Volosinov, 1983), and in the inseparability of the subject and discourse thesis developed by Lacan (1977). In the latter view, social change would have to entail a change in discourse: the Real and the Symbolic Order (Lacan, 1977) are interconnected and hence, change must proceed by considering both. In responding to the question of "How can the subaltern [disenfranchised] speak?" it will not suffice to simply argue, as was the case with those advocating "standpoint epistemology," to privilege the positions and narrative constructions of the disempowered, a process by which we would presumably directly know the harms incurred; for, these narrative constructions still make use of the dominant Symbolic Order and, hence, inadvertently reconstruct the hegemonic order. It would seem, then, that postmodernists ring the bell for the "death of the subject" (Held, 1996). Affirmative postmodernist analysis differs, dismissing these early statements in postmodernist analysis as being the nihilistic/fatalistic forms.

The key question that must be addressed, again, is how to construct alternative discourses, replacement discourses, that allow an expansion in the possibilities of the embodiment of desire and in the construction of more congruent narratives. We are interested in how to overcome the violence of language (Freire, 1972, 1985; Giroux, 1992; Lecercle, 1991). Lacan (1977; 1985) has convincingly described how a male-dominated Symbolic Order maintains itself, and how those who assume the female discursive subject-position are relegated to being "pas toute," not-all, disenfranchised. Our suggestion for change implicates Lacan's analysis of the four discourses (1991; see also Bracher, 1988; Milovanovic, 1992, 1993, 1997; Henry and Milovanovic, 1996; Arrigo, 1995a; see also Arrigo, Chapter 8, this volume); Freire's analysis concerning dialogical pedagogy (see also Giroux, 1992; McLaren, 1994; JanMohammed, 1994); critical race theorists' notions of how harms find themselves in intersections of forces and how "naming" harms becomes crucial for change (Matsuda, et al. 1993); feminist analysis concerning how "contingent universalities" (Butler, 1992) may take form as a basis of creating political agendas; and the notions of chaos, especially concerning dissipative structures and the dynamics of the bifurcation diagram (see also Milovanovic, 1996). Change in the discursive must proceed with change in political economy.

Discourses, as Lacan (1991) has informed us, are structured in one of four forms. When we speak we find ourselves involved in structured dialogues. The "discourse of the master" is one in which the subject assumes a speaking position, a discursive subject-position within which narrative constructions and the embodiment of desire are greatly circumscribed, most often reflecting the dominant hegemonic order. Consider how colonizing powers often inflict their culture, language, and ideals on indigenous populations. Althusser (1971) has referred to this process as *interpellation*, how the subject is constituted in discourse. The "discourse of the university" offers discursive subject-positions where the subject is offered various previously constituted frameworks for the constructions of realities. Consider, for example, the research that was done in various bodies of knowledge: Newtonian physics, Einstein's relativity, Heisenberg's quantum mechanics, and currently, "string theory." Law would be a form of the discourse of the university, although a strong case could be made that it cloaks itself in this form and functions more in the discourse of the master. In the first two discourses, the subject remains "pas toute," incomplete, or in Lacan's words, there remains a surplus of enjoyment (*le plus de jouir*). Consider here how in various contexts—school, media, law—we are often offered a dominant body of knowledge as a given within which to then construct reality. Yngvesson (1993), for example, has shown how the disenfranchised before the courts become further emasculated when their narrative constructions are translated into legalese for further processing (see also Manning's investigation of emergency police calls, 1988). Here the dialectics are such that, on the one hand, the disenfranchised do in fact have their day in court, an empowering experience, but, on the other, are separated from their unique desires and relegated to continuous builders of the contemporary Symbolic Order (i.e., hegemony).

The "discourse of the hysteric" is such that the "hysteric," which we read as the alienated, opposing, revolting subject (and not just the clinical case), is offered clinical diagnoses, stereotypes, clichés, and bureaucratic categories, or master signifiers (signifiers from the dominant Symbolic Order) with which to create narratives and embody desire. S/he finds her/himself in an endless loop along which the given master signifiers provide some understanding and mastery but with great moments of doubt and an endless feeling of *pas toute*. At best, we have an oppositional subject.

The "discourse of the master," for Lacan, provides a vista for change. Here the analyst (read also the "cultural revolutionary," Unger, 1987; or the literacy campaign worker as in Freire, 1972), sensitively reflects to the "hysteric" what is left out in her/his narrative constructions, which provides a basis for further reflection, change, and substitution. In other words, Lacan tells us that the "hysteric" begins to disidentify with old master signifiers and gradually incorporates new master signifiers that better reflect her/his way of being. The discourse of the master is a start, but insufficient by itself.

To better understand the dynamic movement toward the creation of new master signifiers and replacement discourses, we can make use of the works by Freire's dialogical pedagogy and the bifurcation diagram that chaos theory offers us (see the bifurcation diagrams provided by Forker, Chapter 3, Figures 3.1 and 3.2, this volume; see also Milovanovic, 1996, 1997). Our control parameter is the emerging postmodern society characterized by alienation, the intrusion of the hyperreal, and capital logic (the commodification process and the law of equivalence). We assume, for this example, it continues in intensity from left to right. In each phase portrait, we view the x-axis as representing identification with master signifiers, the y-axis as the expression of embodiment of desire in master signifiers, and the z-axis as the rate of change between the two. Desire can be embodied more in the conventional language, *abstract language*—the various formal languages available (i.e., legal, scientific, clinical, street, religious, etc.). Or, desire may be embodied in the *material language* of the body (Lecercle, 1985), a more unstructured language expressed often by the poet, novelist, linguist, as well as by mental patients and those sometimes from alternative lifestyles (see also Kristeva, 1980).

Let us now trace the dynamic system in movement. We could start with the hypothetical situation where the subject finds her/himself in the discourse of the master or university whereby narratives are constructed reconstituting dominant understandings. Here, however, desire does not find full expression. The subject remains *pas toute*. We have a point or limit/periodic attractor whereby movement is toward abstract language, identification with master signifiers, and embodiment of desire within categories available. As we move from left to right in the bifurcation diagram, indicating greater intensity of forces found in the emerging postmodern society, we see bifurcations developing. In Forker's Figure 3.2, Box A, we see the first bifurcation, indicating, in our application, that the otherwise "good" subject is now experiencing a distancing, a disidentification with master signifiers, and a partial movement to the material language of the body. However, the subject returns to a periodic/limit attractor indicated by the greater amplitude. At most we would have the discourse of the hysteric where the subject may occasionally oppose, but eventually resigns her/himself to the dominant offerings, and inadvertently reconstitutes conventional understandings and the dominant order.

As the forces of the emerging postmodern society continue, we see that in Box D a chaos attractor has emerged. Here we see that the subject has greatly disidentified with dominant master signifiers, and greatly resists embodiment of desire in the dominant discourse. S/he finds her/

himself in a situation where vacillation exists between the abstract language and material language of the body. It is here where the literacy campaign worker, or the "cultural revolutionary," becomes a catalyst in dialogical encounters. The cultural revolutionary acts as the "analyst" in Lacan's rendition but remains transparent to the subject. Through a collaborative effort, distancing is created from the previous master signifiers, and new master signifiers that better reflect the socio-economic arrangements begin to take form. A decodification (deconstruction) is followed by a recodification (reconstruction) (Freire, 1972). The butterfly attractor indicates how the subject would vacillate between embodying desire in dominant discourses in creating narratives, and then, move to the other wing, expressing desire and creating narratives in a very different form. The cultural revolutionary, or literacy campaign worker, will collaboratively (dialogically) contribute to the emergence of new master signifiers, a new body of knowledge, and a relatively stabilized discourse more reflective of the subject's situatedness in a political economy.

These new master signifiers, body of knowledge, and replacement discourses would not be static in form, but would be more in the form of dissipative structures. They are emergents. They resist closure. They tend toward what Volosinov referred to as the "multiaccentuality" of the sign (1983). Embedded within the new master signifiers are various differences that remain in dynamic tension. In short, the *pas toute* phenomena begin to wither away. The new replacement discourses offer subjects an alternative form for the embodiment of desire and for the creation of narratives that better reflect the socio-political conditions within which the subject resides. Contrary to Lacan, we see a continuous and necessary tension between the discourse of the hysteric and the analyst, whereby continuous discursive change is produced. The discourses developed could offer the material out of which "contingent universalities" (Butler, 1992) could be constructed. In other words, there is no "death of the subject." The person is a subject-in-process. The sign finds a degree of stability in the active arena of social struggle and change.

Our construction here can benefit from further integration of the works on "border pedagogy" and the creation of a "language of possibility" (Giroux, 1992), and from critical race theory (Matsuda et al., 1993), which stipulates the intersectional nature of domination and the necessity for strategies for "naming" the forces of repression. For Giroux, these replacement discourses are "new languages capable of acknowledging the multiple, contradictory, and complex subject positions people occupy within different social, cultural, and economic relations" (1992: 21). For Matsuda et al. (1993), consistent with Freire, "naming" is a continuous process. "When ideology is deconstructed and injury is named," Matsuda et al. continue, "subordinated victims find their voice" (1993: 13).

As the above has focused on the Symbolic and Real Order (Lacan,

1977), discourse and primordial sense data emanating from historical structures of forces (constellations of iterative loops, or COREL sets), we need to also integrate the Imaginary Order. Here, Cornell's (1991) work is critical (see also Arrigo, Chapter 8, this volume). She describes how alternative imaginary constructions can emerge that do not privilege the male voice. We could also apply her insights for other disenfranchised subjects. Cornell says imaginary play is already in existence in the "slippage" inherent in language. An *excess* always exists. If this is so, we can see how the "free play of the text" can occur through iteration. This is non-linear. Cornell's call is noteworthy: "consciousness-raising must involve creation, not just discovery. We need our poetry, our fantasies and our fables; we need the poetic evocation of the feminine body in Irigaray and in Cixous if we are to finally find a way beyond the muteness imposed by a gender hierarchy in which our desire is 'unspeakable' " (1991: 201). With poetry appears indeterminacy, irony, contradiction, spontaneity, and the free play of the text. We are in the realm of non-linear dynamic systems. We have traveled full circle to the importance of social structures that are based on far-from-equilibrium conditions, the prevalence of coupled dissipative structures, non-linearity dynamics, and tori and strange attractors.

CONCLUSION

This concluding chapter has been suggestive for further research and change possibilities. Ours is an affirmative postmodernism. There is no room for the fatalism and nihilism found in the early forms of postmodern thought. Much has yet to be done. Ours is a perpetually unfinished project. Vision for a better society and the dynamics for its development can surely evolve with the conceptual tools offered to us by chaos theory and other perspectives in the postmodernist paradigm. The chapters included in this book attest to the exciting work that awaits those interested in an alternative and critical understanding in criminology and law, and in social reform.

REFERENCES

Althusser, L. 1971. *Lenin and Philosophy*. New York: Monthly Review Press.
Arrigo, B. 1995a. "Deconstructing Classroom Instruction." *Social Pathology* 1(2): 115–48.
———. 1995b. "The Peripheral Core of Law and Criminology: On Postmodern Social Theory and Conceptual Integration." *Justice Quarterly* 12(3): 447–72.
Balkin, J.M. 1987. "Deconstructive Practice and Legal Theory." *Yale Law Journal* 96(4): 743–86.

Bracher, M. 1988. "Lacan's Theory of the Four Discourses." *Prose Studies* 11: 32–49.

Brion, D. 1991. "The Chaotic Law of Tort: Legal Formalism and the Problem of Indeterminacy." Pp. 45–77 in R. Kevelson (ed.), *Peirce and Law*. New York: Peter Lang.

Butler, J. 1992. "Contingent Foundations: Feminism and the Question of 'Post-modernism.' " In J. Butler and J.W. Scott (eds.), *Feminists Theorize the Political*. London: Routledge.

Cornell, D. 1991. *Beyond Accommodation*. New York: Routledge.

Crenshaw, K.W. 1993. "Beyond Racism and Misogyny: Black Feminism and 2 Live Crew." Pp. 111–32 in M. Matsuda et al. (eds.), *Words That Wound: Critical Race Theory, Assaultive Speech, and the First Amendment*. San Francisco: Westview Press.

Deleuze, G. and F. Guattari. 1987. *A Thousand Plateaus*. Minneapolis: University of Minnesota Press.

Ferrell, J. 1995. "Adrenalin, Pleasure, and Criminological *Verstehen*." Delivered at the Annual Meetings of the American Society of Criminology, Boston, November 21–23.

Freire, P. 1972. *Pedagogy of the Oppressed*. New York: Herder and Herder.

———. 1985. *The Politics of Education*. South Hadley, MA: Bergin and Garvey.

Giroux, H. 1992. *Border Pedagogy*. New York: Routledge.

Gregerson, H. and L. Sailer. 1993. "Chaos Theory and Its Implications for Social Science Research." *Human Relations* 46(7): 777–802.

Held, B. 1996. *Back to Reality*. New York: W.W. Norton.

Henry, S. and D. Milovanovic. 1996. *Constitutive Criminology*. London: Sage.

JanMohammed, A.R. 1994. "Some Implications of Paulo Freire's Border Pedagogy." Pp. 242–52 in H. Giroux and P. McLaren (eds.), *Between Borders*. New York: Routledge.

Katz, J. 1988. *The Seductions of Crime*. New York: Basic Books.

Kristeva, J. 1980. *Desire in Language*. New York: Columbia University Press.

Lacan, J. 1977. *Ecrit*, trans. A. Sheridan. New York: Norton.

———. 1985. *Feminine Sexuality*. New York: Norton.

———. 1991. *L'Envers de la Psychanalyse*. Paris, France: Editions du Seuil.

Lecercle, J.J. 1985. *Philosophy Through the Looking Glass*. London: Hutchinson

———. 1991. *The Violence of Language*. New York: Routledge.

Leiffer, R. 1989. "Understanding Organizational Transformation Using a Dissipative Structure Model." *Human Relations* 42: 899–916.

Love, N. 1986. *Marx, Nietzsche and Modernity*. New York: Columbia University Press.

Lyng, S. 1990. "Edgework: A Social Psychological Analysis of Voluntary Risk Taking." *American Journal of Sociology* 95(4): 851–86.

Manning, P. 1988. *Symbolic Communication*. Cambridge, MA: MIT Press.

Matsuda, M.J., C.R. Lawrence, R. Delgado, and K.W. Crenshaw (eds.). 1993. *Words That Wound*. San Francisco: Westview Press.

Matza, D. 1969. *Becoming Deviant*. Englewood Cliffs, NJ: Prentice-Hall.

McLaren, P. 1994. "Multiculturalism and the Postmodern Critique." Pp. 192–222 in H. Giroux and P. McLaren (eds.), *Between Borders*. New York: Routledge.

Milovanovic, D. 1992. *Postmodern Law and Disorder*. Liverpool, UK: Deborah Charles.

———. 1993. "Lacan's Four Discourses." *Studies in Psychoanalytic Theory* 2(1): 3–23.

———. 1994. *Sociology of Law*. Albany, NY: Harrow and Heston.

———. 1995a. "Inscribing the Body with a Sign." Pp. 47–78 in R. Janikowski and D. Milovanovic (eds.), *Legality and Illegality*. New York: Peter Lang.

———. 1995b. "Moral Philosophy, Social Justice and the Question of Punishment in a Just Society." Pp. 249–82 in R. Janikowski and D. Milovanovic (eds.), *Legality and Illegality*. New York: Peter Lang.

———. 1996. "Postmodern Criminology." *Justice Quarterly* 13(4): 567–609.

———. 1997. *Postmodern Criminology*. New York: Garland.

O'Malley, P. and S. Mugford. 1994. "Crime, Modernity and Excitement." Pp. 189–211 in G. Barak (ed.), *Varieties of Criminology*. Westport, CT: Praeger.

Pashukanis, E. 1978. "The General Theory of Law and Marxism." In P. Beirne and R. Sharlet (eds.), *Pashukanis: Selected Writings on Marxism and Law*. New York: Academic Press.

Pepinsky, H. 1991. *The Geometry of Violence and Democracy*. Bloomington: Indiana University Press.

Reiman, J. 1990. *Justice and Modern Moral Philosophy*. New Haven, CT: Yale University Press.

Schehr, R. 1996a. *Communities of Resistance*. New York: Lang.

———. 1996b. *Dynamic Utopia: Establishing Intentional Communities as a New Social Movement*. Westport, CT: Praeger.

Teubner, G. 1988. *Autopoietic Law*. New York: Walter de Gruyter.

Unger, R. 1987. *False Necessity*. New York: Cambridge University Press.

Uusitalo, J. 1991. "Abduction, Legal Reasoning, and Reflexive Law," Pp. 163–85 in R. Kevelson (ed.), *Peirce and Law*. New York: Peter Lang.

Volosinov, V. 1983. *Marxism and the Philosophy of Language*. Cambridge, MA: Harvard University Press.

Weber, M. 1978. *Economy and Society*, vols. 1 and 2, G. Roth and C. Wittich (eds.). Los Angeles: University of California Press.

Whorf, B. 1956. *Language, Thought and Reality*, J. Carrol (ed.). New York: John Wiley.

Wilhemsson, T. 1989. "Need Rationality in Civil Law." *Scandinavian Studies in Law* 33: 223–33.

Yngvesson, B. 1993. *Virtuous Citizens: Disruptive Subjects*. New York: Routledge.

Young, T.R. 1991a. "The ABC of Crime." *Critical Criminologist* 3(4): 3–4, 13–14.

———. 1991b. "Chaos and Crime." *Critical Criminologist* 3(2): 3–4, 10–11.

———. 1992. "Chaos Theory and Human Agency." *Humanity and Society* 16(4): 441–60.

Index

About the Editor and Contributors

DRAGAN MILOVANOVIC is Professor of Criminal Justice in the Department of Criminal Justice, Sociology and Social Work at Northeastern Illinois University. He has authored, co-authored, and edited 12 books, as well as over 100 other publications. His books include *Weberian and Marxian Analysis of Law* (1989), *Postmodern Law and Disorder* (1992), *The Sociology of Law* (1994), *Constitutive Criminology* (1996), and *Postmodern Criminology* (1997). His co-edited books include *Legality and Illegality: Semiotics, Postmodernism and Law* (1995), *New Directions in Critical Criminology* (1991), *Racism, Empiricism and Criminal Justice* (1990), *Race, Gender, and Class in Criminology* (1996), and *Thinking Critically About Crime* (1996). In 1993 he received the Distinguished Achievement Award from the Division on Critical Criminology of the American Society of Criminology for his service and scholarly contributions to critical theory.

BRUCE A. ARRIGO is Professor of Forensic Psychology and Criminology and Director of the Institute of Psychology, Law, and Public Policy at the California School of Professional Psychology–Fresno. He has written extensively in the areas of law, criminology, and justice studies. His recent books include *Madness, Language, and the Law* (1993), *The Contours of Psychiatric Justice* (1996) and, with T.R. Young, *The Dictionary of Critical Social Science* (1997). He is presently editing an anthology titled *The Margins of Justice: The Maturation of Critical Theory in Law, Crime, and Deviance* (forthcoming).

ALLISON FORKER, in preparation for this work, delivered parts of her research at Northeastern Illinois University's fourth annual symposium.

She has received the "Outstanding Student Paper Award" from the Division of Critical Criminology of the American Society of Criminology for 1996. Allison looks forward to completing her coursework in criminal justice at Northeastern and moving on to graduate school, where she hopes to integrate her interests in criminology, media analysis, and social policy.

HAL PEPINSKY is a member of the Department of Criminal Justice, Indiana University. He has written extensively over the years in sociology and criminology. His books include *Crime and Conflict: A Study of Law and Society, The Geometry of Violence and Democracy* (1991), *Myths That Cause Crime* (1993), *Criminology as Peacemaking* (1991), and *We Who Shall Take No Prisoners* (1994).

ROBERT C. SCHEHR is Assistant Professor of Sociology in the Criminal Justice Program at the University of Illinois in Springfield. His research interests include the areas of peacemaking criminology, conflict mediation, and social movements.

CAREN SCHULMAN is a career public service employee who returned to university life in 1994 to complete her bachelor's degree in Criminal Justice at Northeastern Illinois University. As a speaker on the topic of Chaos Theory and its application to the judicial decision-making process and Critical Legal Studies, she presented a paper, *"Mapping the Terrain,"* at the annual meeting of the American Society of Criminology in the fall of 1996. Upon completing her undergraduate degree Caren will pursue a degree in law and aspires to a second career as a litigator.

GLENNA L. SIMONS is a Ph.D. candidate in the Department of Sociology and Anthropology at Purdue University. She has presented papers concerning the social construction of justice and the use of the "reasonable woman" standard of evidence review by courts as a rhetorical strategy in sexual harassment cases (Society for the Study of Social Problems, New York, 1996). She has also co-authored (with JoAnn Miller) a paper entitled "A Case of Everyday Justice: Free Press vs. Fair Trial in a Burglary Case." *Journal of Crime and Justice* (forthcoming).

WILLIAM F. STROUP II is a Ph.D. candidate in the Sociology and Anthropology Department of Purdue University. He has presented papers about the influence of event sequence discourse on the search for social structure (Midwestern States Anthropological Society, Indianapolis, Indiana, 1995), chaos theory as metaphor for exploring legal systems (South Western Sociological Association, Houston, Texas, 1996), and the potential use of chaos theory in sociology (South Western Sociological

Association, Houston, Texas, 1996). He also has a paper which establishes research protocols for the investigation of chaos in dynamic complex adaptive social systems (forthcoming).

T.R. YOUNG is founder and director of the Red Feather Institute for Advanced Studies in Sociology. He is editor of the Transforming Sociology Series and author of many articles and books oriented to emancipatory knowledge. Young contributes to democratic knowledge processes in politics, criminology, economics, medicine, religion, education, and the arts. Young has written foundational articles on chaos theory and non-linear social dynamics.

ISBN 0-275-95707-1

HARDCOVER BAR CODE